GOOD NEWS

AND

GOOD WORKS

Also by Ronald J. Sider

Cup of Water, Bread of Life
Rich Christians in an Age of Hunger
Christ and Violence
Living like Jesus
Completely Pro-Life

GOOD NEWS

AND

GOOD WORKS

A Theology for the Whole Gospel

RONALD J. SIDER

Baker Books

A Division of Baker Book House Co
Grand Rapids, Michigan 49516

© 1993 by Ronald J. Sider

Published by Baker Books
a division of Baker Book House Company
P.O. Box 6287, Grand Rapids, MI 49516-6287

First printing, February 1999

Previously published by Zondervan Publishing House under the title *One-Sided Christianity? Uniting the Church to Heal a Lost and Broken World*

Printed in the United States of America

Library of Congress Cataloging-in-Publication Data

Sider, Ronald J.
    [One-sided Christianity?]
    Good news and good works : a theology of the whole Gospel / Ronald J. Sider.
        p. cm.
    Includes bibliographical references (p.) and indexes.
    ISBN 0-8010-5845-7 (paper)
    1. Mission of the church. 2. Evangelistic work. 3. Church and the world. 4. Church and social problems. 5. Christianity and justice. I. Title.
    [BV601.8.S47 1999]
    269—dc21   98-42783

For current information about all releases from Baker Book House, visit our web site:
http://www.bakerbooks.com

To
John Stott
Colleen Samuel
Vinay Samuel

Contents

Preface

Over eighty years ago, Walter Rauschenbusch delivered his famous lectures at Yale called "A Theology for the Social Gospel." This exposition of the social gospel by the movement's most prominent spokesperson stands as the classic articulation of one side in the great social gospel–fundamentalism debate that divided the church for much of the twentieth century.

In significant ways, Rauschenbusch's famous book (based on the lectures) offered much needed correctives. He rightly insisted that the church too often has understood both sin and salvation in one-sided individualistic ways, neglected social justice, and ignored Jesus' ethical teaching. But the weaknesses in Rauschenbusch's book—and the reasons theologically conservative Christians needed to challenge this articulation of the social gospel—are equally clear.

Rauschenbusch bluntly insists that the social gospel "plainly concentrates religious interest on the great ethical problems of social life."[1] He belittles "trust in the vicarious atonement of Christ" as rigid dogma (101) and insists that the social gospel has little interest in metaphysical questions about the Trinity or deity of Christ (150–51), not to mention Satan. For the social gospel, "its chief interest is concentrated on those manifestations of sin and redemption which lie beyond the individual soul" (95). Whereas "the non-ethical practices and beliefs in historical Christianity nearly all center on the winning of heaven and immortality," Rauschenbusch gladly predicts that "the more the Social Gospel engages and inspires theological thought, the more will religion be concentrated on ethical righteousness" (15).

This kind of tragically one-sided focus on the ethical aspects of Christian faith significantly contributed to one of the greatest divisions in twentieth-century Christianity. To transcend that division,

9

we need a full-blown biblical theology that affirms both personal and social sin, both personal conversion and structural change, both evangelism and social action, both personal and social salvation, both Jesus as moral example and Jesus as vicarious substitute, both orthodox theology and ethical obedience. In this book, *Good News and Good Works*,[2] I have tried to develop what I believe is a biblical "theology for the whole gospel." In another book, *Cup of Water, Bread of Life*,[3] I describe ten of the best models I know of ministries that combine evangelism and social action. My prayer is that these two books will make at least a small contribution to helping the church in the twenty-first century be more balanced and wholistic—because it is more biblical—than the church has been through much of the twentieth century.

Acknowledgments

I wish to thank those who have contributed to this book in special ways.

First, a special thanks to John Stott, Colleen Samuel, and Vinay Samuel—three dear friends to whom I gratefully dedicate this book. One of God's highly treasured gifts to me has been the privilege of learning from and working with them as friends and partners.

To those who have allowed me to share parts of their journey, I owe a special debt: Addie Banks, Michael Banks, James Dennis, Nelson Diaz, Cassandra and Showen Franklin, David Gitari, Brian Hathaway, Glen Kehrein, and Raleigh Washington.

Many scholars were kind enough to send me some material, provide a key piece of technical information, or respond to a first draft of part of the manuscript. Without attributing to them any blame for what I finally wrote, I wish to thank them for their help: Gerald H. Anderson, David Barrett, Manfred Brauch, Emilio Castro, Jill Renee Duncan, Samuel Escobar, Leighton Ford, Michael Green, David Hesselgrave, Paul G. Hiebert, Andrew Kirk, Tom McAlpine, Thomas McDaniel, David O. Moberg, Bryant Myers, Clark Pinnock, Valdir Steuernagel, John Stott, Miroslav Volf, C. Peter Wagner, and Ralph D. Winter.

For their special efforts in publishing this book, I want to thank Dwight Baker and Robert Hosack of Baker Book House.

Ketly Pierre worked for weeks typing my initial handwritten text. For enduring tight deadlines and my special hieroglyphics, she deserves the special reward reserved for those who do works of supererogation. Rick White and James Moore, my research assistants, tracked down documents, and James prepared the index. Naomi Miller, my secretary/administrative assistant par excellence, was able, as usual, to handle any crisis and accomplish whatever needed to be done. In numerous ways, she contributes enormously to all my endeavors.

To my wife, Arbutus, I owe the deepest debt. Her love and support and our common commitment to Christ and his kingdom provide a bedrock of joy and wholeness that empower all my work.

PART 1

A HOUSE DIVIDED

1

My Pilgrimage

I don't want to be like these white Christians here. They sing about the love of Jesus. But they don't care about justice in South Africa.

A Jewish university student in South Africa

In 1979 I spent two wonderful weeks lecturing in South Africa. One of the most fascinating persons I met was a young university student named James.[1] He came to the annual conference of an evangelical university movement where I was speaking about Jesus' concern for the poor and his resurrection on the third day. Like most other parts of the South African Church then, this evangelical student movement had split into four groups: white Afrikaans-speaking, white English-speaking, colored, and black. The students at the conference were mostly white English-speaking.

James was not a Christian. He was Jewish and an ardent social activist. His passion in life was the struggle against apartheid. Somehow, however, these devout white Christians had caught his attention. James and I quickly became friends during the conference, talking about South African politics hour after hour.

Abruptly one evening after a vigorous three-hour conversation, James said: "Ron, I'm burned out." I wasn't surprised. He was trying to be a full-time activist and a full-time student, but his next comment startled me: "God told me that if I would come to this conference, I would learn something about his Son."

I looked at James and replied, "James, I believe that Jesus Christ died on the cross and rose again for you."

He paused for a second and then astonished me again: "I believe all of that, Ron, I really do."

Still he held back. Something obviously was blocking his acceptance of Christ. After a moment, he said quietly, "I don't want to be like these white Christians here. They sing about the love of Jesus and the joy of heaven, but they don't care about justice in South Africa. If I become a Christian, will I have to give up the struggle?"

"Goodness no, James. Jesus wants to strengthen your passion for justice for all people in South Africa, not take it away. Certainly it will have to be on his terms, but it will be a deeper, more powerful commitment."

I waited quietly for a moment and then added, "I'm not in any hurry, but if you would like to pray together, I'd be glad to do that." Quickly he agreed, and we went to my room. He prayed a beautiful prayer, confessing his sins and accepting Jesus Christ as personal Savior and Lord.

After I finished praying, I looked at James, and his face was shining. I'm sure mine was too. In fact, I was so excited that all I could do for the first few minutes after he left was walk around the room, singing praises to the Lord. It was a special moment of fantastic joy.

The white evangelical students at that conference were typical of a major segment of the Christian church for a good deal of this century: strong on personal evangelism but with little or no passion for justice for the poor and liberation for the oppressed. As a result, even their evangelistic efforts faltered.

Evangelicals aren't the only Christians who are one-sided. In 1981, I was invited to speak at the thirtieth anniversary of the founding of the National Council of Churches in the U.S.A., a group that is often characterized as "liberal" or "mainline." As I looked over the list of workshops, I noticed that about a dozen were devoted to ecumenical affairs. Great. I saw about fifteen workshops on issues of peace and justice. Great. Then I checked carefully to see how many workshops dealt with evangelism, church growth, and cross-cultural sharing of the gospel. Do you know how many there were? Not a single one. Before I gave my lecture, I asked, "Brothers and sisters, how on earth can the NCC be this one-sided in 1981?"

Maybe that's one reason the churches in the NCC are losing millions of members.

During that same period, I happened to meet on a plane one day a man who had been a key leader in ecumenical social action circles in the sixties. He had done great work fighting for civil rights. As we talked, however, I realized that he was no longer a Christian. During seminary he had lost all belief in historic Christian orthodoxy. All he had left was the ethics of Jesus, so he threw himself passionately into the civil rights movement and became a leader in social action for mainline Protestants. But by the time I met him around 1981, he was discouraged. He had lost his hope and his faith.

These stories make me very sad. For a young man to turn away from the Lord because some Christians seemed unconcerned about the evil of apartheid would have been tragic. And to realize that other Christians have put so much emphasis on social action that they almost forget to tell dying sinners about my wonderful Savior is ghastly.

These stories may not provide a comprehensive picture of the groups involved, but they *do* illustrate a terrible division that has plagued the church for much of this century. Some Christian organizations and churches major almost exclusively on evangelism. Others on social action. (Unfortunately most churches in both groups do neither.) Each group uses the other's one-sidedness to justify its own continuing lack of balance, and the division devastates the church's witness and credibility. I believe that both types of one-sidedness are unbiblical and heretical.

We *could* do so much better by returning to the example of Jesus! We must reclaim a full-orbed biblical understanding of the total mission of the church if we are to seize the astounding opportunities for both evangelism and social transformation offered at this moment in history. This book is my attempt to show how, I believe, a genuinely biblical perspective inseparably interrelates and intertwines evangelism and social responsibility without equating or confusing the one with the other. In fact, a growing number of churches are doing just that. They are regularly bringing people to personal faith and also ministering to their physical and social needs.

Nothing excites me more than to hear stories of churches who are leading people to Christ and ministering to the needs of hurting people. I long for the day when every village, town, and city has congregations of Christians so in love with Jesus Christ that they lead scores of people to accept him as personal Savior and Lord every year—and so sensitive to the cry of the poor and oppressed that they work vigorously for justice, peace, and freedom.

There is a real sense in which the central passion of my life and ministry for the last thirty years has been to encourage the whole church to do just that.

I was born into an evangelical farm family in Canada. Mom and Dad demonstrated by word and deed that they loved Jesus Christ more than anything else in the world. At about eight years of age, during one of the regular revival meetings in my home congregation, I knelt at the altar and accepted Jesus Christ.

The Brethren in Christ Church in which I grew up combined the traditions of evangelical revivalism, Wesleyan holiness, and Mennonite Anabaptism. It was thoroughly evangelical but had not experienced the wrenching, early twentieth-century divisions of the social gospel–fundamentalist battles that helped produce the huge gulf between evangelism and social action. In my early years in the faith I just assumed that devout Christians shared the gospel, as my missionary uncle had in Africa, and also cared for the poor, as my church's relief agency was doing.

Then I went to the university, where my faith ran headlong into modern skepticism. I began to question whether an honest thinker in the modern world could accept historic Christian faith. Was not the Enlightenment right in claiming that all miracles, including the central miracles of the incarnation and resurrection, were incompatible with modern science? I struggled and doubted. And in that time of personal turmoil, evangelical historian John Warwick Montgomery replaced the secular agnostic who had chaired my history department for my first two years of college. John Montgomery and I became friends, and he introduced me to the historical evidence for Jesus' resurrection. He convinced me that if one examines the historical data in an objective way without a philosophical bias against the possibility of miracle, the correct historical conclusion is that the tomb was empty and that Jesus the carpenter was alive on the third day. If that happened, of course, it is a strong sign confirming Jesus' claim to be the Messiah and Son of God.[2]

Talk about God's providence (and maybe his sense of humor). Few mortals today would have imagined an alliance between Ron Sider and John Warwick Montgomery, but without John's apologetic zeal and friendship, I shudder to think where I would have ended up.

With renewed faith I eagerly resolved to take on the secular university world with a historical apologetic for Christian faith.[3] That, ironically, is why I went to Yale Divinity School. I wanted to understand fully the strongest arguments against historic Christian orthodoxy. So after two years in the doctoral program in history at Yale, I took a three-year leave of absence and moved up the hill to the divinity school. All along, InterVarsity Christian Fellowship had been the center of my Christian activity at Yale, and I planned, after completing theological studies and the Ph.D., to be an InterVarsity adviser as I worked as a Renaissance-Reformation historian in some secular university.

But God had different plans. A strong call to be active as an evangelical Christian in a renewal of biblically grounded concern for social justice began to grow within me. It was the decade of the sixties. My wife, Arbutus, and I sat with our African-American landlord and his wife, tasting their pain the day that Martin Luther King Jr. was killed. I discovered how the evangelical tradition in the eighteenth and nineteenth centuries had combined a passionate devotion to both evangelism and social concern in great leaders like William Wilberforce and Charles Finney. As a youth delegate I attended the Wheaton '66 Congress on the Church's Worldwide Mission and worked hard to get a short statement on social concern into the final document.

I resolved at that time to do everything in my power to make sure that as evangelicals became more concerned with social issues, they would not lose either their passion for evangelism or their grounding in historic Christian orthodoxy. It was painfully obvious from other students at the divinity school and the deadness of much New England church life that replacing evangelicalism's one-sided preoccupation with evangelism with a social gospel preoccupied with peace and justice was no solution. I did not know what my contribution would be as a Renaissance-Reformation historian, but I was eager to do the little I could to help the church embrace both evangelism and social concern.

As it turned out, I never taught Renaissance-Reformation history. Instead, I accepted a position beginning in September 1968 at Messiah College's new inner-city campus located at the border between Temple University and the black ghetto of North Philadelphia, teaching courses like "Christianity and Contemporary Problems."

Our family lived in the inner city and attended an all-black church. Our sons, Ted and Mike, integrated the local public school. I organized weekend seminars for rural and suburban church leaders so they could listen to African-American leaders share the anguish of racism and poverty. (Most of what I know in my heart about oppression I have learned from African-Americans.) And I encouraged my students both to become involved in the struggle against racism and poverty and also to share their faith as they took classes in the secular academic context of Temple University.

In the spring of 1973, I found myself at the first Calvin College conference on Christian Faith and Politics, sitting in a planning meeting with people like Rufus Jones and David Moberg. In his lectures and books, Moberg was urging evangelicals to reverse the Great Reversal, abandon our neglect of social concern, and return to the nineteenth-century evangelical tradition of people like Charles Finney, who was both the most influential evangelist at mid-century and also one of the leading abolitionists fighting against slavery. As we discussed plans for a Thanksgiving workshop for evangelical leaders on social concern, it was natural, given my sense of call, to accept responsibility for organizing the meeting.

Elder statesmen like Carl Henry, Foy Valentine, Bernard Ramm, Frank Gaebelein, and Paul Rees joined younger evangelicals like Jim Wallis, Paul Henry, Sharon Gallagher, Samuel Escobar, and me in a weekend conference. Richard Ostling of *Time* magazine said to me afterward that it was perhaps the first time in the twentieth century that evangelical leaders devoted an entire weekend exclusively to social issues.

The result was the Chicago Declaration of Evangelical Social Concern, one of the steps on the way to the renewal of evangelical social concern.[4] (It was also probably one of many streams that contributed to the strong insistence at the Lausanne Congress on World Evangelization called by Billy Graham ten months later that the world evangelical movement dare not neglect social responsibility.) The Chicago Declaration sounded a ringing call for repentance:

> We acknowledge that God requires justice. But we have not proclaimed or demonstrated his justice to an unjust American society. Although the Lord calls us to defend the social and economic rights of the poor and the oppressed, we have mostly remained silent. We deplore the historic involvement of the church in America with racism and the conspicuous responsibility of the evangelical community for perpetuating the personal attitudes and institutional structures that have divided the body of Christ along color lines.
>
> We call our fellow evangelical Christians to demonstrate repentance in a Christian discipleship that confronts the social and political injustice of our nation.

One significant result of the Chicago Declaration was a new openness on the part of mainline, ecumenical leaders to dialogue with evangelicals. Ecumenical leaders contacted me (I chaired the committee for the ongoing Chicago Declaration process) expressing gratitude for the Chicago Declaration and seeking dialogue with concerned evangelicals.

Three two-day dialogues resulted. For one of these organized with people from the World Council of Churches (WCC), I prepared a paper on the relationship between evangelism and social concern that was later published in the WCC's *International Review of Mission*.[5] In that earliest version of what is now this book, I urged evangelicals to strengthen their social engagement and ecumenical folk to renew their passion for evangelism.

The Chicago Declaration and the publication of my *Rich Christians in an Age of Hunger* (1977) opened opportunities undreamed of by this Ontario farm boy ten years earlier when the call first crystalized in divinity school to help foster a biblically grounded social

21

concern. My evangelical commitment to biblical orthodoxy opened doors in the evangelical community, and my passion for social justice fostered dialogue with ecumenical leaders.

In 1977, an invitation to join the Theological Commission of the World Evangelical Fellowship (WEF) came my way. With excitement, I plunged into new responsibilities as chair of the Unit on Ethics and Society in the WEF.

Ongoing ecumenical interaction both deepened my passion for peace and justice and renewed my concern that evangelism not get lost in the struggle for justice. Frequently I was moved by the vigorous call, grounded in the prophets and Jesus, for justice for the oppressed. I was encouraged by ecumenical leaders who wanted to ground social action in historic Christian orthodoxy.

But I also met ecumenical leaders whose one-sided concern for peace and justice disturbed and frightened me. For example, the WEF asked me to be one of their observers at the conference of the World Council of Churches (WCC) on Justice, Peace, and the Integrity of Creation at Seoul, Korea, in 1990. I was surprised and pleased to be asked to chair one part of the drafting committee, but their unwillingness to strengthen the biblical foundations of the document was dismaying. And when the plenary body even refused to insert a statement saying that persons *alone* are created in the image of God, I was disturbed. (Do the trees and the flowers also bear God's image?)[6]

Evangelicals tend to be suspicious of the WCC, but we must remember that this organization is vast and diverse. Sometimes, as in their 1983 document, *Mission and Evangelism,* the WCC calls vigorously for evangelism. And let's face it, their criticism of evangelical failure to work vigorously for justice for the oppressed is surely often deserved. Too often, however, as at Seoul in 1990 and the last general assembly in Canberra (1991), the theology expressed at WCC gatherings is inadequate and the primary focus is on peace, justice, and ecology. Focusing one-sidedly on those issues, I am convinced, will not solve the problems of the church or the world at the end of the second millennium.

Thankfully, organizations are made up of individuals, and it is thrilling to see what God is doing through people from all sorts of churches. In fact, one of the most important experiences for me in the last decade has been to meet younger evangelical leaders from developing countries (often called the "Two-Thirds" World). Their ministry and theology often rise above the tragic one-sidedness of so many Western evangelical and mainline churches. During a consultation of the International Fellowship of Evangelical Missions Theologians at Kabare, Kenya (1987), I visited some of the wholistic mission programs of evangelical Anglican bishop David Gitari, now Archbishop of Kenya.

In 1975 Bishop Gitari became the first bishop of the new diocese of Mt. Kenya East, covering two-fifths of Kenya. He placed local evangelists trained to do evangelism and church planting in every parish. He also assigned development workers and educators to each parish. The result has been economic development and exploding church growth. For years, Bishop Gitari has opened at least one (and sometimes two) new churches every month in his diocese.[7] That is the kind of wholistic mission that, I believe, is both faithful to Jesus and capable of attracting a lost and hurting world.

It is that kind of wholistic approach that I work at in my own local church. We don't always succeed. In fact, I must confess that in spite of my wholistic theology, my practice has not always been as balanced as I would wish.

In the seventies, my wife, Arbutus, and I helped found Jubilee Fellowship in a lower income, interracial section of Philadelphia, where we still live. We were young, evangelical, social activists presumptuously convinced that we knew how to reform church and society. Theoretically we believed in both evangelism and social action, but we did precious little direct evangelism. Instead, we worked long hours at social justice. And we truly hoped that our neighbors would see Christ in our lives and in our good deeds, but somehow, we seldom found the time or courage to ask them directly if they knew Jesus. I must confess sadly that my leading James to Christ in South Africa was very much an exception (although a very welcome one) in my life.

From 1981 to 1993, Arbutus and I were actively involved in another interracial, inner-city congregation in the middle of all-black North Philadelphia. The church sought to do both evangelism and community development. Our community center (which I served as president for several years) sponsored things like a health center and an employment referral service. As I write this today, I remember the joy that surged through our congregation last Sunday as a former drug addict shared how his new faith in Christ had helped him kick the habit. As we clapped to thank the Lord, we also clapped for our assistant pastor, Darryl Wallace, because we knew it was his costly, persistent discipling that had been crucial. In our drug-ravaged, crime-tormented section of the city, it is not hard to get people to accept Jesus. People know they need help. Some months ago about fifteen people came forward after a simple evangelistic film. The hard part is the tough love and long hours needed to restore broken lives and disciple mature believers.

Consider, for example, James Dennis, one of my special friends. For several years, we served together as elders in this inner-city church. Twenty years ago, James Dennis was an angry black militant. He hated whites. A few years ago, he said that if he had met me back then, he might have killed me. Thank God, he met Jesus first!

Like so many inner-city young men with few decent job opportunities, James became an alcoholic. His marriage was in trouble, and he landed in prison for a serious crime. While there, someone shared the gospel with him, and he began to experience the transforming grace of Jesus Christ. When he left prison, our pastor walked beside him, supporting and discipling, and James became an active member and then an elder in our church.

James Dennis is a radically different person today. He is still a proud African-American who will not tolerate even the hint of white racism, but God erased his racial hatred and restored his family. He has a good job and owns his own home. Transforming grace has invaded his life.

Anybody who thinks that the best government program on jobs, housing, and prison reform would have been enough to solve James Dennis's problems simply doesn't get it. He needed a personal relationship with Jesus Christ, which has transformed the core of his being, his values, inner convictions, and family life. At the same time, anybody who thinks that being born again, by itself, would have been enough to solve his problems doesn't get it either. James Dennis can be as born again as you like, but if the inner-city school system offers his children a lousy education, if decent housing is unavailable, and there are no jobs to be found, he still has big problems.

Year by year as I struggle with the devastation of America's inner cities, my longing for more Christians and churches who truly combine evangelism and social concern grows deeper and deeper. Brother James needed someone to tell him about Jesus. No social programs could have restored the brokenness at the center of his being, but he and his family also desperately need better employment and educational systems in North Philadelphia. Shouldn't biblical Christians be the ones making sure that people like James are treated fairly?

In God's name, I cry out: Why can't there be thousands and thousands of churches all across our world that meet the needs of the whole person in the name of the Lord whom we worship and follow?

2

Mapping the Terrain: Four Divergent Models

Evangelism and the salvation of souls is the vital mission of the church.

BILLY GRAHAM

God is knowable exclusively in the cry of the poor.

JOSÉ MIRANDA

Most churches today are one-sided disasters. In some suburban churches hundreds of people come to Jesus and praise God in brand-new buildings, but they seldom learn that their new faith has anything to do with wrenching, inner-city poverty just a few miles away. In other churches, the members write their senators and lobby the mayor's office, but they understand little about the daily presence of the Holy Spirit. And they would be stunned if someone asked them personally to invite their neighbors to accept Christ.

One group saves souls. The other reforms structures. That's what I call *lopsided Christianity.*

I remember a troubling conversation with a leading European ecumenical activist in Seoul, Korea, in March 1990. One day, while working together on a committee at an international conference of the WCC, I expressed concern over the sweeping loss of faith in Western Europe. Only about 5 percent of the population goes to church on a typical Sunday in Luther's Germany and many other countries of Europe where the Reformation once shaped society. In spite of widespread church membership, the vast majority of Europeans are no longer confessing Christians.

When I asked my friend how he thought pagan Europe could be won to Christ again, he seemed unconcerned. Things will probably get worse, he shrugged, before they get better. Social action, not evangelizing secularized Europeans, seemed to be his passion.

Similarly, I have discussed with my evangelical colleagues the horrible gaps between, for example, blacks and whites—even within the body of Christ. When topics such as this are brought up, the response is still too often either indifference or outright anger. "Our job is to try to change man's heart, not the structures of society" has been a dominant attitude among evangelicals.

How typical are these attitudes? What are the central themes today in the relationship between evangelism and social concern? And what exactly is the proper biblical relationship between evangelism and social concern?

Twentieth-century Christians have fought ferocious battles over this last question. In fact, in *Transforming Mission,* one of the best books on missiology in decades, David Bosch claims that this question is "one of the thorniest areas in the theology and practice of mission" today.[1]

Most modern views on this question fall within four basic types[2]: Individualistic Evangelical, Radical Anabaptist, Dominant Ecumenical, and Secular Christian. I use an adjective with each type to indicate that the position outlined is not the only possible position that someone using the basic label might adopt. The chart on pages 28–29 outlines the key ideas of each model.

The Underlying Issues

In order to understand these four basic types, it is essential to grasp the underlying issues that shape the different models. They all struggle to answer ten basic questions.

1. How should we understand sin?

Is sin primarily rebellion against God that requires divine forgiveness? Or is it primarily offense against neighbor that demands

27

	Sin	Anthropology	Content of Gospel	Meaning of Salvation	History and Eschatology
MODEL ONE Individualistic Evangelical	emphasis is on personal sins like lying and adultery	people are isolated individuals rather than persons-in-community—strong body-soul dichotomy	salvation of individual	justification and regeneration of individuals	little continuity
MODEL TWO Radical Anabaptist	some emphasis on social sin but main emphasis is on personal sin	people are both individuals personally responsible to God and persons-in-community	Good News of the kingdom	both justification and regeneration of individuals and the new redeemed community of the church	little continuity
MODEL THREE Dominant Ecumenical	personal and social but for many the emphasis falls heavily on the social	a balance of personal and communal	Good News of the kingdom	1) justification and regeneration of individuals 2) church 3) increasing peace and justice in society outside the church is also salvation (for some, this receives the greatest emphasis)	great continuity (in liberal version, there is little emphasis on Christ's return)
MODEL FOUR Secular Christian	offense against neighbor and structural injustice	personal and communal	Good News about the possibility of social progress	justice and peace in society	history is the only reality

Source of Theological Truth	Object of Evangelism	How Is the Gospel Shared?	How Is Society Changed?	Locus of God's Activity
Bible	only persons	largely proclamation of Word	as converted individuals are salt and light	primarily the church (all saving activity occurs there)
Bible	only persons	both word and deed (i.e., the visible demon-stration of the common life of Jesus' new redeemed community, the church)	by converted individuals and the example of the church	primarily the church (all saving activity occurs there)
Bible, reason, tradition, human experience (especially each local context)	persons and social structures	word and deed (which includes both life of church and political action in society)	through conversion, the life of the church, and restructuring societal institutions (in the liberal version, the last is most important)	God's redeeming activity occurs in both the church and the world
reason and human experience are decisive	only social structures	the gospel of social progress is shared via politics	only through restructuring society	only the world

transformed social relationships? Does sin manifest itself primarily in the form of personal sins (such as lying or adultery) directed largely against individuals? Or do we encounter sin primarily in unjust social structures and oppressive societal systems like apartheid, economic injustice, and dictatorships?

2. How should we understand people?

Is the essence of a person her immortal soul that lives for a time in the body and then is released to live in an immaterial heaven? Or is the person a body-soul unity destined to live on a transformed earth? If the soul is the most important aspect of persons, then presumably, "spiritual" things are vastly more important than "physical" or "secular" concerns. Is that distinction biblically inadequate?

Are persons primarily individuals or primarily persons-in-community? Do individual ideas and inner values shape history, or does our environment mold us in powerful ways? In other words, is it only by inner conversion that society is changed, or does societal change create new persons?

3. What is the gospel?

Is it more biblical to summarize the gospel as the Good News of forgiveness or as the Good News of the kingdom of God? Is the core of the Good News that God forgives and regenerates individuals through the cross of Christ? Or is it that the messianic kingdom foreseen by the prophets broke into history in the ministry and person of Jesus, creating a new redeemed community in which all the evils of the world are being corrected? And if the gospel is properly understood as the Good News of the kingdom, does the kingdom come only when people confess Christ, or does it also emerge wherever peace, liberty, and justice develop in society?

4. What is salvation?

Is salvation something that happens only to individuals? Or should we speak of salvation as a social reality in the redeemed community of believers? Or even more widely, should we think of salvation occurring when social structures and societal systems become more just and free whether or not the people in those societies know or confess Jesus Christ? And is there a cosmic character to salvation so that even the "groaning creation" participates in salvation, at least at the end?

When persons experience salvation, will they continue sinful patterns? Or does salvation include a turning away from the distorted, oppressive ways of sinful habits and evil status quos?

Is salvation largely escape from wrath to come or personal and social wholeness now? Is it escape from the world's evil or escape out of the world?

Are people lost without Jesus Christ? Is he the only way to salvation? Will everyone eventually be saved or will some be separated eternally from the living God?

5. *What is the connection between our work now for justice and freedom and the perfection of the coming kingdom that comes only at Christ's return?*

In more technical theological language, what is the connection between history and eschatology? Is the world a sinking ocean liner from which we must rescue as many souls as possible? Or does God intend to conquer the evil that has invaded the good creation and transform the world? Is "heaven" more like sailing with one's grandchildren in an unpolluted Delaware River in a transformed world that is free of all evil? Or is heaven the spiritual bliss of immortal souls in an immaterial world of ideas?

Is the only continuity between life now and life eternal the fact that our response of faith to God's offer of salvation now determines our future destiny? If so, are words and deeds intended to encourage people to accept Christ our only actions that have eternal significance? Or is there some sense in which God cleanses the best of human cultures and incorporates it into the coming kingdom in such a way that our work for peace and justice now has continuity with God's eternal reign?

6. *What is the ultimate source and authority for answering such tough questions?*

Is it God's revelation in the Bible? Tradition? Reason? Or is it found in the historical context of being poor, black, female, or oppressed?

31

Twentieth-century Christians have debated these perennial questions in the context of their search to understand the proper relationship between evangelism and social concern. In the process, they have struggled with four other questions.

7. Who or what is the object of evangelism?

Do we only evangelize persons, or can we also evangelize social systems like multinational corporations and governments?

If we only invite persons to repent and believe, do we only address the gospel to individuals, or can whole villages or communities accept Christ together?

8. How is the gospel shared?

Is it only by words or also by actions? Are deeds of mercy, acts of justice, worship, and fellowship in the church all means of sharing the gospel?

9. How is society changed?

Only as individuals are converted? Only as social systems are changed? What about the alternative lifestyle of Jesus' new community?

10. Where is the primary location of God's activity today?

Is God's primary work occurring now through the church so that worship and fellowship, evangelism, and church planting become the Christian's central concerns? Or is the world the focus of God's activity so that humanizing the social structures becomes a major or even primary occupation? Does the world set the agenda for the church, or does the church question the world on the basis of God's revealed truth? Is the church the exclusive bearer of salvation to a lost world, or is the church merely a preliminary illustration and halting interpreter of what God has already done, is doing, and will do in the world?

These ten questions focus many of the most decisive (and controversial) issues shaping every contemporary idea of how the church should operate in the world today. As we look at the four dominant models on the relationship between evangelism and social concern, these basic questions will surface again and again.

The Individualistic Evangelical Model

Evangelism is the primary mission of the church in the individualistic evangelical model. The most basic concern is the salvation of individual souls.

Billy Graham is the best-known representative of this view. In his keynote address at the International Congress on World Evangelization at Lausanne in 1974, Graham defined evangelism as the announcement of the Good News that "Jesus Christ, very God and very Man, died for my sins on the cross, was buried, and rose the third day." *Evangelism and the salvation of souls is the vital mission of the church.*[3] Like many others in this first category, Graham believes that born-again Christians should challenge racism and oppression and work to improve society. But social justice is "not our priority mission."[4] As the Lausanne Covenant insists, "Evangelism is primary" (section 6).

Within this model, there are two sub-groups. Many, while believing that evangelism is primary, insist that evangelism and social responsibility are both important. Mission includes both. Others want to focus largely, if not exclusively, on evangelism. They argue that mission equals evangelism.

John Stott and the Lausanne Covenant reflect the majority viewpoint. In a keynote at the International Congress on World Evangelization in Lausanne (1974), Stott acknowledged that he had abandoned his earlier view that mission only includes evangelism. Rather, he argued, mission includes all that Christians are sent into the world to do.[5] In the words of the Lausanne Covenant, "evangelism and socio-political involvement are both part of our Christian duty" (section 5). To be sure, "in the church's mission of sacrificial service, evangelism is primary" (section 6). But evangelism and social concern are both crucial and both are part of mission.[6]

A minority disagrees. "Historically, the mission of the church is evangelism alone," Arthur Johnston insisted in his *Battle for World Evangelism.*[7] He believed that evangelicals at Lausanne conceded too much to the World Council of Churches and overemphasized social action.[8] "Evangelism [is] . . . the biblical mission of the church."[9] Donald McGavran, the influential founder of the Church Growth Movement, certainly cared about the poor and oppressed, but his central passion was evangelism and church planting. He, too, defined mission largely as evangelism.[10]

In this model the understanding of persons, sin, the gospel, and salvation all tend to be individualistic. Unconsciously, the Enlightenment's individualism has helped shape this model's view of persons as primarily isolated individuals rather than persons-in-community. The sins usually condemned are personal sins like lying and adultery rather than participation in social evils like economic oppression or institutionalized racism.

For the individualistic evangelical, the gospel is about the justification and regeneration of individuals rather than the dawning messianic kingdom where all areas of life are being redeemed in Jesus' new community of believers. The Wheaton Congress (1966) defined the Good News as "the Gospel of individual salvation."[11] Sometimes this individualism emerges (especially in Lutheran circles) with the claim that the forgiveness of sins in justification "is *the* heart of the gospel message."[12] Salvation is primarily spiritual and eschatological according to Donald Bloesch: "Jesus came to offer deliverance from the power of sin and death rather than from political and economic bondage."[13]

In this model there is virtually no continuity between social justice now and the coming kingdom. Dispensationalism, which has shaped so much of twentieth-century evangelicalism, considered social concern insignificant because society will get worse and worse until Christ's return. According to some popular exponents like Hal Lindsey, that event has often been predicted to be just a few years away. "Christianize the World? Forget it! Evangelize the world, Christian. That is your mission in the world."[14] Dwight L. Moody, the most popular evangelist at the turn of the century, summarized this perspective vividly: "I look upon this world as a wrecked vessel. God has given me a lifeboat and said to me, 'Moody, save all you can.'"[15] The world is doomed, but if we focus on evangelism, individual souls can be rescued for heaven.

From this perspective one can only evangelize persons, not social structures.[16] Communication of the gospel is largely if not entirely through verbal proclamation. The church is the center of God's concern, and the world changes only as converted persons act as salt and light in society.

What do people who adopt this model care most passionately about? Nothing in the world, not even life itself, they believe, is as important as coming to saving faith in Jesus Christ that leads to life eternal in the presence of the risen Lord. The crucified and risen Jesus, the only Son of God, is the one mediator between a holy God and sinful persons. Without him, all are lost. Therefore, nothing dare weaken evangelistic zeal. Tragically, modern skepticism and an exaggerated emphasis on dialogue with other religions have produced a loss of nerve and a neglect of evangelism among many Christians. Equally serious, they believe, is the tendency of liberal Christians to substitute social concern for a lost orthodoxy, seeking to create new persons through transformed social structures. Such utopian schemes forget that the root of evil in the world lies far deeper than oppressive social systems. It comes from humanity's defiant rebellion against God. Only divine grace can create new persons. That process begins now but will only reach completion at Christ's return.[17]

A full critique of this model is premature, but I'd like at least to raise a few questions:

First, with regard to the poor and oppressed, how does this model square with the Bible? In most evangelical churches, you seldom feel the surging passion of Amos's or Isaiah's demand for justice. And little is said about the hundreds of biblical texts on God's concern for the poor. I will never forget a conversation with Frank Gaebelein, one of the great evangelical leaders of this century. Once, toward the end of his life, he told me sadly that he had attended evangelical Bible conferences for six decades but never once had heard a sermon on justice. Many evangelicals have reacted so strongly against a "social gospel" that they have, according to Pentecostal evangelist Peter Kuzmic, combatted "one heresy with another."[18]

Second, does the individualistic understanding of sin and salvation come more from the Enlightenment or the Bible?[19] In fact, isn't it this individualistic understanding of persons that often leads to the naive assumption that converted persons automatically change society? True, converted persons are less likely to do destructive social things like steal, betray their spouse, and refuse to work. But the sociologists are surely right that we are social beings molded in powerful ways by the societal structures that surround us. Exclusive attention to inner conversion is inadequate. One of the most obvious demonstrations of that is the tragic fact that some of the most racist places in South Africa, Northern Ireland, and the United States have been precisely those areas with the highest percentage of born-again Christians. Without a call to costly discipleship and biblical teaching on what discipleship demands in the face of racism and oppression, conversion offers no automatic guarantee of social transformation.

Third, does the sharp division between "spiritual" and "physical" (and the preference for the former) come more from Greek thought than from the Bible? Plato certainly considered the body evil and the soul good (and therefore more important). But did the Hebrew thinkers? Would Amos and Jesus understand and affirm the claim of Harold Lindsell that "the mission of the church is preeminently spiritual [and] revolves around the non-material aspects of life"?[20] In biblical thought is not the person a body-soul unity? And, if Yahweh is Lord of all, is one area of reality less "spiritual" than another?

The Radical Anabaptist Model

In this model, the primary mission of the church is simply to be the corporate body of believers. Anabaptists view sin in much the same way that evangelicals do, but they place more emphasis on being persons-in-community, not lone rangers. As a result, there is greater emphasis on the church. The gospel is the Good News of the kingdom. To be sure, forgiveness and regeneration are still central to the gospel, but they are not all of it. The church is also part of the gospel. By their words, deeds, and life together, Christians evangelize the world by announcing the Good News that by grace it is now possible to live in a new society (the visible body of believers) in which all relationships are being redeemed. The church refuses to live by the social, cultural, and economic values of the Old Age. Instead it lives out the values of Jesus' messianic kingdom in its life together. Consequently it offers to the world a visible model of redeemed (although not yet perfect!) personal, economic, and social relationships. Salvation is therefore personal *and* social. The Good News is that people can now enter this strikingly new community, the church.

Evangelism is very important in this model. In fact, the sixteenth-century Anabaptists were the first Protestant missionaries. They called every Christian to carry out the apostolic mandate to evangelize non-Christians, at a time when Luther and the other Reformers argued that the first-century apostles had fulfilled the Great Commission.[21] But verbal proclamation, however central, is not the only way to evangelize; the loving fellowship of the church is also a powerful evangelistic witness. Evangelism happens by the word of proclamation and the life of discipleship.

Unlike the first model, the radical Anabaptist model's understanding of the gospel and salvation is not individualistic, but it does not equate salvation with socio-political liberation. Sin always has and always will radically corrupt all political programs of social justice designed and implemented by human beings. The church, to be sure, has relevance for social justice in the surrounding society, especially as it provides a model for secular society. But political activity is not the primary task of the church. As John Howard Yoder puts it, "The very existence of the church is her primary task. The primary social structure through which the Gospel works to change other structures is that of the Christian community."[22]

Some radical Anabaptists find no place for political engagement. Jesus proclaimed the kingdom and invited all people to join his new messianic community, but he did not organize Christians for Social Action to lobby the Roman senate. Therefore, say some Anabaptists, Christians today should not engage in direct political activity. Living as converted individuals and offering fallen society the new model of the church are the only ways to change the world.[23]

Other Anabaptists find a small place for direct political engagement, but as Yoder says, "The primary social structure through which the Gospel works to change other structures is that of the Christian community."[24]

Most people in this model care deeply about all the things individualistic evangelicals do. In addition, they want to insist that Jesus' new redeemed community of disciples is part of the gospel of salvation.

What questions should we ask radical Anabaptists?

Does their position not too often result in an exclusive, ethnic, ingrown community? Are not even the most faithful members of Jesus' dawning kingdom also citizens of this world until history ends and Christ returns? Radical Anabaptists may very well be right that Christians have wrongly abandoned Jesus' kingdom ethics for the sake of political "effectiveness." But does the claim that believers dare never sacrifice Jesus' ethics in their political engagement mean that they have no responsibility directly to reshape the larger structures of the world? Might it not be the case that some valid differences between Jesus' situation and ours mean that Christians today should vote and lobby senators even though Jesus did not?

The Dominant Ecumenical Model

Right at the core of this third model is the claim that the conversion of individuals and the political restructuring of society are both central parts of evangelism and salvation. We *can* evangelize both persons and social structures. Salvation includes both what happens when people come to personal faith in Jesus Christ and also what happens when China, Iran, or the United States attain greater justice, freedom, peace, and ecological wholeness. Salvation therefore is personal and social. Unlike model two, in which social salvation refers only to what happens *within* the redeemed community of confessing Christians, social salvation in model three includes socioeconomic liberation in secular and non-Christian society. Therefore the World Council of Churches declared in an important meeting on "Salvation Today" (Bangkok, 1973): "Salvation is the peace of the people in Vietnam, independence in Angola, justice and reconciliation in Northern Ireland."[25]

Both persons and social structures are objects of evangelism, according to an important official document, *Mission and Evangelism,* published by the WCC in 1982. The conversion of individuals is important: "The proclamation of the Gospel includes an invitation to recognize and accept in a personal decision the saving Lordship of Christ. It is the announcement of a personal encounter, mediated by the Holy Spirit, with the living Christ, receiving his forgiveness and making a personal acceptance of the call to discipleship."[26] Few could

38

argue with this position, but the dominant ecumenical says that we must also convert social structures: "The call to conversion, as a call to repentance and obedience, should also be addressed to nations, groups, and families" (section 12). And further: "The Evangelistic Witness will also speak to the structures of this world; its economic, political and societal institutions" (section 15).

The *understanding* of persons and sin is also wholistic. Persons are not isolated individuals but persons-in-community embedded in complex socioeconomic structures. Sin is both personal and social in the WCC's *Mission and Evangelism:* "Sin, alienating persons from God, neighbor and nature, is found in both individual and corporate forms, both in slavery of the human will and in social, political, and economic structures of domination and dependence."[27]

This model is the dominant one in ecumenical circles today. Liberation theologians endorse it.[28] And much Roman Catholic and mainline Protestant thinking runs in parallel lines.

To understand this model, however, it is crucial to see that it has three distinct sub-types: a liberal, a conservative, and a Roman Catholic version.

The Liberal Sub-type

This version de-emphasizes the vertical side of sin and salvation. Sin is primarily ignorance and alienation from neighbor expressed in oppressive social structures. Salvation may take a liberationist or a technological character. At the WCC's Geneva Conference on Church and Society (1966), Richard Shaull looked for salvation primarily in a revolutionary overthrow of what he saw as neo-colonialist imperialistic capitalism. Emmanuel Mesthene hoped for technological progress so that the world's poor could share in the material blessings of the Industrial Revolution already enjoyed in the West.[29] But for both, the primary locus of salvation is global society now, not the church, or life after death.

This liberal version of model three is reflected in the continuing tendency of the WCC to neglect evangelism and major on sociopolitical engagement. Raymond Fung, Secretary for Evangelism at the WCC until 1991, noted a few years ago that within the WCC, the evangelism agenda is "not at all strong."[30]

Much (but certainly not all) Latin American Liberation Theology reflects the liberal version of model three. The sin that liberation theologians usually denounce is social sin—oppressive, socioeconomic structures.[31] According to Gustavo Gutiérrez, the God who liberates in history "can be proclaimed *only with works, with deeds*—in the practice of solidarity with the poor."[32] The distinction between the church and the world largely disappears. That part of salvation that receives the most emphasis is economic liberation in the here and now as democratic socialism replaces capitalist oppression.[33]

The Conservative Sub-type

Not all those who use the broader definitions of evangelism and salvation neglect or de-emphasize the vertical relationship with God. A number of younger evangelical leaders deeply committed to evangelism, the full authority of the Scriptures, and historic Christian orthodoxy argue for this broader terminology.

In *Political Evangelism,* Richard Mouw, now president at Fuller Theological Seminary, uses this broader definition of salvation and evangelism. Mouw by no means abandons or even de-emphasizes the importance of calling persons to faith in Jesus Christ who justifies and regenerates individuals. But salvation is not limited to these areas. The heart of the gospel is that Jesus saves. And Jesus came to save "the entire created order from the pervasive power of sin."[34]

Mouw argues that since the redemptive work of Christ has cosmic implications, therefore all political activity is a part of evangelism.

> The *scope* of the evangelistic activity of the people of God must include the presentation of the *fullness* of the power of the Gospel as it confronts the cosmic presence of sin in the created order. *Political* evangelism (i.e., political activity) then, is one important aspect of this overall task of evangelism.[35]

The late Orlando Costas came to the same conclusion: "The Good News of [Christ's] triumph must be proclaimed in the political, economic and social structures. . . . These, too, must be redeemed by the liberating power of the Gospel."[36]

Indian evangelical theologian, evangelist, and activist Vinay Samuel has argued vigorously for this broader terminology. Samuel is actively engaged in evangelism and church planting among the poor. In a recent conversation, I remember his joy and excitement as he told me about a Sunday service the previous week at which more than two dozen people came forward to accept Christ.

Samuel argues that the kingdom comes and salvation emerges both when people confess Christ and when justice increases. He rejects the traditional distinction between creation and redemption: "Wherever God works in the world, that work is based on the victory Christ won over sin and evil on the cross."[37] To think otherwise is to ignore Colossians 2:14–15, which teaches that Christ disarmed the principalities and powers at the cross.[38]

The kingdom arrives "wherever Jesus overcomes the evil one. This happens in fullest measure in the church, but it happens in society also." We can therefore speak of salvation emerging as Christ works in the world to overcome injustice.[39] At the same time, Samuel does *not* mean that anyone who experiences social justice will also enjoy eternal life with Christ. Rather, he distinguishes the experience of "salvation" enjoyed by non-Christians whose societies improve, from the experience of "salvation" enjoyed by believers who confess Jesus Christ and enter the way of faith that leads to eternal life.[40]

The Roman Catholic Sub-type

The official Roman Catholic viewpoint is very close, at most points, to the conservative sub-type of model three just described. It views sin as personal and social. The kingdom is central to the gospel and is realized in church and society. It defines salvation in broad terms without neglecting the personal and transcendent aspects. Christ is the unique and only Savior of all.

Paul VI's 1975 encyclical, *On Evangelization in the Modern World (Evangelii Nuntiandi [EN])* and John Paul II's (1991) *Mission of the Redeemer (Redemptoris Missio [RM])* and his recent *To the Nations (Ad Gentes)* are, along with earlier documents from Vatican II, the most important statements.[41]

Evangelization is the central concept (especially in *EN*) and it means taking the gospel into every area of society so that persons and cultures are truly transformed by divine grace. "Evangelizing means bringing the Good News into all the strata of humanity." The gospel converts "both the personal and collective consciences of people, the activities in which they engage, and the lives and concrete milieux which are theirs."[42] We start by evangelizing persons, but we can also evangelize cultures and thereby build the kingdom (19–20).

Evangelization happens via the lifestyle of the Christian community (41), verbal proclamation (42), the liturgy (43), catechetical instruction of new Christians (44), and socioeconomic liberation (29–31). The laity evangelize as they transform economics, politics, the media, family, art, and education according to the gospel (70).

Catholic teaching defines salvation broadly without de-emphasizing the transcendent: "Salvation . . . is liberation from everything that oppresses man but . . . is above all liberation from sin and the Evil One" (9). Any reduction of salvation to mere socioeconomic well-being ignores two crucial things: the conversion of individuals and eschatological salvation in the life to come (27, 32). "The church links human liberation and salvation in Jesus Christ, but never identifies them" (35; also *RM,* 11, 17).

Thus far, the Catholic position clearly parallels the conservative sub-type of model three. Some statements of John Paul II, however, might on first reading seem to bring the Catholic position much closer to the liberal view that all people everywhere are saved. John Paul II stated unequivocally in his first encyclical that "every person, without exception, has been redeemed by Christ, and with each person, without any exception, Christ is in some way united, even when that person is not aware of that."[43] This is not a rejection of the uniqueness of Christ. He is the only Savior of the world. But "since salvation is offered to all, it must be made concretely available to all." And many people even today do not hear the gospel. To those, God mysteriously offers salvation through Christ's sacrifice even though they know nothing about Christ or the church (*RM,* 10).

To interpret these statements properly, however, one must remember the Catholic theological distinction between God's offering salvation and our actually appropriating it. The official *Catechism of the Catholic Church,* published in 1992 with the Pope's endorsement as "a sure norm for teaching the faith," clearly and explicitly teaches that some people are condemned to hell, which is "eternal separation from God" (section 1034).[44] The Catholic position is rightly viewed as a conservative sub-type of model three.

What are the central concerns of folk in model three?

They want passionately to insist that working for peace, justice, and the integrity of creation is an essential, central Christian responsibility, grounded in the core of Christian theology. They believe that solidarity with the poor and oppressed is a central criterion of faithful discipleship and mission. They believe that biblical faith is wholistic and that the individualistic ideas about persons, sin, and salvation that have undermined Christian social action actually come from Greek thought and the Enlightenment, not from the Bible.

Difficult questions also surface for model three. Does the Bible make a strong case for using salvation language (and kingdom language) to talk about the emergence of justice or peace in society? And what about the claim that all people—believers and nonbelievers alike—experience salvation when justice increases? Doesn't this lead to either universalism (all will be saved) or a two-tiered concept of salvation (Salvation I: enjoyed by non-Christians when society improves; Salvation II: enjoyed by those who confess Christ)?

Is this two-tiered understanding of salvation really helpful? Might not the older language of justice based in creation and salvation grounded in redemption be less complex and confusing?

Similarly, does the Bible support the notion of evangelizing social structures? Should we ask secular (or Islamic) government institutions to repent of their sins, seek baptism and church membership, and enter on the path to eternal life with Christ? If evangelism is defined to include development and politics as well as activities designed to lead nonbelievers to faith in Christ, then again we face a dilemma. Either the question of balance between evangelism and social ministry is moot because they are identical, or we distinguish between Evangelism I (development and social action in the name of Christ) and Evangelism II (activity whose primary purpose is inviting non-Christians to accept Christ). Again one must ask whether this two-tiered definition of evangelism is really more illuminating than the older distinction between evangelism and social action.

The liberal sub-type of model three raises further questions. Is it not a substantial departure from biblical teaching to understand sin as primarily social and salvation as primarily socioeconomic liberation? Dare Christians make the search for peace and justice more important than spreading the gospel to those who do not know Christ? From the biblical perspective is there not a sharp distinction between the church and the world? Is solidarity with the poor *the* criterion of faithful discipleship?

To those who tend toward universalism, we must ask, Does the Bible really teach that everyone is or will be saved? If not, on what authority dare we make such claims?[45]

The Secular Christian Model

In this model, evangelism is merely politics and salvation is only social justice. This fourth model abandons the uniqueness of Christ and in some cases even belief in God. Horizontal concerns totally eclipse the vertical. Sin is injury to neighbor, not offense against God. What salvation we dare hope for arrives in history through restructuring society. Knowing God is nothing more than seeking justice for the oppressed. In the words of José Miranda in *Marx and the Bible*, "To know Yahweh is to achieve justice for the poor."[46] Or again, "The God who does not allow himself to be objectified, because only in the immediate command of conscience is he God, clearly specifies that he is knowable *exclusively* in the cry of the poor and the weak who seek justice."[47]

Several roads lead to model four.

Western secularism is one. The Enlightenment's rejection of the supernatural and the stunning triumph of modern science and technology led many to abandon the transcendent and look for meaning in technological progress. In *Christianity in World History,* Arend Van Leeuwen promoted a theology of secularization. The modern technological revolution, he argued, is the source both of material abundance and secularism's rejection of traditional Christian beliefs. Therefore Christians should, Van Leeuwen concluded, embrace this secularism as the essence of Christian faith, focus on the search for peace, justice, and human well-being, and be totally unconcerned if, for example, India remains Hindu forever.[48]

The preparatory documents for the WCC's Uppsala assembly (1968) come close to this perspective. In earlier times, they acknowledged, Christians assumed that "the purpose of mission

44

was Christianization, bringing man to God through Christ and his church." Today the goal of mission is the humanization of society: "What else can the churches do than recognize and proclaim what God is doing in the world?"[49]

Gibson Winter expressed it powerfully:

> Secularization recognizes history and its problems of meaning as the sphere of man's struggles for salvation. . . . The categories of biblical faith are freed from their miraculous and supernatural garments. . . . Why are men not simply called to be human in their historical obligations, for this is man's true end and his salvation?[50]

Another path to the same result is the rejection of the uniqueness of Christ. In the 1930s William Hocking led an ecumenical commission to rethink Christian mission and concluded that Christians should abandon evangelism and join all religions in the search for God and a decent world.[51] John Hick, Paul Knitter, and Marian Bohen come to the same conclusion today. After years of living among Muslims, Bohen has concluded that any claim to an absolute truth that seeks to evangelize leads to intergroup violence. We should listen to the songs of Hindus and Muslims and try their dances but never urge them to abandon their own music. The God of Abraham, Sarah, Jesus, Muhammed, and Buddha created all humankind to live in solidarity. That is mission enough.[52]

People who adopt model four seek honestly to listen with integrity to people of other faiths. They also confront squarely the implications of modern science as they understand it. But can a person abandon the uniqueness of Jesus Christ and still maintain the substance of Christian faith?

Certainly there is much to learn from each of these models but all are inadequate. I make that judgment on the basis of what I believe to be the biblical understanding of the gospel, salvation, conversion, and social concern. In the next six chapters we will explore what the Bible says about those themes. Then, in chapters nine and ten, I will offer a fifth model, one that I call Incarnational Kingdom Christianity.

PART 2

THE GOSPEL
OF THE KINGDOM

3

The Dawning Kingdom

I must preach the good news of the kingdom of God . . . because
that is why I was sent.

LUKE 4:43

When I first visited Te Atatu Christian Fellowship in Auckland,
New Zealand, in 1986, I glimpsed a miniature of Christ's dawning kingdom.

White and black, rich and poor, uneducated and educated worshiped the risen Lord together in the joy of the Holy Spirit. For the
decade of 1978–1988, vigorous evangelism resulted in over one
thousand conversions! Many of the new converts were poor and
jobless, so the congregation began developing a variety of ministries
to assist both these new believers and other needy folk as well. A
drug rehabilitation farm, a modestly priced housing cooperative,
emergency accommodation, a trust providing interest-free loans,
and a Christian bookstore are all a part of Te Atatu's community
life. So are miraculous signs and wonders. In the power of the Spirit,
bodies are healed, drug addicts are restored, broken marriages are
renewed, and non-Christians come to know Christ.

My wife, Arbutus, daughter, Sonya, and I visited Te Atatu again
in August 1990. Again we witnessed the presence of the kingdom.
We stayed with one of the eldership team, Brian Hathaway, and his

wife, Noeleen. Their daughter, Sharon, quickly included our daughter, Sonya, in her youth group's activities of worshiping, playing, and evangelizing. Arbutus and I will be forever grateful for the way God used that time with Sharon to touch Sonya's life in a powerful way.

Out of the experiences of this congregation, Hathaway has recently written an excellent book, *Beyond Renewal: The Kingdom of God*.[1] He is not satisfied with congregations that focus exclusively on social action, or exclusively on evangelism, or exclusively on charismatic renewal. All belong together, he argues, insisting that a biblical view of the gospel of the kingdom shows how all three fit together.

Differing Views of the Kingdom

Have you noticed the growing use of the word *kingdom*? Social activists, charismatics, and advocates of world evangelization often refer to the kingdom and sometimes even cite the same texts to support their different (frequently one-sided) concerns.[2]

Social activists quote Luke 4:16ff. to prove that faithful Christians, like Jesus, must meet the physical and social needs of the poor, blind, lame, and oppressed.

Charismatics quote Luke 4:16ff. to demonstrate that faithful Christians, like Jesus, should be "filled with the power of the Spirit" and therefore perform miraculous signs and wonders.

Proponents of world evangelization cite Luke 4:16ff. (less often, however, until recently) to show that faithful Christians, like Jesus, will preach Good News to those who have not yet heard.

Tragically, each group sometimes ignores or even rejects the concerns of the others.

The different interpretations of specific texts, of course, result from fundamentally divergent understandings of the kingdom.[3] Medieval Catholicism, on the one hand, tended to identify the kingdom with the institutional, visible church. Modern social activists, on the other hand, have viewed the kingdom largely as a socioeconomic-political reality that human beings can create through politics—whether democratic politics in the social gospel movement or Marxist revolution in some liberation theology. Many twentieth-century evangelicals understand the kingdom largely as an inner spiritual reality in the souls of believers: "The kingdom of God is the present inner rule of God in the moral and spiritual dispositions of the soul with its seat in the heart."[4] Other conservative Christians (in the dispensationalist tradition of Darby and the *Scofield Reference Bible*) have seen the kingdom as entirely future. They believe that when Jesus' Jewish contemporaries rejected him as Messiah, the kingdom was postponed. Therefore the kingdom will come only at the end of history, when the one thousand years of millennial reign occur. Not until then will Jesus' kingdom ethics be normative.[5]

Such contradictory views cannot be fully reconciled. It may be possible, however, to discover correct insights in each as we look again at the New Testament and seek anew the full biblical understanding of the kingdom.

The Centrality of the Kingdom

Unless Matthew, Mark, and Luke are totally wrong, all who want to preach and live like Jesus must place the "kingdom of God" at the center of their thought and action. This phrase (or Matthew's equivalent, the "kingdom of heaven") appears 122 times in the first three Gospels—most of the time (92) on the lips of Jesus himself.[6]

Jesus points to the kingdom as the purpose of his coming. Both his preaching and his miraculous healing are signs of the kingdom. And he sends out his disciples to announce the kingdom.

For Mark, the kingdom is the best summary of his entire Gospel: "After John was put in prison, Jesus went into Galilee, proclaiming the good news of God. 'The time has come,' he said. 'The kingdom of God is near. Repent and believe the good news'" (Mark 1:14–15). Jesus explicitly defines his own mission in these terms: "I must preach the good news of the kingdom of God to the other towns also, because that is why I was sent" (Luke 4:43).

Jesus' response to John the Baptist demonstrates that Jesus viewed his preaching and healing as signs of the kingdom. In Luke 7:18–28, we read the story of the visit to Jesus by the disciples of John. They ask whether Jesus is the "one who was to come"—i.e., the long-expected Messiah who will usher in the messianic kingdom of God. For his answer, Jesus points to his preaching and his healing of the blind, the lame, and even the socially ostracized lepers.[7] Later, in his argument with the Pharisees, he makes the same claim, insisting that his miraculous casting out of demons is visible proof that the kingdom has begun (Matt. 12:28).

When Jesus sends out his disciples, he commands them to preach and demonstrate the kingdom in the same way. "As you go," he commissions the Twelve, "preach this message: 'The kingdom of heaven is near.' Heal the sick, raise the dead, cleanse those who have leprosy, drive out demons" (Matt. 10:7–8). The seventy-two disciples receive the same instructions: "Heal the sick . . . and tell them, 'The kingdom of God is near you'" (Luke 10:9).

If anything is clear in Jesus, it is that the announcement and demonstration of the kingdom are at the very core of his message and life. As New Testament scholar Norman Perrin has said, no scholar today doubts that "the central aspect of the teaching of Jesus was that concerning the Kingdom of God."[8]

The Expectation of the Kingdom

To understand what Jesus meant by the kingdom of God, we must recall the prophets' messianic hope.

When God called his chosen people out of Egypt, he wanted them, *as a society,* to be a visible demonstration of God's will for all: "You will be for me a kingdom of priests and a holy nation" (Exod. 19:6). Therefore God gave the law, showing them how to worship God, do justice, share the land, enact fair laws, and maintain strong families. Tragically, they preferred idolatry and oppression. The result was God's blazing anger and refining fire, which sent first Israel and then Judah into foreign captivity.

The prophets, however, looked beyond devastating national destruction. They foresaw a future day when God's Messiah would come to pour out the Spirit in a new way (Joel 2:28–29) and restore God's people as a visible community living in right relationship with God, neighbor, and earth.

Jeremiah 31:31–34 shows that right relationship with God was at the center of the messianic hope. In the messianic time when God makes a new covenant with Israel and Judah, God promises to "forgive their wickedness and . . . remember their sins no more" (v. 34).

With forgiveness goes inner transformation because God also pledges to "put [his] law in their minds and write it on their hearts" (v. 33). A renewed relationship with God was central to the messianic hope.

Equally important was the ringing declaration that the Messiah would restore right relationships with neighbor. "In the last days" (the prophets' shorthand for the messianic time), "they will beat their swords into plowshares and their spears into pruning hooks" (Isa. 2:4). The parallel passage in Micah also foresaw a productive, just economic order: "They shall all sit under their own vines and under their own fig trees, and no one shall make them afraid" (Micah 4:4 NRSV). Not just inner hearts or individual relationships with a few neighbors but the whole social order will be transformed (Isa. 42:1–4).

> For to us a child is born,
> to us a son is given,
> and the government will be on his shoulders.
> And he will be called
> Wonderful Counselor, Mighty God,
> Everlasting Father, Prince of Peace.
> Of the increase of his *government* and peace [shalom]
> there will be no end.
> He will reign on David's throne
> and over his kingdom,
> establishing and upholding it
> with justice and righteousness
> from that time on and forever.
>
> ISAIAH 9:6–7, EMPHASIS ADDED

The prophets had long taught that God was especially concerned for the poor, weak, and marginalized.[9] Therefore it is hardly surprising that justice for the poor was central to their vision of the new messianic society. Of the messianic shoot from the stump of Jesse, the prophet predicted: "With righteousness he will judge the needy, with justice he will give decisions for the poor of the earth" (Isa. 11:4).

In their soaring messianic vision, the prophets even dared to hope for renewed relationships with the nonhuman creation:

53

"The infant will play near the hole of the cobra and the young child put his hand into the viper's nest. They will neither harm nor destroy on all my holy mountain, for the earth will be full of the knowledge of the LORD as the waters cover the sea" (Isa. 11:8–9).

The Hebrew word *shalom* (peace) is probably the best single word to capture the fullness of the messianic hope. *Shalom* means wholeness and right relationships with God, neighbor, and earth.[10]

In the midst of oppression, idolatry, and captivity, the prophets looked to the future messianic time. In that day, in the power of the Spirit, the Messiah would bring transformed relationships with God, neighbor, and earth. There would be a new society genuinely living according to God's righteous laws finally inscribed on people's hearts and wills.

The Fulfillment of the Prophetic Hope for the Kingdom

The early church declared Jesus to be the fulfillment of these breathtaking messianic prophecies. Matthew 4:15–16 quotes Isaiah 9:1–2 in connection with the beginning of Jesus' proclamation of the coming of the messianic kingdom. Paul refers to Isaiah 11:1 and 10 in Romans 15:12. In Luke 1:68–79, Zechariah announces that John the Baptist will prepare the way for Jesus, the Messiah. Quoting Isaiah 9:2, Zechariah points with eager anticipation to the Messiah who will "guide our feet into the path of peace" (Luke 1:79). When the angels (Luke 2:14) announce Jesus' birth with the choral shout "on earth peace," they simply confirm the dawning fulfillment of the prophetic vision of messianic *shalom*.

Shivers of excitement must have raced through first-century Jewish listeners when Jesus announced the ringing words: "'The time has come. . . . The kingdom of God is near. Repent, and believe the Good News.'" I believe that Jesus meant two things: He meant that he was the long-expected Messiah, and he meant that the messianic age was breaking into the present.[11]

Present and Future

Vigorous scholarly debate has raged over whether Jesus thought the kingdom was entirely future or entirely present, or partially future and partially present. Some (such as C. H. Dodd) have argued that the kingdom was entirely present in his life and work. Others (such as Albert Schweitzer) have insisted that for Jesus the kingdom was exclusively future. It would come only at the end of the age. Dispensationalists long believed that the kingdom was postponed until the millennium because Jesus' Jewish contemporaries rejected him as Messiah.

There is a growing consensus, however, that Jesus viewed the kingdom as both present and future. Jewish eschatology (belief about the "last things") looked forward to a supernatural convulsion when the Messiah would come to destroy Israel's national enemies in a bloody battle and initiate the new age of messianic peace. In Jewish expectation, on the one hand, there was a fundamental, almost total, break between the old age and the new messianic age. Jesus, on the other hand, taught that the messianic age had actually broken into the old age. Its powers were already at work in this old age in his person and work, even though the kingdom would come in its fullness only at the end of history.

Several incidents from the Gospels support the view that Jesus considered the messianic kingdom to be already present. In Luke's account of the visit to the synagogue at Nazareth, Jesus read from Isaiah 61:1–2, widely accepted as a messianic passage. A tremor of anticipation must have surged through the synagogue as they listened to the words about the coming Messiah who would, in the power of the Spirit, release captives, heal the blind, and liberate the oppressed. When he was finished, Jesus informed the audience, "Today this scripture is fulfilled in your hearing" (Luke 4:21).

Earlier, we examined Jesus' response to John the Baptist's question about whether he was the expected Messiah. Using language that echoed Isaiah 1 and pointing to his ministry to the poor, sick, and marginalized, he said that his actions were answer enough.[12]

And after a dispute with the Pharisees about the source of his power over demons, Jesus declared: "If I drive out demons by the Spirit of God, then the kingdom of God *has come* upon you"

(Matt. 12:28, emphasis added). These incidents suggest the kingdom is truly present.[13]

In Jesus' thinking, a fundamental break in history was occurring: "The Law and the Prophets were proclaimed until John [the Baptist]. Since that time, the good news of the kingdom is being preached" (Luke 16:16). The messianic kingdom has begun.

Yet, Jesus knew that the kingdom had not reached its culmination. The parables of growth demonstrate that the kingdom grows slowly now. Only in the future will the harvest (a symbol of consummation) arrive (Mark 4:3–8).[14] Sin and evil continued to flourish so Jesus looked ahead to the close of the age when the kingdom would come in its fullness (e.g., Luke 21:27). And, as his response to the thief on the cross reveals, when, before that time, death overtakes those who trust in Jesus, they promptly enter his eternal kingdom. The thief on the cross pleaded, "Jesus, remember me when you come into your kingdom." Jesus responded: "Today you will be with me in paradise." Mortimer Arias's comment on this exchange is superb: "Jesus, who had announced the Good News to the poor in this life, still had Good News for the poor beyond this life, when nothing could be expected from history. Jesus' evangelization, therefore, is truly holistic—for this world and for the world to come!"[15]

The kingdom then had broken decisively into history in the person and work of Jesus the Messiah. But it would come in its fullness only at the return of the Son of Man on the clouds of heaven (Matt. 24:30). On that day, people will come from East and West to celebrate the messianic banquet in the final kingdom (Matt. 8:11).

Entering the Kingdom

Jesus' teaching differed sharply from that of his contemporaries. The Pharisees believed that the Messiah would come if all Jews would obey the law perfectly. The violent revolutionaries of the time thought that the Messiah would come if all Jews would join in armed rebellion against Roman imperialism.[16] Jesus' way was (and still is) radically different. The kingdom comes as sheer gift. We enter not by good deeds or social engineering, but only as we repent and accept God's forgiveness.

In parable after parable, Jesus underlined God's acceptance of sinners (e.g., Luke 18:9–14). The merciful Father in heaven is like the father who forgives the prodigal son. Even though this foolish upstart had squandered half the family fortune on extravagance and prostitutes, the father welcomed his repentant son back as a full member of the family (Luke 15:11–32). Jesus dealt gently with the adulteress (John 8:1–11). To the intense disgust of the Pharisees, he publicly embraced and dined with scandalous sinners like tax collectors and harlots.[17]

It is not the self-righteous Pharisee but the greedy, oppressive tax collector agonizing over his wickedness whom God forgives (Luke 18:9–14). Only as we come as humble children with no claims can we enter Christ's kingdom: "Unless you change and become like little children, you will never enter the kingdom of heaven" (Matt. 18:3). When we do, we experience the boundless, eager mercy of God: "Do not be afraid, little flock, for your Father has been pleased to *give* you the kingdom" (Luke 12:32, emphasis added). That same understanding of God led Jesus to die as the ransom for our sins (Matt. 20:28). Central to any biblical understanding of the kingdom is that we enter it by sheer grace and divine forgiveness. The kingdom comes as gift.

The Kingdom Becomes Visible

Jesus was not a lone ranger. He did not travel around the countryside declaring God's forgiveness to isolated hermits. Jesus formed a new society. He gathered a new community of forgiven disciples, who challenged evil and proclaimed the gospel.

A Forgiven and Forgiving Community

Zacchaeus symbolizes Jesus' new community of forgiven sinners. As a tax collector for imperialistic Rome, Zacchaeus was an affluent oppressor and a despised social outcast, but Jesus' astonishing acceptance and forgiveness overwhelmed him. In gratitude he offered the same love to others, making fourfold restitution for dishonest profit and giving half his goods to the poor (Luke 19:2–10).

Jesus' repeated linkage of God's forgiveness and our forgiving others underlines the point. Jesus tells the parable of the unforgiving servant (Matt. 18:21–35) to answer Peter's question about how often he must forgive other brothers and sisters in the community. Peter thought seven times might do! Jesus said seventy times seven—i.e., *indefinitely.* That is the context for Jesus' powerful parable of the unforgiving servant: "The kingdom of heaven is like a king . . ." (v. 23) who forgives a prominent servant millions of dollars. Incredibly that same servant instantly turns around and callously tosses one of his own obscure servants into jail for a few dollars. Furious, the king commands prison and torture for the merciless rascal. Jesus ends the story with the disturbing words: "So my heavenly Father will also do to every one of you if you do not forgive your brother or sister from your heart" (v. 35 NRSV).

Again and again Jesus repeats this point. In the Lord's Prayer we ask God to "forgive us our debts, as we also have forgiven our debtors" (Matt. 6:12). Immediately after the prayer, Jesus emphasizes the point in the strongest way: "If you forgive others their trespasses, your heavenly Father will also forgive you; but if you do not forgive others, neither will your Father forgive your trespasses" (vv. 14–15 NRSV).

Jesus is not teaching that our good deeds earn God's favor. But the Creator who made us for community has decided that divine forgiveness will not remain with those who violate community by withholding forgiveness from the offending neighbor.[18] The foundation of Jesus' new community is radical divine forgiveness grounded finally in Jesus' cross. And that sweeping forgiveness, as Ephesians 2:11–16 demonstrates, creates a new community of forgiving sinners.

Jesus' New Community

Jesus, the kingdom, and all the blessings of the kingdom are inseparable. One cannot have the ethics of the kingdom or the forgiveness of the kingdom apart from Jesus.

Matthew reports a whole string of instances in which Jesus summons people with the simple words: "Follow me."[19] Jesus tells the rich young man to give all his wealth to the poor, "then come, follow me" (Mark 10:21). In verse 29, Jesus identifies himself with the gospel he proclaims. Anyone who surrenders all "for me and the gospel," Jesus promises, will enjoy the eternal kingdom.

The kingdom's forgiveness that Jesus announces is inseparable from his person. In Mark 2:10, Jesus heals the paralytic explicitly to demonstrate that he has authority to forgive sins—an authority grounded finally in the fact that at the center of his entire mission was his intention to die as a ransom for our sins (Mark 10:45).

Jesus, the kingdom, and the forgiven kingdom community are inseparable. John Paul II is right: "The kingdom of God is not a concept, a doctrine, or a program subject to free interpretation, but it is before all else *a person* with the face and name of Jesus of Nazareth, the image of the invisible God. If the kingdom is separated from Jesus, it is no longer the kingdom of God which he revealed."[20]

4

A Disturbing Kingdom Community

I thank Thee Lord, that Thou hast not made me a Gentile . . .
Thou hast not made me a slave . . . Thou hast not made me
a woman.

FIRST-CENTURY PRAYER FOR JEWISH MEN

There is neither Jew nor Greek, slave nor free, male nor female,
for you are all one in Christ Jesus.

GALATIANS 3:28

I get uncomfortable whenever I see people who profess to be
Christians growing complacent with sin. Whether it's an issue
of personal immorality (marital infidelity, for example) or corporate immorality (unfair labor practices, for another example), followers of Christ ought to abhor wrongdoing. In fact, Jesus and
his new community of disciples challenged evil wherever they
found it. This wasn't merely some inward spiritual challenge or a
gauntlet thrown down to the religious leaders. To be sure, it
included that because he regularly denounced hypocrisy and
blasted the religious leadership. But he also challenged the economic establishment, overturned social values and customs about
women, and defied the political leadership. Precisely because Jesus
knew how good the Creator intends culture and civilization to
be, he challenged surrounding society wherever sin had introduced brokenness.

Battling the Kingdom of Darkness

Although Jesus challenged the evil of his day, it would be wrong to think of him as a sort of celestial consumer advocate. In other words, he wasn't just interested in challenging the status quo. Behind wicked persons and twisted social patterns, Jesus saw the work of Satan and his demonic forces. At the heart of his announcement of the kingdom is total warfare with the Evil One who has introduced devastation into the good creation.

Remember, Jesus battled Satan in the wilderness before he began his public ministry (Luke 4:1–13). In Mark, Jesus' first miracle resulted when a demon-possessed man recognized Jesus as "the Holy One of God." Quickly Jesus ordered the evil spirit to leave (Mark 1:21–26). Again and again, Jesus cast out demons. In fact, he cited his victory over the demonic forces as a sign that the messianic kingdom had broken in (Luke 11:20). And when the seventy-two disciples returned rejoicing over their power to cast out demons, Jesus said, "I saw Satan fall like lightning from heaven" (Luke 10:18). Jesus saw himself as the strong man binding the demonic powers (Luke 11:22) that moved behind the broken social values and patterns he confronted.

Challenging the Evils of the Status Quo

Rich and Poor

Jesus shocked the rich with his words about sharing. He told the rich young man who came inquiring about eternal life (and, probably, membership in Jesus' new circle as well) that he would have to sell his vast holdings and give all his wealth to the poor. As the wealthy youth turned away sadly, Jesus added a comment that still jars all of us who are rich: "It is easier for a camel to go through the eye of a needle than for a rich man to enter the kingdom of God" (Luke 18:25). When another wealthy person responded in obedient repentance, he gave half of his vast riches to the poor (Luke 19:2–10). Jesus urged the rich to make loans to the poor, even if there was no reasonable hope of repayment (Luke 6:34–35). Those who do not feed the hungry and clothe the naked, he said, go to hell (Matt. 25:31–46). If, as a number of modern scholars argue, Jesus understood his ministry as an implementation of a messianic Jubilee (cf. Lev. 25), that simply underlines what is unmistakably clear in any case.[1] Jesus offered a sweeping challenge to an uncaring wealthy establishment.

The other side of this challenge to the rich was a powerful identification with the poor. Born in a stable, introduced to the agony of refugees as a child, Jesus, the wandering teacher, had no house of his own (Matt. 8:20). The poor flocked to him. He fed and healed the needy.

It is especially important to understand Jesus' teaching that his messianic kingdom is especially for the poor.

> Blessed are you who are poor,
>   for yours is the kingdom of God.
> Blessed are you who hunger now,
>   for you will be satisfied.
>
> LUKE 6:20–21[2]

When John the Baptist asked if he was the Messiah, Jesus pointed to the fact that he healed the sick and preached the gospel of the kingdom to the poor (Luke 7:21–22). The inaugural address in the synagogue at Nazareth includes the same statement about preaching to the poor (Luke 4:18). One simply does not understand Jesus' teaching on the kingdom unless one sees that he was especially concerned that the poor realize that the kingdom breaking into history was particularly good news for them. Our proclamation of the gospel is simply unbiblical unless we, like Jesus, focus special attention on the poor.

That does not mean, however, that "*the* missionary yardstick is the relation of the Church to the poor."[3] Nor does it mean, with liberation theologian Leonardo Boff, that "the poor are the *primary* addressees of Jesus' message and constitute *the* eschatological criterion by which the salvation or perdition of every human being is determined."[4] A proper concern for and relationship to the poor is not *the* (i.e., the only decisive) measure of faithful discipleship and faithful communication of the gospel of the kingdom.[5] At the same time, one dare not spiritualize Jesus' announcement of the Good News and blessing to the poor and suggest that Jesus was directing the poor to take comfort in the treasures of heaven where moth and rust do not corrupt.[6]

The heretical neglect of the poor by many affluent Christians is a flat rejection of the Lord of the church. If Jesus is the norm, then faithful Christian sharing of the gospel will make the poor *one* major priority in such a way that the poor in the world today are as convinced as the poor in Jesus' day that the gospel is fantastic news for them—precisely because Jesus' new kingdom community embraces the poor, invites them to personal faith, welcomes them into their fellowship, and shares economically so that, in the words of Acts, "there is no poor among them."

We have already seen that at the center of Jesus' proclamation was the announcement that the long-expected prophetic hope for the Messiah was now being fulfilled in his own life and work. At the core of the prophetic promise was the belief that the Messiah would bring justice to the poor. Jesus and his new community did precisely that. The common purse of Jesus and his followers was, in part, in order to share with the poor.[7] Jesus assured his disciples that those who give up everything for him and his gospel of the kingdom "will receive a hundred times as much in *this present* age (homes, brothers, sisters, mothers, children, and fields)" (Mark 10:30). He meant that the messianic time of justice was breaking in and his messianic community was already sharing in such a sweeping way that the resources of all were available to any who were in need. The result, as Acts 2 and 4 demonstrate, was that there were no poor among Jesus' circle of disciples. It is no wonder that the poor rejoiced. Nor is it surprising that Jesus called them blessed.

The Marginalized

Jesus' special concern for the poor extended to all the marginalized, weak, and socially ostracized. In sharp contrast to his contemporaries, Jesus demonstrated a special interest in the disabled, children, drunkards, prostitutes, and lepers (cf. Luke 7:32–50; 19:1–10). In Jesus' day, lepers experienced terrible ostracism (Luke 17:12), living alone in awful poverty, shouting "unclean, unclean" lest anyone accidentally touch them. Jesus gently touched the lepers and miraculously healed them (Mark 1:41).

From the Dead Sea Scrolls, we learn that the Essenes, a Jewish religious group of Jesus' day, actually *excluded* the disabled from the religious community:

> No one who is afflicted with any human impurity may come into the assembly of God. . . . Anyone who is . . . maimed in hand or foot, lame or blind or deaf or dumb or with a visible mark in his flesh. . . . These may not enter or take their place in the midst of the community.[8]

Jesus, by contrast, commands the members of his new messianic community to invite *precisely* these people: "When you give a banquet, invite the poor, the crippled, the lame, the blind" (Luke 14:13). In the parable of the great banquet, Jesus repeats the lesson, teaching that his kingdom is for "the poor, the crippled, the blind and the lame" (Luke 14:21). Jesus was directly defying contemporary norms and social practices.

The frequent charge that Jesus offered table fellowship with "sinners" underlines the way Jesus reached out to social outcasts. The Pharisees drew a sharp line between those who kept the law and those who did not. The word *sinners* in the Gospels often refers to the non-observant folk (including many poor people) who regularly failed to keep the law to the Pharisees' satisfaction. The Pharisees called such folk "sinners" and refused to eat with them.[9] Tax collectors, who collaborated with the oppressive Roman imperialists, were among the most despised. Their occupation was one of seven occupations in Jesus' time that automatically deprived persons of Jewish civil and political rights.[10] (Since shepherds were also in this list, the angel's appearance to the Bethlehem shepherds was a clear signal that Jesus would identify with the marginalized.)

Jesus frequently ate with these outcasts. The Pharisees just as regularly objected! "Now the tax collectors and sinners were all gathering round to hear him. But the Pharisees and the teachers of the law muttered, 'This man welcomes sinners and eats with them'" (Luke 15:1–2; cf. also 7:34; 19:7; Mark 2:15). Jesus' response was to tell the parables of the lost sheep, lost coin, and lost son (Luke 15:3–32). God is like the shepherd who seeks the lost sheep and the father who forgives the prodigal. Therefore Jesus welcomes the socially marginalized into his kingdom where God's transforming power will change them. He even chooses "Matthew the tax collector" (Matt. 10:3) as one of his twelve disciples. What outrage!

Women

Jesus' attitude toward women reflects the same sweeping challenge to the status quo. In Jesus' day, it was a scandal for a man to appear in public with a woman. A woman's word was considered useless in court.[11] It was better to burn a copy of the Torah (the first five books of the Old Testament) than to allow a woman to touch it. Indeed, according to one first-century statement, "If any man teach his daughter Torah, it is as though he taught her lechery."[12] Women were excluded from most parts of the temple. Nor did they count in calculating the quorum needed for a meeting in the synagogue.[13] The Jewish prayer I quoted at the beginning of this chapter is not a joke![14] First-century Jewish men regularly thanked God that they were not Gentiles, slaves, or women.

Jesus and his new community rejected centuries of male prejudice and treated women as equals. Jesus appeared with women in public (John 4:27) and taught them theology (Luke 10:38–42). He allowed a woman that everybody knew was a sinner to wash his feet with her tears, wipe them with her long hair, kiss and perfume them—all in public (Luke 7:36–50)! When Mary abandoned her traditional role of cooking food to listen to Jesus' theology lesson, Martha objected. But Jesus defended Mary (Luke 10:38–42). Jesus rejected Moses' teaching on divorce, which allowed a man (but not a woman) to dismiss his spouse if she did not find favor in his eyes (Deut. 24:1–2). Jesus called both husband and wife to live together in lifelong covenant (Mark 10:1–12).[15] It was surely no accident that Jesus granted the first resurrection appearance to women!

Luke 8:1–3 describes what Mortimer Arias calls the "first and most amazing evangelistic team ever assembled in the history of Christian mission."[16]

> Jesus traveled about from one town and village to another, proclaiming the good news of the kingdom of God. The Twelve were with him, and also some women who had been cured of

evil spirits and diseases: Mary (called Magdalene) from whom seven demons had come out; Joanna, the wife of Cuza, the manager of Herod's household; Susanna; and many others. These women were helping to support them out of their own means.

What a shocking spectacle. This is not the normal homogeneous unit of a male rabbi with his male students. Rather, it is women and men together publicly announcing the kingdom. Arias wonders what King Herod's budget director thought about his notorious wife's scandalous activity.[17] And the women look more like breadwinners than cooks. "They were as heterogeneous as they could be: men and women, clergy and laity, fishermen, tax collectors, matrons, former prostitutes, the affluent and the poor!"[18] Centrally involved in this radical demonstration of Jesus' new kingdom community were women, publicly and actively ministering with him.

In its attitude toward women, the early church continued to live Jesus' messianic challenge to the status quo. Messianic prophecy had foretold that in the last days, daughters and sons, women and men would prophesy (Joel 2:28). That happened in the early church. Women prophesied (Acts 21:9; 1 Cor. 11:5) and corrected the theology of men (Acts 18:24–26).[19] Liberated from the restrictions of the synagogue, women participated enthusiastically in the early church's worship services. Paul joyously boasted that in Christ, there is "neither Jew nor Greek, slave nor free, male nor female" (Gal. 3:28).

One understands this incredible claim about early Christian community only when one remembers that Paul is probably referring explicitly to the common Jewish prayer quoted above where men thank God that they are *not* Gentiles, slaves, or women. What an astonishing upsetting of the status quo! Jesus and his new community of women and men were indeed an upside-down kingdom.[20]

Jesus' challenge to current society did not end, however, with his approach to the poor and marginalized. Jesus also summoned the powerful to repent and change. Leaders should be servants. Love for enemies should replace vengeance.

Political Leadership

Jesus must have infuriated Herod. When someone warned him that Herod wanted to kill him, Jesus shot back his response: "Go tell that fox . . ." (Luke 13:32). In Jesus' day, that word meant about the same thing as the slang use of the word *skunk* does today.[21]

In Jesus' time as today, rulers enjoyed dominating their subjects. Jesus was bluntly descriptive: "You know that those who are regarded as rulers of the Gentiles lord it over them." Jesus' kingdom model for his new community is strikingly different: "Not so with you. Instead, whoever wants to become great among you must be your servant, and whoever wants to be first must be slave of all. For even the Son of Man did not come to be served, but to serve, and to give his life as a ransom for many" (Mark 10:42–45).

Jesus points to the cross, on which he dies as the substitute for our sins, as the model for servant leadership in his new community.

Violent Revolutionaries

Jesus also defied the violent liberation movement of his time. Most first-century Jews expected the coming Messiah to be a military conqueror in the tradition of King David, who would throw off the yoke of the oppressive Romans. Whether there was an ongoing organized guerrilla movement, or only repeated, spontaneous outbursts by different messianic pretenders is not clear.[22] But the violent path to the messianic kingdom was attractive in the first century.

When Herod the Great died just after Jesus' birth, three different messianic pretenders provoked armed rebellion.[23] The Roman governor of Syria rushed to Jerusalem and crucified two thousand rebels. In 6 A.D. an uprising led by a man named Judas attracted widespread support. Guerrilla bands operated in the caves of the Judean desert. In the forties, two sons of Judas were crucified as proponents of messianic violence. Finally, in 66 A.D., the revolutionaries persuaded the whole nation to rebel against Rome. Four years later, Roman legions demolished Jerusalem stone by stone.

The violent revolutionaries hated Roman imperialists, rejected payment of Roman taxes, and urged violent revolution. "Whoever spills the blood of one of the godless is like one who offers a sacrifice" was their maxim.[24] They believed that if they could persuade the entire Jewish nation to rebel against Rome, the Messiah would come.[25]

Jesus rejected their whole approach. His messianic strategy was one of love for enemies not massacre of opponents. "You have heard that it was said, 'Love your neighbor and hate your enemy.' But I tell you: Love your enemies and pray for those who persecute you, that you may be sons of your Father in heaven" (Matt. 5:43–45). In this passage, Jesus rejects the standard Jewish interpretation, which limited neighborly love to fellow Israelites.[26] Instead, he condemns retaliation and vengeance and extends neighborly love to anyone in need, even oppressive Roman imperialists.

Jesus fit the humble, peaceful view of the Messiah that was described in Zechariah 9:9–10. The crowds shouted messianic slogans as Jesus made his triumphal entry into Jerusalem (Matt. 21:9; Luke 19:38). But the Messiah rides on a humble donkey, not a warhorse![27]

Jesus sensed that the nationalistic passions and violent messianic hopes surging through his people would result in disaster. Again and again there are premonitions and warnings of pending catastrophe.[28] Just after disappointing popular messianic hopes with his peaceful triumphal entry, Jesus weeps over Jerusalem:

> As he approached Jerusalem and saw the city, he wept over it and said, "If you, even you, had only known on this day what would bring you peace—but now it is hidden from your eyes. The days will come upon you when your enemies will build an embankment against you. . . . They will not leave one stone on another, because you did not recognize the time of God's coming to you."
>
> LUKE 19:41–44

Jesus' peaceful path to messianic shalom was a radical alternative and direct challenge to the popular, religious revolutionaries of his day.

Religious Leaders

We have seen how Jesus' challenge to the status quo included economics, social life, and politics, but he did not overlook the religious establishment. He denounced them as blind, hypocritical guides, whitewashed tombs, snakes, and vipers. He condemned the way they meticulously tithed little things like mint and dill but neglected "the more important matters of the law—justice, mercy and faithfulness" (Matt. 23:23).

Jesus' cleansing of the temple fits perfectly into this pattern of constantly challenging the unjust status quo. Outraged that the wealthy priestly aristocracy collected huge sums from their monopolistic sale of animals for sacrifice, Jesus called their economic practices robbery: "It is written," he said to them, " 'My house will be a house of prayer'; but you have made it 'a den of robbers'" (Luke 19:46).

Jews who traveled from afar to Jerusalem to worship had to purchase their animals to sacrifice at Jerusalem. The priestly aristocracy took over the court of the Gentiles reserved for prayer for non-Jews and used that area to charge exorbitant, monopolistic prices for sacrificial animals. Furious, Jesus drove them out. This was not an armed attack on the temple, but it was a dramatic act of civil disobedience designed to protest both the economic oppression and the desecration of the temple going on there. The very next verse following this account of Jesus' nonviolent civil disobedience in the temple says that the chief priests and other religious leaders were trying to kill him (Luke 19:47).

That is hardly surprising. It is important to see that the religious establishment moved to destroy Jesus for two reasons: because of his radical socioeconomic challenge to the status quo and because of his alleged blasphemy. It is quite understandable that the religious, economic, and political establishment viewed Jesus' attack on the status quo as highly threatening. They obviously had to change their values and actions fundamentally or get rid of this disturbing prophet.[29] We simply misunderstand what led up to the cross if we miss the fact that Jesus' execution is "the punishment of a man who threatens society by creating a new kind of community leading a radically new kind of life."[30]

Jesus' theological claims also infuriated them. When he claimed divine authority to forgive sins, they objected (Mark 2:6–11). When he set his own authority above that of Moses, they were offended (Matt. 5:31–39). When he told the parable of the tenants who destroyed the master's vineyard and identified himself as the special Son sent by the Master (Luke 20:9–18), they began looking for a way to arrest him (v. 19). When he broke their rigid rules by healing on the Sabbath, they decided to destroy him (Matt. 12:9–14). When, at the trial, he acknowledged that he was "the Christ, the Son of the Blessed One," they tore their clothes and pronounced him a blasphemer (Mark 14:62–64).

Blasphemer, social radical, and messianic pretender. That was the charge. That is why the political and religious leadership conspired to kill him. When they forced Pilate to admit that Jesus' messianic claims were a political threat to Rome (John 19:12–13), Pilate agreed to crucify him. The inscription on the cross ("King of the Jews") shows that the alleged crime was Jesus' messianic claim. Roman governors regularly crucified Jewish messianic pretenders in the first century.

In fact, Pilate and the priestly aristocracy were right. Jesus was a threat to their unjust, oppressive, unfaithful power and system. Jesus came, claiming to be the Messiah of the Jewish people. He urged the whole society to accept God's radical forgiveness and begin living his new kingdom values. But to do that, they would have to adopt Jesus' radical challenge to the way they exercised power and leadership and the way they treated the poor and marginalized. Equally serious, they would have to accept Jesus as God's Messiah and only Son. They preferred to kill him.

Dismissing Jesus' Challenge

Too often, Jesus' sweeping challenge to the status quo is dismissed. Some brush it aside as a view taught by social-gospel folk who ignore Jesus' deity and atonement. Others misread Jesus' statement, "My kingdom is not of this world" (John 18:36). Still others like Albert Schweitzer see Jesus' eschatological claims as confused and mistaken and therefore irrelevant for faith today. All are wrong.

Jesus' messiahship, deity, and atonement are inseparable from his radical challenge to the status quo. It was precisely the fact that he came to die for our sins that he could offer God's unconditional forgiveness. This same forgiveness was the foundation of his radical new community of forgiven and forgiving sinners. It is precisely because he is more than a prophet, indeed Messiah and only Son of God, that his sweeping challenge to the status quo is normative for Christians rather than esoteric subjectivity or bizarre megalomania.

Jesus explained that his kingdom was not of this world in *one* specific sense—namely that his disciples should not fight to establish it (John 18:36). The values of Jesus' new kingdom do not derive *from* this world, but his kingdom is very much *in* this world.

To say otherwise is to make nonsense of all that we have seen earlier about the central teaching of Jesus that the messianic kingdom is now entering history in his person and work. Precisely his meeting the physical needs of people and identifying with the poor and marginalized are signs of that arriving kingdom.

Radical scholarship has, in this century, often claimed that Jesus' eschatology was simply mistaken. Jesus allegedly thought the fullness of the eschatological kingdom would come in his lifetime and he was wrong. But even the professional New Testament scholarly community is changing its mind.[31] As we have seen, Jesus believed the kingdom was actually dawning in his person and work, but he certainly looked to the future for its fulfillment.

The core of Jesus' radical ethical thrust, however, is precisely his summons to begin living now in this fallen world according to the values and demands of the dawning kingdom. In the power of the Holy Spirit who works signs and wonders, it is now possible to live out Jesus' new challenge to the status quo. Jesus' gospel of the kingdom does indeed produce a disturbing community. But it is a community that lovingly challenges the evils of the status quo precisely because it shares the Creator's love for the good creation and dares to strive now toward that wholeness in personal, socio-economic, and political life that Christ will bring in its fullness at his return.

Communicating the Gospel of the Kingdom

Jesus preached and healed. He taught and acted. The eternal Word-become-flesh was the perfect combination of word and deed.

Peter Wagner notes that many social activists insist that Jesus cared for the poor and oppressed, and then neglect the fact that he performed miracles and cast out demons.[32] Some charismatics, of course, do the reverse. Jesus obviously did both and so should we.[33]

Matthew 9:35 summarizes Jesus' entire public ministry under the three headings of teaching, preaching, and healing: "Jesus went through all the towns and villages, teaching in their synagogues, preaching the good news of the kingdom and healing every disease and sickness." When he sent out the Twelve, Jesus gave them the same wholistic commission "to preach the kingdom of God and to heal the sick" (Luke 9:2). Both words and wonders, both preaching and miracle, both gentle invitation and sharp confrontation, were central to Jesus' communication of the kingdom.

Jesus modeled what he taught. He not only announced the arrival of the messianic time of justice and shalom for the poor and oppressed, he also fed the hungry and welcomed the socially ostracized into his new community. His diverse circle of men and women, rich and poor, crippled and well, was a visible demonstration of the kingdom that he announced.

In fact, the reality of Jesus' new redeemed community was part of the gospel of the kingdom. To be sure, Jesus nowhere says that explicitly. Paul, however, does. Ephesians 3:1ff. explicitly says that the existence of the multi-ethnic church is part of the gospel.[34] But what Jesus says and does leads to that same conclusion.

C. H. Dodd says that Jesus' purpose was to form a "community worthy of the name of a people of God"; in fact, "the new Israel under his own leadership."[35] Jesus' choice of precisely *twelve* disciples underlined this intention. Jesus led an incredibly diverse community of prostitutes who had repented, tax collectors who had renounced oppression, disabled who had been healed, women who were no longer ostracized, poor who were no longer hungry, and revolutionaries who had forsaken violence. This new community of redeemed riffraff was a living demonstration that the messianic kingdom of justice and shalom was dawning. Its very existence both confirmed Jesus' announcement of the gospel of the kingdom and constituted one central part of its content.

Jesus ministered to whole persons.[36] Sick bodies, broken spirits, and disrupted relationships with God all received his gentle healing touch. Forgiving sins, welcoming social outcasts like lepers and fallen women into community, miraculously healing the blind and lame, confronting powerful economic and religious leaders with the demand to repent and change, Jesus brought a comprehensive healing to body and soul, individual and community. Many, to be sure, rejected his message and healing. But as the Jewish Messiah, he invited his entire people to enter the messianic kingdom and experience its comprehensive, Spirit-given wholeness.

The Early Church and the Kingdom

Most of Jesus' contemporaries, however, found it hard to believe that the carpenter's small circle of forgiven tax collectors, prostitutes, and fishermen was truly the beginning of the glorious messianic kingdom promised by the prophets. Jesus' circle was too weak and insignificant. His teaching was too demanding and costly. His claims were too presumptuous if not indeed blasphemous.

To prove he was wrong, the religious and political leaders had him crucified. That, as Jürgen Moltmann rightly insists, destroyed the credibility of Jesus' fantastic messianic claims.

> For the disciples who had followed Jesus to Jerusalem, his shameful death was not the consummation of his obedience to God nor a demonstration of martyrdom for his truth, but the rejection of his claim. It did not confirm their hopes in him but permanently destroyed them.[37]

But then God raised him from the dead! The resurrection proved to the discouraged disciples that Jesus was truly the Messiah and that his messianic kingdom had begun. Pentecost confirmed it. As one reads Peter's sermon in Acts 2, one sees clearly that it was the raising of the crucified One and the pouring out of the Holy Spirit that convinced the early church that the messianic age predicted by the prophets had truly begun (Acts 2:17ff., 29ff.). Jewish messianic hope had expected the giving of the Spirit when the Messiah came. The messianic prophecy of Joel (Joel 2:28–29) came true at Pentecost, thus confirming Jesus' messianic claim.

The New Testament uses two interesting words to express the early Christian belief that the messianic age had truly begun even though it was not yet fully present. They are the words *aparche* (firstfruits) and *arrabon* (pledge or down payment). In 1 Corinthians 15:20 and 23, Paul says that Jesus' resurrection is the firstfruits of the general resurrection that Jewish messianic hope expected at the coming of the Messiah. In 2 Corinthians 1:22 and 5:5, Paul describes the Holy Spirit as a down payment or guarantee (cf. also Rom. 8:23; Eph. 1:14).

The word *firstfruits* is used in the Old Testament to talk about the early harvest festival that celebrated the first arrival of the new crops (see Exod. 23:16, 19; Deut. 26:2, 10). The full harvest was not yet present, but the beginnings of the harvest had already arrived. The presence of those firstfruits caused rejoicing for they were visible, tangible evidence that the full harvest would surely come. Jesus actually rose from the dead on precisely the day when, in Jewish worship, the first ripe sheaf of the harvest was presented to the Lord.[38]

Arrabon (down payment or guarantee) is a loan word from the Semitic. It comes from the arena of commerce and means a deposit that pays part of a total debt and gives a legal claim for the full repayment. It is a present tangible pledge that ratifies a contract. As the *Theological Dictionary of the New Testament* says, "It always implies an act which engages to something bigger."[39]

These words were particularly suited to express the early Christian belief that the resurrection and Pentecost were visible, tangible evidence that the messianic kingdom had begun. Like the firstfruits of the harvest, the messianic age had truly dawned. The early Christians had already tasted the powers of the age to come (Heb. 6:5). Therefore, in spite of the powerful evidence that the Old Age was still very active, the early Christians were certain that the fullness of the messianic kingdom would surely arrive in God's good time.[40]

The Cosmic Dimensions of the Kingdom

It is crucial to understand that the kingdom expectations of the New Testament are all encompassing.[41] The dawning kingdom that Christ will complete at his return does not pertain only to the soul or only to the church or only to individuals. It relates to persons and social structures, indeed even to the nonhuman creation.

It was the present reality of the already dawning messianic kingdom that anchored this breathtaking cosmic hope of the early Christians. They dared to believe that the crucified and risen Carpenter was the key to history. They dared to believe that at his return he would complete his victory over every rule and authority, even death itself (1 Cor. 15:20–26) and bring all things into subjection to God.

They even believed that "the creation itself will be liberated from its bondage to decay and brought into the glorious freedom of the children of God" (Rom. 8:21). Even though they were an almost infinitesimally insignificant minority in a powerful pagan empire, they dared to proclaim that God would reconcile all things in heaven and on earth through the cross of this Jewish carpenter (Col. 1:15–20). They dared to hope for that cosmic completion of the kingdom that Jesus announced precisely because the life, death, and resurrection of Jesus, plus Pentecost, were solid, tangible evidence that the messianic reign had already begun.

The Difference It Makes

Defining the gospel as the Good News of the kingdom rather than merely the Good News of forgiveness or the Good News of personal salvation matters a great deal.[42] For one thing, people who confess Jesus as the way, the truth, and the life ought to be careful not to abandon his central teaching! For another, understanding the central Christian message as the gospel of the kingdom helps provide a comprehensive, wholistic framework that transcends one-sided, partial perspectives.

Jesus' kingdom is clearly wholistic. Thank God that it *does* bring forgiveness with God and personal, inner sanctification in the power of the Spirit. But it also challenges and changes the social order.[43] The kingdom impacts soul and body, individual and society. The church properly communicates the Good News of Jesus' kingdom by word and deed: by proclamation, miracles, acts of mercy and justice, and living out the gospel as a winsome example to others.

The Good News of the kingdom precludes an inward-looking preoccupation with the church. Howard Snyder puts it pointedly: "Church people think about how to get people into the church; kingdom people think about how to get the church into the world. Church people worry that the world might change the church; kingdom people work to see the church change the world."[44]

The church, to be sure, is important. Indeed so important that Jesus' new redeemed community is part of the Good News. God wants the church to be a little miniature now of the coming kingdom. For that reason, it should, like Jesus' first community, be a disturbing challenge to every kind of evil rather than a comfortable club of conformity to the world. The church has learned the awesome secret of God's cosmic design to restore the whole creation to wholeness. Therefore Christians go forth into the world both to lead people to faith in Christ and also to erect signs of the coming kingdom within the broken kingdoms of the world, confident that the Messiah will one day return to complete the victory over the kingdom of darkness.

We can now see more clearly the difference it makes when we define the gospel the way Jesus did; i.e., not *merely* as forgiveness of sins, but that and much more. Jesus' gospel includes the fact that the messianic reign has in fact begun and there is now a reconciled and reconciling community whose visible life is a powerful sign of the kingdom that has already begun and will some day arrive in its fullness. I will focus on seven differences—in addition to the important concern that surely Christians ought to define Jesus' central teaching the way Jesus himself did.

1. If the gospel is not just forgiveness of sins, but the Good News of the kingdom of God, we cannot separate a reconciled relationship with God and a reconciled relationship with brothers and sisters in Christ's body. I am not saying that the two relationships are identical—they are distinct. But they are also *inseparable*. We cannot continue in reconciled relationship with God if we refuse to be reconciled to other members of Christ's body. The gospel of the kingdom protects us from an unbiblical, individualistic spiritualism that reduces salvation just to the forgiveness of the individual soul.

2. If the gospel is not just forgiveness of sins, but the Good News of the kingdom of God, we better understand that reconciled social and economic relationships in the body of Christ are one part of salvation. That is what the story of Zacchaeus shows us so clearly. Economic sharing and racial reconciliation in the body of Christ are not some optional things we can choose if we feel like it. They are essential parts of what it means to embrace the gospel. When the church fails to live that way, the church is a visible denial of Jesus' proclamation that the messianic kingdom has already begun.

3. If the gospel is not just forgiveness of sins, but the Good News of the kingdom of God, we understand more clearly that ministering to both the physical and spiritual needs of people is not some

optional possibility, but essential to the gospel. In the messianic time, the prophets promised the Messiah would bring reconciled relationships with God and neighbor. Both spiritual and material needs would be met. Jesus the Messiah came, announcing and demonstrating his dawning kingdom by word and deed. Both his preaching and his healing were evidence that the kingdom was arriving. Tenderly ministering to the material needs of people in the name of Jesus is part of how faithful disciples share the gospel of the kingdom.

4. If the gospel is not just forgiveness of sins, but the Good News of the kingdom of God, we see more vividly that the Christian community, if it is faithful, will always challenge what is wrong in the status quo. Jesus' messianic community can never comfortably fit into any fallen society. Guided by the vision of the dawning kingdom and empowered by the Holy Spirit, the faithful church will always be a loving critic, a countercultural community. They will treasure what is good in their society and challenge what is broken, precisely because they know the Creator of all is also the Redeemer who desires that Satan's inroads into this good creation be rolled back.

5. If the gospel is not just forgiveness of sins, but the Good News of the kingdom of God, then any sharing of the gospel that does not include a significant concern for the poor is unbiblical. That is not to say, however, either that God cares more about the poor than the rich or that every evangelistic effort must include a word or action empowering the poor. God cares equally about everyone. Unfortunately, almost all comfortable people care more about themselves than about the needy and marginalized. God has an equal concern that every person accept Christ and enjoy the wholeness intended by the Creator. Since sinful persons regularly neglect or oppress the poor, God's people will regularly appear to be on the side of the poor precisely because they share God's equal concern for everyone.

Concern for the poor does not need to find explicit expression in every evangelistic act. But every extended sharing of the gospel by a congregation or mission agency must make it as clear as Jesus did that the gospel is for the poor and that part of the Good News they share is that there is now a new Christian community in which human dignity, social empowerment, and economic justice for the least and poorest are now being modeled and promoted in the power of the Spirit. Anything less is a denial of Jesus' gospel.

6. If the gospel is not just forgiveness of sins, but the Good News of the kingdom of God, we perceive more clearly that there must always be a sharp distinction between the church and the world. One of the greatest temptations of Christians over the centuries has been to slowly conform to surrounding society rather than live in faith-fulness to Jesus' kingdom norms. Because we are not just forgiven but are also being sanctified by the power of the Spirit, Christians can and should live reconciled lives that make Christians stand out in stark contrast to the broken world around them. In the early church, Jews and Gentiles, slaves and masters, men and women were reconciled—not completely, to be sure, but in such powerful ways that their pagan neighbors saw the radical change and were aston-ished. In amazement their neighbors asked why they were so dif-ferent. In response, the early Christians told them about Jesus. Today, the church looks so much like the world that neighbors seldom ask such questions. So we lose the opportunity for evangelism.

A clear distinction between the church and the world is crucial in a second way too. The fact that the reign of God becomes visible in the church in a way that it does not in the larger world does not mean that social change in the larger society is irrelevant. It just means we do not expect as much reconciliation in the world as in the church. Two things follow: First, our first task is to make sure the church is really Jesus' new reconciled community. Just doing that has a great impact on society. Second, we also work to improve the larger society. Some day Jesus will come back and the kingdoms of this world will become the kingdom of our Lord. Therefore we work now to nudge society in the direction of that coming whole-ness, justice, and reconciliation because we know it will come fully at Christ's return.

7. Finally, if the gospel is not just forgiveness of sins, but the Good News of the kingdom of God, we cannot share the gospel adequately just by preaching. We have to live it too. Words and deeds must go together.

I am absolutely convinced that this full biblical gospel is what our broken world needs. It certainly needs the fantastic news of forgiveness. But it also longs to hear and see the amazing truth that right now there is a reconciled and reconciling community that broken people can enter and be loved and nurtured toward wholeness. If even a quarter of the world's Christians would both preach and live Jesus' full gospel of the kingdom, we would see revival and church growth on a scale never before seen. In addition, the world would become a better place. Brothers and sisters, as we prepare for the third millennium, let's embrace Jesus' whole gospel of the kingdom of God.

Few statements have captured the wholistic, comprehensive meaning of Jesus' Good News of the kingdom as well as one from the first Lausanne Congress on World Evangelization, so I'll close this chapter with it:

> The evangel is God's Good News in Jesus Christ; it is Good News of the reign he proclaimed and embodies; of God's mission of love to restore the world to wholeness through the Cross of Christ and him alone; of his victory over the demonic powers of destruction and death: of his Lordship over the entire universe; it is Good News of a new creation of a new humanity, a new birth through him by his life-giving Spirit; of the gifts of the messianic reign contained in Jesus and mediated through him by his Spirit; of the charismatic community empowered to embody his reign of shalom here and now before the whole creation and make his Good News seen and known. It is Good News of liberation, of restoration, of wholeness, and of salvation that is personal, social, global and cosmic. Jesus is Lord! Alleluia![45]

PART 3

OVERCOMING ONE-SIDED VIEWS ABOUT SALVATION

5

Embracing the Fullness of God's Salvation

If God has reconciled us to himself but cannot reconcile us to each other, then the whole thing is a fraud.

ADDIE BANKS

By the fall of 1991, racial tension and other problems had brought most of us in my troubled, interracial, inner-city congregation to near despair. As a last resort, denominational leaders invited an African-American couple, Reverend Michael Banks and his wife, Addie, to come from the Bronx to lead a weekend series on reconciliation.

One evening, Reverend Banks shared the story of their conversion. Twenty years ago, their marriage was ready to self-destruct. He was drinking a lot to reduce the tension produced by his work as an inner-city drug counselor. He and Addie had wounded each other so deeply that it often appeared that the only reason they stayed together was to destroy each other.

Then one day Addie accepted Christ. Her anger didn't disappear, but her responses were new and different. This first surprised and puzzled then powerfully attracted Michael. Drawn to her new faith, he, too, opened his life to Christ. But Jesus did not produce a quick fix in their marriage. Old pain reinforced old patterns.

Quarrels and fighting continued until Michael finally lost all hope that God could restore their marriage. One day he said to Addie, "Why don't you go your way and I'll go mine?"

Addie's instant retort was theologically brilliant: "If God has reconciled us to himself but cannot reconcile us to each other, then the whole thing is a fraud."

Whether or not Addie Banks's response was theologically sound depends on one's definition of salvation. The word *salvation* means very different things to different people in the church today. For some individualistic Christians, salvation means forgiveness of sins and a one-way ticket to heaven. They do not see much connection between salvation and their broken marriages, racial prejudice, or economic injustice. For secular Christians, salvation is only what happens when society becomes more peaceful and just. Salvation understood as eternal life after death is no longer relevant or believable. Between these two extremes lie a variety of middle positions.

If the gospel is only or largely forensic justification, then salvation is only or largely God's unmerited forgiveness of sinners.[1] Whether or not those forgiven sinners live any differently than before they accepted Christ has nothing to do with their salvation. If the gospel is only justification, then Michael and Addie can become Christians and experience salvation without any change in their self-destructive bitterness and anger. Nor should we expect blacks and whites in my inner-city congregation to overcome racial mistrust and hatred just because they have believed the gospel.

But if the gospel is the Good News of the dawning messianic kingdom, then Addie Banks was right. If, as Mark 10:23–26 suggests, entering the kingdom and experiencing salvation are interchangeable, then salvation is more (although certainly not less!) than mere unmerited forgiveness. Salvation also includes the sweeping transformation that the Holy Spirit works both *within* persons and *between* persons. Salvation then includes the transformed marriage of new Christians like Michael and Addie Banks. Salvation includes an inner-city congregation at Seventeenth and Diamond Streets in North Philadelphia where I used to worship, where blacks and whites love and respect each other, allowing Jesus Christ to create a new, redeemed humanity that transcends the tragedy and oppression of

American racism. Within the circle of those who confess Jesus Christ, salvation is personal and social, individual and corporate.

But what about the larger society? We saw in chapter two that those who adopt model three (Ecumenical Christians) want to speak of salvation when a new Philadelphia mayor creates greater justice for minorities, or when democracy emerges in Eastern Europe. And what about the polluted Schuylkill River whose fish I cannot eat? Is God going to restore the groaning creation (at least at Christ's return)? And should that, too, be called salvation?

Our definition of salvation is crucial for our understanding of the relationship between evangelism and social concern. In this chapter, then, I will briefly sketch a biblical view of salvation. Please bear with me. I don't want to pick out just one part of what the Bible says; I want to listen to all of it. Two things will be especially important to explore: first, the biblical words for salvation; and second, the New Testament understanding of the saving work of Jesus (the atonement).

Biblical Words for Salvation

Salvation in the Old Testament[2]

Yasha', *yeshu'a*, and *yesha'* are by far the most commonly used words to convey the idea of salvation in the Old Testament. (They also provide the Hebrew root of the name Jesus that the angel told Joseph to give to Mary's baby: "Because he will save his people from their sins" [Matt. 1:21].)

Two things are especially important in the Old Testament understanding.

First, salvation is the work of God. God is always seen as the author of salvation. The people are rescued by God (Hosea 1:7), who alone can save the flock (Ezek. 34:22), for there is none other who can do it (Isa. 43:1). He alone merits the lofty title, "God our Savior" (Ps. 68:19). Humble, trusting faith is the way to receive God's salvation.

Second, salvation happens in history and is social, corporate, and communal. Exodus 14:30 is typical: "That day the LORD saved Israel from the hands of the Egyptians." Michael Green comments: "It is no exaggeration to say that this rescue from Egypt, the land of bitter bondage under the threat of imminent death at the hand

85

of harsh taskmasters determined the whole future understanding of salvation by the people of Israel."[3] For Israel, God's single most important act of salvation was a concrete historical event that liberated the whole community.

Justice in the courts and salvation are closely linked together. Psalm 72 begs God to give his divine justice to the king of Israel so that "he will defend the afflicted among the people and save the children of the needy" (v. 4). The idea of salvation as vindication for the poor and the oppressed runs throughout the passages dealing with Israel's legal system.[4]

In the Old Testament, salvation is clearly social and corporate and includes every aspect of life.[5] God's salvation pertains to material prosperity, justice for the poor and needy in the judicial system, and the continued historical existence of the people of Israel. The very center of God's saving activity in the Old Testament was the calling forth of a redeemed community, the people of Israel.

At the same time, the vertical dimension is equally important and everywhere present. God is the author of salvation. God took the initiative to effect salvation at the Exodus. Both persons and the people of Israel continue to enjoy salvation only as they trust in Yahweh.

In fact, the Old Testament rarely, if ever, talks about the presence of God's salvation except in the context of the covenant community who trust in Yahweh. Certainly Yahweh is Lord of all nations. And God works there as well as in Israel to accomplish his will, including justice for the poor (e.g., Dan. 4:27). But the Old Testament does not speak of God's salvation as present apart from his covenant with his chosen people where he is consciously confessed as Lord.

Salvation in the New Testament

Salvation in the Gospels

Three things are particularly important for us. First, Jesus links salvation inseparably with the kingdom of God. When the rich young man asked how to inherit eternal life, Jesus told him to sell all his goods, give to the poor, and follow him. And when the young man sadly declined this costly invitation, Jesus explained that it is almost impossible for a rich person to enter the kingdom of God. To that, the disciples said: "Who then can be saved?" (Mark 10:17–26). Receiving salvation and entering the kingdom are virtually identical.[6]

Second, salvation is communal. A new redeemed community was central to God's salvation in the Old Testament. So, too, Jesus called out a new community of disciples who received the salvation of the dawning kingdom and began to live out Jesus' kingdom values.

Experiencing the salvation of the kingdom that Jesus announced meant a total transformation of values, actions, and relationships. Sometimes, as in the case of the rich young man, people rejected the kingdom's salvation because they were unwilling to abandon wealth and give to the poor. Sometimes, as in the case of Zacchaeus, they repented of sin (dishonesty, official corruption, and injustice) and righted those unjust relationships by returning unjustly obtained money and giving to the poor. "Today," Jesus said, "salvation has come to this house" (Luke 19:9). The text does not say explicitly that Jesus announced forgiveness to the sinful Zacchaeus, although the context makes it abundantly clear that Jesus' whole action of visiting the home of this public sinner was an act of forgiving acceptance. But the salvation that happened was not merely some vertical forgiveness of sin although it certainly included that important component. Also central to salvation in the story of Zacchaeus is the new social relationships that grace made possible in the life of this repentant, forgiven oppressor. The salvation of Jesus' dawning kingdom is corporate and social as well as personal and individual.

Third, physical healing is part of salvation. We saw in the Old Testament that the word *salvation* pointed to wholeness or *shalom* in every area of life. The same is true in the Gospels. The concept of salvation in the Gospels includes the forgiveness of sins—and more. The language about salvation in the Gospels is applied to more than what we normally think of as "spiritual concerns."

In almost one out of four times where Jesus' healings are recorded in the synoptics, the word *save (sozo)* is used to describe physical healings.[7] The Samaritan leper was "saved" (Luke 17:19), as was blind Bartimaeus (Mark 10:52), as were the man whose withered hand was restored (Mark 3:4–5) and the liberated demon-possessed man (Luke 8:36). The word *save* is also used to describe physical rescues from the danger of death by drowning (Matt. 8:25; 14:30). Salvation then includes the transformation of broken, physical bodies when the messianic kingdom breaks into history in the person of Jesus.

Does that mean that if we have enough faith we will have no illness? Is salvation nothing more than physical or emotional wholeness? Is physical healing just as much a fruit of the cross and just as readily available for Christians as forgiveness of sins?[8] No. Paul clearly teaches that death is the *last* enemy to be destroyed (1 Cor. 15:26). Until Christ's return, believer and nonbeliever alike will suffer death and the illnesses that bring death. Again and again, fully obedient, Spirit-filled Christians are forgiven and on their way to eternal life, while dying of poverty or cancer. The atonement does not guarantee physical healing now for Christians.

On the other hand, the texts we have just examined show that God, in his sovereignty, sometimes chooses to heal our physical bodies as a sign of the kingdom that has begun and a foretaste of the total salvation that will come at Christ's return. Since the New Testament sometimes uses salvation language in this connection, Christians today should do the same. It helps us reject the unbiblical body-soul dualism in which salvation is only for the soul and not for the body.[9] It underlines the fact that God's saving agenda is to correct the full devastation of sin, not just in some inner, immaterial realm but in the total created order.

Fourth, right relationship with God is also at the center of salvation. We would be grossly distorting the Gospels if we focused exclusively or primarily on the horizontal aspects of salvation. Right at the heart of salvation is a right relationship with God made possible because Jesus died for our sins on the cross. The Son of Man, whom Jesus identified as none other than himself, came to suffer for our sins.[10] Jesus bore vicariously the wrath of God upon sin. Jesus' cross brings together God's wrath and God's mercy. That is absolutely central to the gospel's portrayal of salvation.

It is equally crucial for the Christian life. Christians fail—in our marriages and churches. We could not survive without the wonderful knowledge that God continues to love and forgive us as we repent.

Earlier, I referred to the struggles in my inner-city church. Sadly, as I proofread this book in Soweto, South Africa, I must report that our church has abandoned its interracial vision, and Arbutus and I

88

have left. I am sure that God wants an interracial body of believers at Seventeenth and Diamond in North Philadelphia. But a long, sad history of prejudice and woundedness apparently makes that impossible for the present. Thank God that when our efforts to live the kingdom—whether in our churches or our marriages—fail because of sin, we can cling to the glorious truth of divine forgiveness.

The Gospel of Luke offers a powerful integration of the various interrelated aspects of salvation we have been discussing.[11] Luke uses salvation language to describe the healing of a Gentile soldier's servant (7:3), the forgiveness of a fallen woman (7:50), the restoration to wholeness of a demented man (8:36), and the provision of new life for a dead girl (8:50). Luke intends these as illustrations of salvation. He wants us to understand that this is what salvation is like—new life, wholeness, forgiveness, and healing. Physical healing can be called salvation in the context of the presence and acknowledgment of Christ. But the mighty acts of Jesus were not merely acts of compassion. They were also signs of the presence of the kingdom of God in his very person. Salvation is what happens when people respond in faith to Jesus' preaching (8:15), and this preaching is nothing other than the proclamation of a person, Jesus the Messiah, and the announcement of his dawning kingdom.[12]

Salvation in St. Paul and the Rest of the New Testament

For Paul, salvation refers to the past, present, and future redeeming activity of God in Christ.[13] It includes the sacrifice of the cross; the experience of justification, regeneration, and sanctification; the reality of Jesus' new community; and the ultimate cosmic restoration of all things in Christ. As in the Gospels, then, salvation in Paul is individual and corporate, vertical and horizontal. And it is virtually always related to conscious confession of Christ.[14]

The past tense of salvation. Salvation as a past event focuses especially on the redeeming act of Christ on the cross. Paul uses three different key words.[15] We obtain *soteria* (salvation) as we hear the gospel, are justified by faith rather than works (Rom. 1:16–17), and are freed from the wrath of God because of the cross (Rom. 5:9). *Apolutrosis* (redemption) similarly is the forgiveness of sins

(Rom. 8:23; Col. 1:13–14) that has been granted to us because of the expiation of the blood of Christ at the cross (Rom. 3:24–25). And *katallage* (reconciliation), which as we shall see has a powerful horizontal component, is grounded in the cross on which Christ was made sin for us so that we could be reconciled to God (2 Cor. 5:18–21).

The present tense of salvation. St. Paul captures much of the *present reality* of salvation with his grand word *dikaiosune*. But what does the word mean? Was Michael or Addie Banks right? Does God forgive us without changing us?

St. Augustine and much of the Catholic tradition understood *dikaiosune* to mean that genuine righteousness that the Holy Spirit creates in persons as they are conformed more and more to the image of Christ.[16] Martin Luther, on the other hand, viewed *dikaiosune* primarily as justification, namely God's act of declaring sinners forgiven for their sins and thus justified "by faith alone" as they trust in Christ's merits reckoned to them through the cross.[17] Which does Paul mean?

A careful reading of St. Paul suggests that the answer is both. Paul does use *dikaiosune* to refer sometimes to what Luther called "forensic justification" (e.g., Rom. 4:5–8). At other times, this word points to genuine sanctification of persons (Rom. 6:1–20).[18]

Nor is the word *righteousness (dikaiosune)* limited to the forgiveness and sanctification of the individual. In Romans 14:17, *dikaiosune* refers to the transformed social relations in the redeemed community of believers. In verses 13ff., Paul acknowledges that no foods are unclean in themselves, but if a sister or brother considers some food unclean, we dare not destroy that weak brother or sister by continuing to eat it. "For the kingdom of God is not a matter of eating and drinking, but of righteousness *[dikaiosune]*, peace and joy in the Holy Spirit" (Rom. 14:17). In this passage righteousness and peace refer to that wholeness of right relations within the Christian community.[19] Living now as members of Jesus' dawning kingdom, they are enjoying shalom, wholeness, genuine social salvation.

Ephesians 2:11–3:7 also illustrates the corporate dimension of salvation in a striking way. Ephesians 2:11ff. describes the vertical and horizontal dimensions of salvation through the cross. At the cross, God reconciled both Jews and Gentiles to God and therefore also made possible the horizontal reconciliation of the two most hostile social groups in the ancient world. Paul first underlines the way this twofold reconciliation (with God and with other believers) has broken down the dividing wall between Jews and Gentiles in Christ (2:11–17). Then he proceeds to discuss the "mystery" of Christ that had been revealed to him and that he preached: "This mystery is that through the gospel the Gentiles are heirs together with Israel, members together of one body, and sharers together in the promise of Christ Jesus. I became a servant of *this gospel*"(Eph. 3:6–7). The reality of the new redeemed community in which two hostile social groups are now, in fact, reconciled in the body of Christ is part of the gospel and thus part of the salvation that Paul announced.

For St. Paul, the present tense of salvation includes forgiveness, sanctification, and the new redeemed community.[20]

The future tense of salvation. Salvation also has a strong *future* aspect in Paul. God, who has begun a work in us, will continue it in the present and will complete it in the future (Phil. 1:6). The salvation that we have already experienced is a down payment of the complete inheritance that will be ours at the return of Christ (Eph. 1:13–14). Then, even our bodies will experience *redemption* (Rom. 8:23).

In fact, the redemption Paul describes in Romans 8:18–23 includes far more than just whole persons.[21] It includes the whole creation! At Christ's return, Paul says, God will also restore the physical world.

Cosmic salvation. Romans 8:18ff. is a most amazing text. In verse 20, Paul's starting point is the fact that the creation had been "subjected to frustration." Perhaps Paul is referring to Genesis 3, which says that human sin also caused disruption and evil in nature (vv. 17–18). But Paul was familiar with the prophetic hope. As we saw in chapter three, the prophets believed that eventually even nature itself would be restored (e.g., Isa. 11:6–10).[22] Paul reaffirms that hope: "The creation waits with eager longing for the revealing of the children of God" (Rom. 8:19 NRSV). Indeed "the whole creation has been groaning as in the pains of childbirth right up to the present time" (v. 22). Paul, however, knows that when the children of God are "revealed"—when Christ returns and we

91

experience the resurrection of the body—then the whole created order will also be made new: "The creation itself will be liberated from its bondage to decay and brought into the glorious freedom of the children of God" (v. 21).[23]

Evangelical scholar F. F. Bruce concludes: "If words mean anything, these words of Paul denote not the annihilation of the present material universe on the day of revelation, to be replaced by a universe completely new but the transformation of the present universe so that it will fulfill the purpose for which God created it."[24]

The first chapter of Colossians contains another breathtaking claim about the cosmic character of salvation.

> For God was pleased to have all his fullness dwell in him, and through him to reconcile to himself all things, whether things on earth or things in heaven, by making peace through his blood, shed on the cross.
>
> 1:19–20[25]

Here the scope of salvation reaches beyond persons to "all things in earth and heaven."[26]

Equally astonishing is the beautiful, symbolic language of Revelation 21:22–22:2. Here, God's Word declares that the glory of human civilization will be purged of evil and taken up into the future kingdom. "*The kings of the earth* will bring their splendor" into the new Jerusalem (21:24) and "the glory and honor of the *nations* will be brought into it" (v. 26).

The evil in human civilization must be removed, of course. That is the function of the tree of life that stands beside the crystalline river that flows from the throne of God. "The leaves of the tree are for the *healing of the nations*" (22:2).

Standing within history, we cannot understand all that these words mean. But at a minimum they surely tell us that the best of human civilization will find its place, purged of evil, in the coming kingdom.[27] It will be part of the cosmic salvation that comes at Christ's return.

Three questions immediately surface. Do these texts mean that everyone will eventually be saved (universalism)? Is there no discontinuity between history and the coming kingdom? Finally, is growing democracy or economic justice in Russia, China, or the United States also salvation?

Other New Testament texts, I believe, exclude universalism. Paul certainly did not believe that everyone was already reconciled to God because of the cross. Immediately after stating that God had reconciled the world to himself in Christ, Paul added that we are Christ's ambassadors, begging people on Christ's behalf, "Be reconciled to God" (2 Cor. 5:19–20).[28] Paul does not suppose they only need to be told that they are already reconciled. Rather, he teaches that all have sinned and stand under God's wrath. As we will see in chapter seven,[29] Jesus talked about eternal separation from God more than any other person in the New Testament. To say, then, that God plans a cosmic salvation in which eventually all things will be reconciled to God does *not* mean that every person will be saved. Rather, it means that all parts of the created order— persons, human civilization, and even the nonhuman creation— will participate in God's ultimate salvation.

But what of a passage like 2 Peter 3:10–13 that says the heavens will be destroyed by fire and the earth "laid bare"? And Revelation 21:1, which says the first heaven and earth will pass away?

Is there no connection at all between history now and the coming kingdom? Is there no connection between social action now and the wholeness that comes at Christ's return?

John Courtney Murray tells a story about an early Christian hermit.[30] This hermit painstakingly wove a basket for a whole day, then the next day he just as carefully unwove it chord by chord. The hermit did not care at all that at the end of the second day he had nothing at all to show for two days of tedious labor. All that mattered was the inner sanctification of his soul and his preparation for eternity. The basket had no other significance. Is history and all Christian social action merely such "basket weaving"? Or is there a connection between the good that we do on earth and the coming kingdom?

The Bible clearly does not teach that we will create better and better societies through brilliant political action until finally we construct utopia. Only the mighty intervention of God at Christ's return will bring the cosmic salvation that the New Testament promises. Human effort cannot create the coming kingdom.

But unless we think that 2 Peter 3:10–13 and Revelation 21:1 contradict the other texts we have examined, we must think in terms of continuity as well as discontinuity.[31] And in fact even these two texts point to continuity. Second Peter 3:13 promises both a new heaven and a new *earth*. Revelation 21:1–5 also foretells a new *earth* and a new *Jerusalem* where God dwells with us and wipes away our tears. Furthermore, it is precisely into the new Jerusalem that the same author later in the same chapter says the kings of our earth bring the glory of the nations.

The resurrected body of Jesus of Nazareth is probably our best clue about continuity and discontinuity.[32] It was the carpenter from Galilee who arose bodily from the tomb on Easter morning and appeared to talk and eat with his startled disciples. But his body was certainly no longer subject to death and decay. And it could do things that we do not understand.

But it is precisely the bodily resurrection of Jesus and the fact that the Incarnation continues that is the capstone of an incredible biblical truth: Creation is so good that God intends to purge it of evil and bring it to perfection.[33]

We should not claim to know the detailed geology or geography of this transformed earth for which we hope. It is enough to know that the Creator who is also the Savior intends to bring the entire creation to wholeness. In summarizing his careful analysis of the relationship between resurrection and creation, Murray Harris, New Testament professor at Trinity Evangelical Divinity School, puts it well:

> Humans are one with creation. . . . The destiny of the individual is interlocked with the destiny of the whole created universe and cannot be considered apart from it without seriously undermining the testimony of the New Testament. The emancipation of creation must be involved in our emancipation, for, given our oneness with creation, the redemption of simply that small segment of creation which is humanity is inconceivable. . . . The entire material universe will share the destiny of Christ's people. . . . Since there is this indissoluble unity between humanity and nature in the future as in the past, there can be no dualism of spirit and matter. No New Testament writer envisages the salvation of the soul or spirit with the visible material world abandoned to oblivion.[34]

The Book of James says it all in a short phrase: Persons who believe in Christ are "a kind of firstfruits of all he created" (James

1:18). In God's cosmic plan of salvation, the whole creation is destined for wholeness.

Does that mean that we should speak of salvation when the environmental movement creates greater ecological wholeness, or when democracy or economic justice grow in China, Russia, or the United States? Not at all. Nowhere does the New Testament use salvation language for what happens before Christ's return except where persons consciously confess Jesus Christ. If Vietnam was in some sense saved when the war ended, then one would suppose that the Vietnamese people were in some sense in the church. But that approach moves toward universalism and a loss of the biblical distinction between the church and the world.

As I argue in the appendix, salvation refers to what happens when persons accept Christ and join his new redeemed society, the church. It also refers to that cosmic transformation at Christ's return. Until then, Christians should work hard to change unjust structures in the larger society beyond the church. But we should call even the best results social justice, not salvation.

That does not mean salvation is only individualistic. It is personal and corporate, individual and social—within Jesus' new community of believers where all relationships are now being redeemed by the power of the Holy Spirit.

The Atonement, Salvation, and Mission

A brief look at the doctrine of the atonement confirms the broad understanding of salvation we have discovered.

In the New Testament, there is no single understanding of Christ's saving work. Rather, we have several sets of words and images that theologians have used to develop three dominant theories or models of the atonement: the moral, the substitutionary, and the classic view.[35]

The Moral Model[36]
In this model, Jesus' basic role is that of teacher and example because the fundamental human problem is ignorance. The locus of Jesus' activity is Galilee where he teaches and Golgotha where he reveals God's love on the cross. The focus is on expanding our knowl-

edge and understanding by activities that teach and model God's love and will. The outcome is the illumination of clouded minds by Jesus' words and example so that we learn to love God and neighbor.

This model is obviously rooted in key New Testament teachings.[37] The Gospels feature in a prominent way Jesus' teaching ministry in Galilee (and elsewhere). At the cross, too, Jesus continues to offer revelation: "This is how we know what love is: Jesus Christ laid down his life for us" (1 John 3:16). This model focuses well the ethical demands of Christian faith and the importance of the proclamation of the kingdom.

By itself, however, this theory of the atonement is inadequate. Unfortunately, evil in the world lies much deeper than mere ignorance. It rests in radically self-centered persons who need not just knowledge but divine forgiveness and power to change. Evil also resides in demonic forces and the social structures they have helped distort. We need a powerful Savior who can conquer the forces that enslave us.

The Substitutionary Model[38]

In this model Jesus' role is that of substitute because our basic problem is that sinners stand condemned as guilty before a holy God. The locus of saving activity is Calvary and the focus is on the reconciliation of God's love and justice accomplished by Christ who takes our guilt upon himself to turn aside God's deserved wrath and punishment of sinners. The outcome is forgiveness, renewed relationship with God, and life eternal rather than eternal separation from the Holy One.

A great deal of biblical material supports the substitutionary view of the atonement. St. Paul explicitly teaches that all who sin stand under God's wrath and condemnation (Gal. 3:10–13). But "God made him who had no sin to be sin for us, so that in him we might become the righteousness of God" (2 Cor. 5:21). As John Stott argues so well, not all of the ways Christians have explicated the substitutionary theory are helpful. But God's "self-satisfaction by self-substitution" is at the heart of the New Testament understanding of the atonement.[39] The fact that the One hanging limp on the middle cross was the Second Person of the Trinity shows that God himself took our place at the cross to reconcile his love and holiness. Without that understanding of the cross, we either trivialize sin or despair of hope.

Taken *by itself,* however, the substitutionary view of the atonement is also inadequate. By itself, the substitutionary model largely ignores Christ's example of teaching and proclaiming the kingdom in Galilee, and his victory over the forces of evil during his life and at Easter. If one reduces the atonement merely to Jesus' death for our sins, one abandons the New Testament understanding of the gospel of the kingdom and severs the connection between the cross and discipleship. The result is the scandal of professing Christians whose sexual practices, business dealings, and political attitudes are no different from those of non-Christians.

But such a view is not biblical. We have seen that the gospel is more (although certainly not less!) than justification by faith. Jesus' teaching ministry and call to costly discipleship were one part of his atoning work.[40] "We may have all the right words and be an expert on the doctrine of the atonement, but if we do not share in his sufferings, 'becoming like him in his death' (Phil. 3:10), we reject the cross."[41]

The Classic Model

In this view of the atonement (sometimes called the *Christus Victor* model), Jesus' primary role is conqueror of evil because the central problem is the power of evil, whether seen in demonic beings, corrupt social structures, or death itself. Gustav Aulen's book, *Christus Victor,*[42] provides the most common label for this model. Aulen argued that it was the dominant model in early (hence the term "classic") Christianity. It is also central to theologies of liberation today. The central locus is twofold: Galilee where Christ cast out demons, and Easter morning when Christ conquered death. Here the focus is not on canceling guilt but on defeating the forces of evil. Christ does that by casting out demons, healing the sick, challenging an unjust status quo, and finally conquering death.

Again, this model is rooted solidly in the New Testament. First John 3:8 is very clear: "The reason the Son of God appeared was to destroy the devil's work." Hebrews says the Son became flesh "so that by his death he might destroy him who holds the power of death—that is, the devil—and free those who all their lives were held in slavery by their fear of death" (2:14–15). The *Christus Victor* motif gets beyond an exclusively individualistic understanding of sin and salvation and points to the social and cosmic aspects of salvation. And it focuses Jesus' work in Galilee and Jerusalem. Above all, it highlights the victory of Easter morning.

René Padilla underlines the importance of this model:

> The church today urgently needs to experience the cross as far more than the cultic symbol of a privatized faith. It needs to experience it as God's victory over the powers of darkness and therefore as a basis to challenge every dehumanizing power that is destroying life in the modern world, be it militarism or consumerism, statism or materialism, individualism or hedonism.[43]

Taken *by itself*, however, this view too is inadequate. Because this model points to the evil forces *outside* the individual, it is easy for proponents of this view to underemphasize the personal side of sin, guilt, and responsibility. This is especially obvious in some theologies of liberation where sin, as we have seen, resides largely in unjust social structures. The result is utopian schemes for building a new person and a new society without realizing that the radical evil in persons undermines such dreams.

Are these three different views of the atonement complementary or contradictory? Some people seem to think they are incompatible, but I see no need whatsoever to reject one biblical perspective in order to affirm another. It is only when we take one view and emphasize it in a one-sided or exclusive way that we have problems. Rather, we need to see how the three views complement each other. Placing them in the context of the kingdom theology outlined in the previous chapter helps us do that.

A Messianic Model of the Atonement[44]

A messianic (or kingdom) approach to the atonement emphasizes Jesus' interrelated roles as teacher, victor, and substitute.

As messianic proclaimer of the kingdom of God, Jesus taught a radical kingdom ethic. He shook the status quo to its roots. From his

Sermon on the Mount through his death on the cross, he taught and modeled the way of love, even for enemies. Living his costly ethics, however, is possible only as forgiven sinners empowered by the Spirit.

As nonviolent messianic conqueror, Jesus did battle with Satan and all the forces of evil. He conquered diseases and demons in his public ministry. On the cross, he broke the power of Satan and on Easter morning he arose triumphant over death itself, promising to return and complete his cosmic victory over all of Satan's distortion of the good creation. As his followers, we join in his battle against the kingdom of darkness, secure in our knowledge of his grand design and in our assurance that we are forgiven when we fail.

As Isaiah's Suffering Servant, Jesus forgave sinners and then died on the cross as their substitute. No matter how sinful and broken, no matter how poor, oppressed, and malnourished, we can repent of our sins, receive divine forgiveness, and enter into a personal living relationship with the holy Creator. Precisely because Jesus died as the substitute for our sins, we can, even as we are dying of starvation, oppression, or war, enter into the joy of a reconciled relationship with Almighty God and know the hope of life eternal. As forgiven daughters and sons, we receive the Spirit's power to live now according to Jesus' kingdom teaching and do battle against every evil, whether personal, demonic, or structural.

Finally, precisely the messianic approach to the atonement underlines the community-building aspect of Jesus' saving work. As we saw in chapters three and four, Jesus not only preached the gospel of the kingdom, he formed a new kingdom community of women and men, prostitutes and royal servants, tax collectors and respectable folk. From the calling together of Israel as a redeemed community, through Jesus' circle of disciples to the community of the early church, establishing a reconciled community is central to God's plan of salvation.[45] That's why Ephesians 3 says the new multi-ethnic church of Jew and Gentile is part of the gospel. It's why Titus 2:14 says that Christ "gave himself for us to redeem us from all wickedness and to purify for himself a *people*."[46]

The messianic model integrates the insights of the moral, substitutionary, and classic views of the atonement. Christ's saving work took place not only at the cross but also in his public ministry in Galilee and on Easter morning.[47] Our problem is not just our guilt but also our ignorance and powerlessness. We need enlightened minds, victory over Satan, new power to live what we know, restored relationships with neighbor, as well as divine forgiveness. In Jesus, therefore, God forgives our sins, fills us with the empowering Holy Spirit, defeats Satan, and creates a new people. Jesus our Savior is exemplary Teacher, victorious Conqueror, forgiving Substitute, and Head of a new redeemed community. Hallelujah, what a Savior!

Our examination of biblical salvation language and the doctrine of the atonement has demonstrated that salvation is personal and communal, individual and corporate.[48] We dare not reduce salvation to interpersonal transformation of relationships with the neighbor because right at the center of salvation is a renewed relationship with God. Christians are forgiven sinners enjoying a reconciled relationship with a holy, loving God. We dare not reduce salvation to a personal relationship with God in justification and sanctification because right at the heart of salvation is the new redeemed community. Christians are members of Jesus' new redeemed society in which the Holy Spirit is now transforming all relationships whether emotional, social, or economic. Nor dare we reduce our future hope of salvation to an invisible, immaterial world of souls, because right at the center of our hope is God's promise to make all things new. We wait in eager expectation for God's cosmic salvation when with transformed bodies in the new Jerusalem, we will revel in the glory of the nations and the splendor of creation itself, now freed of the bondage and corruption that our sin introduced.

If we understand this full-orbed biblical picture of salvation, how can we help but throw ourselves enthusiastically into the work of both evangelism and social action?

6

Conversion That Transforms

Churches today are tragically split between those who stress conversion but have forgotten its goal, and those who emphasize Christian social action but have forgotten the necessity for conversion.[1]

Jim Wallis

One Sunday while I was writing this book, an interracial group of young women from Teen Challenge visited my inner-city church. One beautiful young woman shared a wrenching story of incest, physical abuse, and the terrifying bondage of drugs. Regina felt worthless. She was deathly afraid of God because she thought God would treat her the same way that all men had. She was nothing. After a wretched life and eight abortions, she wanted to die. Again and again she tried to commit suicide.

Then she met Jesus. In Teen Challenge's marvelous Spirit-filled drug rehabilitation program, God began to put her life back together. She now feels pure and clean, "more innocent than when she was born."

After she shared her story, she and the others sang a powerful song about the new dignity and transformation that conversion brings: "It's not because of what I've done, it's because of who I am. I've been adopted by the King."

At least once a year Teen Challenge brings a group to our church to share their testimonies. This morning, as usual, the pain of their wrenching histories and the joy of their transformed lives made me weep.

What an awesome gift conversion is. It would be silly, to be sure, to suppose that Regina's struggles are over, but her relationship with God has brought a new sense of dignity, worth, and hope. Her other relationships are also beginning to change.

Jim Wallis tells a different story. He grew up in a devout evangelical family and accepted Christ at an early age. But his faith and the life of his suburban evangelical church had no perceived relationship at all with racism and the plight of black Americans living just a few miles away in inner-city Detroit. Somehow as a teenager, Jim found himself drawn to the city, and he became friends with black inner-city youth, but when Jim tried to involve his church in the struggle against racism, he met cold resistance. "Would you really want your sister to marry one?" was the response. His church leaders saw no connection between conversion and social problems like racism, economic oppression, and militarism.[2] Jim was so disappointed that for a time, he lost his faith in Christ.

For some Christians today, conversion relates primarily to our vertical relationship with God. It brings forgiveness of sins and assurance of eternal life. For many more, it also means significant inner transformation in our personal lives. God's grace empowers us to turn from stealing, lying, and sexual promiscuity. Personal ethics and family relations change. Like Jim Wallis's evangelical church, however, conversion has little impact on questions of racism, economic oppression, environmental pollution, and militarism.

Conversely, there are many secular people and some secularized Christians who care passionately about peace and justice in society but see no connection between their political activity and conversion. If we merely change social structures and promote good education, they believe, we can create new people.

A careful look at the biblical understanding of repentance and conversion will show how one-sided both views are. In the New Testament, conversion involves a radical change, a complete turning around. Accepting Christ includes accepting his kingdom approach to everything. It means letting Jesus be Lord of our politics and economics just as much as our church attendance.

A biblical understanding of conversion demonstrates with equal clarity how foolish it is to think that mere knowledge or political change can solve social problems. Social injustice is grounded finally in human selfishness and sinful rebellion against the Creator. All of us need God's transforming grace in order to live what Jesus taught. A biblical understanding of conversion is crucial if we are to understand the complex interrelationships of evangelism and social action.

The Biblical Understanding

The New Testament uses three basic word groups to talk about repentance and conversion. *Epistrepho* literally means "to turn around."[3] Behind this Greek word stands the Hebrew word *shub*, which appears about 1050 times in the Old Testament. Like *epistrepho*, *shub* often has the simple secular meaning of physically turning around. But in about 120 cases, *shub* has the very important theological meaning of Israel's turning from sinful rebellion against Yahweh to total submission to God's will expressed in the covenant.[4] Similarly, *epistrepho* also has a theological meaning and refers to turning from the ways of Satan to faith in and submission to Christ.[5]

Metanoia (often translated "repentance") represents a second crucial word group. This Greek word means "to change one's mind."[6] According to the *Theological Dictionary of the New Testament,* Jesus' call to *metanoia* demanded an "unconditional turning to God" and an "unconditional turning from all that is against God."[7] "It involves the whole walk of the [person] who is claimed by divine lordship."[8]

The third (less common) word group is *metamelomai*. It means to change one's mind or regret something.[9]

These three word groups carry slightly different meanings. But for our purposes, we can focus on the common reality to which they point. They all refer to that process of radical transformation of thoughts and actions (initiated by divine grace) that happens when a person is drawn to faith in Jesus and submits to him as unconditional Lord. Regret for past sin, the experience of forgiveness, baptism, and a life of growing discipleship are all a part of biblical conversion.[10]

The call to repentance and conversion is at the very center of the preaching of both Jesus and the early church. Mark links repentance and the kingdom in his first summary of Jesus' whole message: "'The time has come,' he said. 'The kingdom of God is near. Repent and believe the good news'" (Mark 1:15).[11] Jesus said that the purpose of his coming was to call us to repentance (Luke 5:32). Repentance is the only faithful response to Jesus' announcement of the kingdom. In Luke's account of the Great Commission, Jesus commands his disciples to preach "repentance and forgiveness of sins" in his name (Luke 24:47). Preaching at Athens, Paul said: God "commands all people everywhere to repent" (Acts 17:30). "Godly sorrow," Paul told the Corinthians, "brings repentance that leads to salvation" (2 Cor. 7:10). Repentance, according to the Bible, is an essential part of the process of salvation.[12]

Biblical repentance and conversion involve a radical transformation of our relationships both with God and neighbor. They certainly involve genuine sorrow for sin against God. Those who truly repent enjoy a new forgiven and reconciled relationship with the Holy One.[13] But repentance, as the story of Zacchaeus shows, just as surely involves radical changes in relationships with the neighbor. Repentance for Zacchaeus, the oppressive tax collector, meant turning from his social sins and forsaking his unjust oppression. Only then did Jesus announce that salvation had come to his house (Luke 19:9). As Paul told Agrippa, Christians should "prove their repentance by their deeds" (Acts 26:20).

One can hardly improve on the way René Padilla put it in his plenary address at Lausanne: "Repentance is much more than a private affair between the individual and God. It is the complete reorientation of life in the world . . . in response to the work of God in Jesus Christ."[14]

If we understand and practice genuinely biblical repentance, then we establish an important, inseparable link between conversion and Christian social responsibility.[15] Biblical repentance includes turning from all sin including *social* sins.[16] That means abandoning racist attitudes and neglect of the poor, indeed all that distorts human community. The tragedy of so much modern evangelism is that it has operated with a biblically inadequate view of sin seeing only the personal side. Consequently, it also operated with a biblically inadequate understanding of repentance and conversion focused only on turning from personal sins and restoring the vertical relationship with God.

This one-sided, individualistic understanding of repentance contributed to an equally one-sided, individualistic understanding of discipleship that neglected the link between conversion and social justice.

Divorcing Reconciliation with God and Neighbor

The wholistic biblical view of repentance and conversion is grounded in the pervasive biblical teaching that right relationship with God is inseparable from right relationship with neighbor. That is not to say that they are identical. But they are inseparably related in such a way that right relationship with God inevitably also involves more just, loving relationships with sisters and brothers in the church and the larger human family.

Perhaps the most pointed way that the Bible teaches this truth is in Jesus' persistent word that God simply does not forgive those who refuse to forgive others.

> For if you forgive others their trespasses, your heavenly Father will also forgive you; but if you do not forgive others, neither will your Father forgive your trespasses.
>
> MATTHEW 6:14–15 NRSV

In the one explicit prayer that Jesus gave to his disciples, he told us to ask God to "forgive us our debts, as we also have forgiven our debtors" (Matt. 6:12). In the astonishing parable of the unmerciful servant, the king angrily throws the ungrateful wretch into prison for failing to imitate the king's mercy. Jesus' conclusion is pointed for anyone who wants justification without conversion: "So my heavenly Father will also do to every one of you, if you do not forgive your brother or sister from your heart" (Matt. 18:35 NRSV).[17]

105

Both testaments clearly teach that true knowledge of and love for God is inseparable from concern for others, especially the poor and downtrodden.[18] In Jeremiah 22:13–14, the prophet denounces oppressive King Jehoiakim for building his magnificent palace by oppressing his workers. Then he turns to Jehoiakim's father, good King Josiah, who defended the cause of the poor and needy. "'Is that not what it means to know me?' declares the LORD" (v. 16). Knowing God properly is inseparable from doing justice for the poor. First John 3:17 says almost the same thing: "If anyone has material possessions and sees his brother in need but has no pity on him, how can the love of God be in him?" If we claim to love God and do not love our neighbors, we are liars.

Even our worship infuriates God if done at the neglect or expense of the poor. When the people of Amos's day tried to please God with liturgical worship at the same time they oppressed the poor, God angrily declared: "I hate, I despise your religious feasts" (Amos 5:21; cf. also Isa. 1:10–15; 58:3–7). Jesus was equally harsh with scribes who "devour widows' houses and for a show make lengthy prayers" (Mark 12:40).

Matthew 25:31ff. draws the inevitable conclusion. Those who fail to feed the hungry and clothe the naked "go away to eternal punishment" (v. 46). It is impossible to have a right relationship with God while persisting in neglecting or oppressing the needy neighbor.

These texts do not teach works-righteousness. As we saw in chapter three, other parts of Jesus' teaching make it very clear that the kingdom comes as a gift. We cannot earn God's forgiveness. Luke 12:32 says explicitly that "your Father has been pleased to *give* you the kingdom" (emphasis added). But the very next verse is a command: "Sell your possessions and give to the poor."

Paul says the same thing. Forgiveness is a gift from God received by faith. But we are "created in Christ Jesus to do good works" (Eph. 2:10).[19]

The Creator has made us for community. Therefore God refuses to offer his mercy and forgiveness to those who persistently destroy community by neglecting or oppressing sisters or brothers in the human family. J. Deotis Roberts is right. There can be no proper "expression of love between man and God which does not include the brother."[20]

Some Christians sometimes sound as if they think that if their doctrine of Christ and the atonement is orthodox, all else is secondary. Such a view is heretical. Douglas Webster is right.

> Earlier I argued that the supernatural incarnation is incredible to modern men and women. But is not costly discipleship incredible to many conservatives? The language of losing one's life for Christ's sake may be as symbolic and mythical to conservatives as the Virgin Birth and substitutionary Atonement are to liberals.[21]

Sixteen times the New Testament refers to Jesus as Savior. Four hundred twenty times it refers to him as Lord.[22] Costly obedience is inseparable from saving faith. Right relationship with neighbor must flow from a proper relationship with the Creator of human community. Our doctrine is unbiblical and our life disobedient if repentance and conversion do not involve fundamentally transformed relationships with neighbors, business associates, employees, employers—anyone with whom we associate.

Neglecting this side of repentance and conversion, however, is only one way that we can fall into serious error. It is equally possible to discuss conversion as a new lifestyle in which one seeks peace and justice in such a way that one neglects his or her relationship with God.[23] That, too, is heretical. Sin is first of all sin against our holy God as Psalm 51:4 says so pointedly. We dare never forget that right at the heart of repentance must be the sinner's anguished plea for forgiveness and reconciliation with Almighty God.

Cheap Grace, Exorbitant Grace, and Conversion

I'll never forget an intense, late-night debate with church growth specialist Peter Wagner in Atlanta in 1977. Peter had come to a national conference on racial reconciliation organized by evangelical social activists like myself both because he cared deeply about the issue and also because he wanted to understand us. Somehow—to nobody's surprise—we quickly got into a vigorous exchange on the ethical content of conversion. What, specifically, are we converted *from*?

Many have accused Donald McGavran, Peter Wagner, and other church growth thinkers of cheap grace. They are, it is alleged, so preoccupied with statistical growth that they weaken or ignore the gospel's costly demands in order to add members.[24] Furthermore, goes the argument, their distinction between discipling (bringing persons to initial faith in Christ) and perfecting (nurturing sanctification and ethical growth) is exegetically and theologically problematic.

In response, Peter has charged evangelical social activists like me with promoting "exorbitant grace" and "spiritual exploitation." He says that when we demand that potential converts must first oppose militarism or economic injustice in the Third World, we manipulate evangelism in order to promote a particular political agenda. It is wrong for social activists "to load their favorite cause on repentance."[25]

You can be sure that the arguments during that late-night session flowed fast and furiously. One part of the debate, as I recall, centered on the content of repentance. Of what must a new convert repent? And who or what defines the sins to be confessed?

Peter, of course, stressed the importance of starting with the "felt needs" of the person considering Christ. Every person has different needs and the evangelist must present the gospel as Good News that will heal that person's concrete brokenness.

I agreed, but I had another question: What if the person has no sense of sin in a large area where the Bible speaks strongly? Suppose a very oppressive businessman feels guilty for his sexual affairs at the office but has no guilt for his unjust, racist employment policies. Certainly the evangelist should joyfully explain that coming to Jesus Christ will bring liberating forgiveness for his sexual promiscuity. But, I insisted, the evangelist must also explain that God abhors racism and economic injustice. Therefore coming to Jesus will mean repenting of his social sins of racism and exploitation and submitting his business practices to the Lordship of Christ.

Peter disagreed. The evangelist, he said, must stick to the person's "felt needs" and trust the Holy Spirit to sensitize his conscience at some later time. "Does that not let the sinner and fallen society define sin rather than the Bible?" I asked. "And is it not a basic characteristic of theological liberalism when we let society rather than Scripture define sin?"

I don't remember Peter's answer, but I can assure you it was a lively one.

Before and after that friendly, vigorous exchange, many theologians and missiologists have debated this central question. Some real progress and growing understanding have developed.

On both sides there is now agreement on at least four points. First, nearly everyone, including church growth advocates like Peter Wagner and Donald McGavran, believes that there must be an essential ethical element in the evangelistic invitation. It must be clear that believing in Jesus Christ means not only trusting him to forgive one's sins but also submitting obediently to him as unconditional Lord.[26] No convert, of course, understands everything that obedient discipleship will involve, but evangelism must explain that accepting Jesus includes accepting him as Lord.

Second, we all agree that conversion is a lifelong process. No one who comes to Christ can know at the time of initial faith the full ethical implications of a lifetime of obedient discipleship. Therefore *some* distinction between initial acceptance of Christ and becoming more like him is necessary. Walking with Christ means learning year by year more about what it means to be transformed into his image "from one degree of glory to another" (2 Cor. 3:18 NRSV).

Third, the specific "felt needs" of the person to whom the evangelist speaks are important. There should be a primary concern to present the gospel as Good News that will bring God's shalom to the person's specific area of perceived brokenness.

Fourth, a much deeper awareness of the pervasive influence of Western culture has underlined the importance of contextualized evangelism. Leslie Newbigin and many others have rightly lamented the fact that Western missionaries have sometimes imposed their own cultural values rather than biblical essentials as requirements for baptism.[27] We can only repent sadly of the tragedy of polygamists being compelled, before receiving baptism, to send away all but their first wife (often condemning the others to poverty and sometimes to prostitution).[28] The evangelist, especially the cross-cultural evangelist, must trust the living Christ, as Newbigin says, to speak "through the Scriptures . . . directly to the new convert in a way that is not just an echo of the words of the missionary."[29] There is no available, universally applicable list of sins for which the evangelist must be certain to ask repentance before inviting someone to come to Christ in saving faith.

On the above, we agree, but disagreement persists in some important areas.

First of all, to contrast "discipling" (bringing persons to initial confession of Christ) with "perfecting" (ethical growth) is exegetically wrong and potentially misleading. Church growth writers have tried to ground their use of these words on Matthew 28:19: "Therefore go and make disciples of all nations, baptizing them in the name of the Father and of the Son and of the Holy Spirit, and teaching them to obey everything I have commanded you."[30] Their terminology and distinction, however, simply do not fit with careful exegesis.

In the Greek, the phrase "make disciples" is an imperative. Two participles ("baptizing" and "teaching") give specific content to what it means to "make disciples." Teaching them to obey all Christ's commands belongs every bit as much to "making disciples" as the initial activity of confessing Christ, experiencing baptism, and joining the church.[31] Therefore, to use the word *discipling* for the initial activity of conversion and to distinguish that word from ethical growth in sanctification has no exegetical basis whatsoever in this text.

Worse, it fails to capture the essential thrust of Jesus' understanding of the word *disciple.* The *Theological Dictionary of the New Testament* says that the word *disciple (mathetes)* "always implies the existence of a personal attachment that shapes the whole life of the one described as *mathetes.*"[32] The core of Jesus' teaching on discipleship was total, lifelong, unconditional submission to him as Master: "If anyone would come after me, he must deny himself and take up his cross and follow me" (Matt. 16:24). By discipleship, Jesus meant the entire life of obedience, not some initial decision.[33]

To limit the word *discipling* to the initial acceptance of Christ runs the danger of minimizing or losing the full ethical concern of Jesus.[34] Every biblical evangelist should be primarily concerned with doing exactly what Jesus commanded—i.e., making disciples in the way he said. That includes a central emphasis on teaching Jesus' kingdom ethics.[35] The distinction between initial conversion and a lifetime of growth in ethical awareness and obedience is important. But *discipling* and *perfecting* are the wrong words.

We do need words to talk about the difference between the initial task of inviting people to faith and the lifelong process of promoting growing sanctification. But "discipling" and "perfecting" are misleading. It would be better to speak of the initial task as evangelizing non-Christians and the second as nurturing believers to become more and more conformed to the image of Christ. The result of the first activity is an initial conversion and the result of the second is a growing sanctification.

I sense another problem. Some in the "mega-church" movement place a high priority on "reaching people where they are" without raising troublesome ethical questions. They want the seekers' sense of need to define what they seek from Jesus. They are glad when new converts feel good that Jesus "meets their needs," but they hesitate to talk about painful conversion, hidden sins that require confession, and costly discipleship. That might offend folk and slow down church growth![36]

Unless we insist on the central role of God's revelation in defining the sins of which converts must repent, we fall into ethical relativism and theological liberalism. White racists may never understand that racism is a terrible sin if their sense of need defines sin. The oppressive businessman may never acknowledge that callous, unjust treatment of workers is sin if his sense of need defines sin. The liberal bureaucrat may never understand how his arrogance betrays his purpose as a community servant. Only if we let the Scriptures play the decisive role in defining the sin from which converts must repent and turn away can we avoid liberalism and cheap grace.

I have not forgotten the danger of loading one's personal political agenda into the evangelistic task. That must be avoided. Nor does the oppressive business leader or blatant racist or liberal bureaucrat need to know all that following Jesus will involve. But the evangelist had better tell them up front that racism, economic oppression, and arrogance are sins against God Almighty.

Consider Jesus' example. The rich young inquirer who fell at Jesus' feet was seriously contemplating becoming a disciple (Mark 10:17ff.). But Jesus did not ask him where he felt guilty! Jesus declared God's Word—first the Ten Commandments and then a powerful prophetic word on riches and sharing with the poor. Even though the inquirer had said nothing about it, Jesus promptly put his finger on the toughest area of sin for this particular person—his idolatrous materialism. Rather than make it easy to join his circle of disciples, Jesus made it exceedingly costly.

Jesus was more gentle with the Samaritan woman, but he pointedly asked about her husband and thereby evoked her confession of marital sin even though she preferred to discuss ethnic differences (John 4:15–18). And just when "church growth" began to explode during his popular Galilean crusade, Jesus went out of his way to underline the cost of discipleship.

> Large crowds were traveling with Jesus, and turning to them he said: "If anyone comes to me and does not hate his father and mother, his wife and children, his brothers and sisters—yes, even his own life—he cannot be my disciple. And anyone who does not carry his cross and follow me cannot be my disciple.
>
> Suppose one of you wants to build a tower. Will he not first sit down and estimate the cost to see if he has enough money to complete it? . . . In the same way, any of you who does not give up everything he has cannot be my disciple.
>
> Luke 14:25–28, 33

The inner-city preacher must tell the young black male that following Jesus means becoming a responsible husband and father. The suburban pastor needs to demand that the congregation's investment bankers stop supporting companies that oppress the poor and exploit the helpless.

In other words, inviting people to come to Christ without truthfully telling them about the cost will eventually lead to a church that is ethically no different from the world. Or to state it more positively, telling potential converts that there are major areas where accepting Christ will demand fundamental change will produce a church that could change the world.

That leaves the question of culture. To what extent should an evangelist from one culture demand changes among new converts from another culture? This has always been a sticky issue for missionaries, but our multicultural society has brought the issue into our own churches. There are no simple rules, but generally, we need a combination of appealing to the "felt needs" of individuals and calling their attention to Scriptures that focus on sins that may be of particular importance to the new convert. The cross-cultural evangelist knows her own understanding of God's Word is limited by her culture in ways she even fails to grasp. We must trust the Holy Spirit to apply the Word to receptive hearts in the new culture. Cross-cultural settings call for particular caution.

Within one's own culture there is somewhat less danger of mis-understanding what areas of biblical ethics to highlight for specific persons. Even within one culture, however, situations vary greatly.

The generality of Billy Graham's preaching is appropriate for vast and diverse crowds but would be inappropriate for a one-to-one conversation with a longtime acquaintance exploring conversion. Furthermore, Reverend Graham is careful to point out that conversion demands a turning away from all sin.

In Western countries, at least, the greater danger today is cheap grace, not exorbitant grace. Our churches are full of people who somehow made a decision for Christ, or joined the church without any clear understanding or commitment to submit their total life to Jesus as Lord. The result is a materialistic, sexually disobedient church that is so culturally conformed to the dominant values of Hollywood and Wall Street that one can hardly tell the difference between the church and the world. Surely our desperate need in this kind of society is for Jesus' blunt, convicting word to the rich young inquirer.

The Power of Conversion

Two-Thirds World evangelists Vinay and Colleen Samuel offer insight into the transforming power of conversion.[37] Vinay Samuel has been called a "theologian of dignity." Vinay's and Colleen's theology and ministry demonstrate the incredible way that personal faith in Christ transforms precisely the most marginalized, oppressed people in India.

Massive poverty exists in India. Women suffer more than men. The lowest castes suffer most of all. Taught by their Hindu faith that their poverty and oppression are the result of sins in a previous incarnation, the lowest castes suffer passively in grinding poverty and oppression, hoping that patience in this life will lead to a better status in their next reincarnation.

113

These are the people the husband-and-wife team of Vinay and Colleen serve. For the first seven years after returning from graduate study at Cambridge University, Vinay pastored large, affluent St. John's Anglican Church in Bangalore. Vinay and Colleen, however, soon began a ministry in a slum called Lingarajapuram at the edge of the city. In 1983, his entire family moved with him to this slum to pastor the growing church.

Their tailoring program provides jobs for destitute women who otherwise would be forced into prostitution. Their school offers education to the poorest children. Their Bridge Foundation has provided loans and management training to over one hundred small businesses. They do it all in the name of Christ in the context of the Christian church. The result has been hundreds of conversions in the last decade. It has also meant repeated invitations to Colleen to run for high political office, including mayor of Bangalore and member of the Indian Parliament. (She declined.)

When Vinay visited my home last year, he was still overwhelmed with joy at the more than twenty-five people who had come forward to confess Christ the previous Sunday. As he looked at those coming to faith, he saw the wife of a very prominent Indian military official kneeling next to a prostitute. Both gave their lives to Christ that morning!

Most of those who came forward that day had been helped by a two-year-long program with a large group of impoverished folk pushed out of their slum housing. Vinay's and Colleen's Divya Shanthi Christian Association helped them find a new place to live, provided literacy classes, and leadership training. By training the group's own non-Christian leaders in the context of prayer and Bible study, they offered help with dignity in the name of Christ. Many of the leaders have become Christians—some of them on that Sunday morning.

Vinay's theological reflections on dignity help explain the power of conversion. "The [Hindu] outcaste is taught by tradition that his or her life is a judgment of God. The longing for dignity as a child of God is to be met not by an endless cycle of rebirths but by new birth in Christ."[38] Samuel insists that economic development by itself cannot break the power of caste and the resulting sense of worthlessness. But when outcastes accept Christ and join his new family, everything changes. Each person understands himself or herself as a son or daughter of God, made in the very image of the Creator and called to be a steward of God's creation. This God is opposed to caste, oppression, and poverty. This God calls the oppressed themselves to change history. As women and outcastes are empowered by faith in Christ and share in the Lord's table with other "respectable folk," they find a new dignity and power to change. It was precisely this new dignity and transforming power in Christ, Samuel believes, that encouraged the mass movement of Untouchables to Christianity in the early part of this century. They could escape their despised status in Hindu society by coming to Christ, accepting a biblical worldview, and joining a new kind of community that treated them with dignity.[39]

Anglican missionary Stephen Neill has similar reflections on the way personal faith in Christ produced enormous change among low-caste Indians.

> Things will not change until men begin to believe that they can change. The outcaste Christian saw them change before his very eyes, as he and his friends ceased to drink, began to work, cared more for their wives and children, realized within the limits of an unjust system great changes could be brought about.[40]

Without insisting that the sequence is universally normative, Neill pointed out that direct evangelism led to recovery of human dignity, which led to socioeconomic transformation, which led to new hope and finally political engagement.

Many people reflecting on diverse historical and cultural contexts make the same point. In a speech at Atlanta in 1991, Latin American liberation theologian José Miguez Bonino argued that the transforming power of conversion to Christ is probably the most important contribution evangelicals are making to the growth of democracy in Latin America:

> Possibly the most important relation of Protestantism to democracy, however will be found in Latin America in its evangelization, the creation of congregations and the pastoral service at the popular level. The call to conversion invites a decision in

115

which poor people (many times uprooted and threatened by anomia) claim their freedom and decide on the direction of their lives. The caring community, in recognizing them, provides a sense of personal dignity and worth which no declaration of human rights could convey. Active membership in the congregation opens the possibility of participation, an experience of self-realization and of democratic decision-making.[41]

African-American theologians J. Deotis Roberts and James Cone have said similar things about the history of African-American slaves. "The Christian faith gave the black man a sense of 'somebodiness' in spite of circumstances to the contrary."[42]

Harvard professor James Q. Wilson has claimed a correlation between periods of revival and reduction of crime in American history. He points out that the economic and social pressures of rapid urbanization that occurred in the middle of the nineteenth century would have been expected to lead to mounting crime. On the contrary, crime rates dropped from the mid-1800s to 1920. Nevertheless, during the prosperous 1920s, crime rates rose. His explanation? The widespread spiritual awakenings that had helped lower the crime rate in the earlier period did not continue in the same way in the twenties.[43]

Even national opinion polls seem to confirm the transforming power of an intimate, personal faith in Christ. A Gallup Poll discovered that church members in general (37%) are more likely to help the poor, sick, and elderly than people who are not members of churches (22%). Furthermore, evangelical Christians who regularly pray and study the Bible are more likely (42%) than other Christians (30%) to do social ministry. A more recent Gallup Poll discovered that the "highly spiritually committed" are twice as likely to work among the poor, sick, and elderly as the "highly uncommitted."[44] In a large survey of members of the United Church of Christ, the "pious" (devotionally oriented) members were more committed to working for civil justice than others were.[45]

The conversion of individuals is centrally important to Christian social responsibility. Earlier, I told the story of my friend from my church, James Dennis, who went to prison for a major crime. It is dangerous nonsense to imagine that some brilliant political program of structural change could have solved his problems. He needed radical surgery and new creation at the core of his life. He needed a personal encounter with the living God in Jesus Christ and the renewing power of the Holy Spirit. He needed that genuine biblical conversion that again and again has produced sweeping change not just in individual lives but in society.

Coming to faith in Christ, however, does not guarantee that we will have a major impact on society. Tragically we so often weaken, or even largely destroy, the transforming power of genuine conversion in many ways by becoming one-sided: by focusing exclusively on its vertical (or horizontal) dimensions; by neglecting the social (or personal) side of sin; by failing to see that love for God is inseparable from (but not identical with) love for neighbor; by neglecting Jesus' call to surrender unconditionally every area of our lives (not just the private sphere) to his Lordship; by failing, as a church, to be Jesus' new redeemed society, embracing and empowering the broken ones who come seeking help.

But when conversion is truly biblical, it is an explosive reality that transforms persons, families, and nations. It does that because it combines several crucial things for you and me who experience this divine gift.

First, it brings a restored relationship with the One who made me so that my heart would be restless until it rests in him.

Second, it brings liberating freedom from the paralyzing power of guilt and shame.

Third, it brings a new supernatural power from beyond myself, which empowers me to begin to abandon self-centered, destructive behavior. My brokenness is so severe that I need more than good ideas. I need help.

Fourth, it brings a dynamic new sense of dignity and worth. In conversion, I discover that the Creator of the galaxies loves me so much that he was willing to suffer the hell of Roman crucifixion *for me,* and now wants to have a living, personal relationship with me, live with me (John 14:23), and call me friend (John 15:15). That brings me a powerful new sense of value and importance.

Fifth, I discover that this loving Savior is also the God of justice. I learn that he abhors oppression, injustice, tyranny, racism, and environmental destruction. To my astonishment, God calls me to be a steward of his good creation and join him in correcting the oppressive structures and systems that mar his creation and trample his people.

Finally, in conversion I discover that that last terror, death itself, will be but for a moment. In joyful amazement I learn that however imperfect may be the personal or social transformation experienced now, I am destined to live forever in a redeemed world in the presence of the risen Lord.

PART 4

GO YE: THE BIBLICAL MANDATE FOR MISSION

7

Why Evangelize?

Woe to me if I do not preach the gospel!

1 Corinthians 9:16

As I reflect back on the last three decades of my life, I must confess that I wish I had done more personal evangelism. I wish that year by year I had had the joy of leading at least one person to Jesus.

That does not mean that I think I missed my central calling. I believe that God has called me to be an evangelical social activist.

I'll never forget a weekend with British evangelist David Watson that confirmed this call. Toward the end of a wonderful weekend with David and his wife, Anne, in 1980, David shared a special word for me that he believed came from the Spirit. He told me that God had led him to pray daily for the Spirit-filled gift of evangelism. (And God answered that prayer, using David to lead thousands around the world to Christ.) David said he sensed the Spirit telling him to urge me to pray in the same way for the Spirit-filled gift of working for justice. I have tried to do that. And I believe that my special call has been in the area of biblically shaped social action.

I think, however, that biblical social activists should not only talk about the importance of evangelism. They should also do it. I want to do more direct evangelism in the next twenty years than in the last twenty.

Stories like the one Anastasios of Androussa shared at a WCC gathering on evangelism have strengthened my resolve to really *do* more evangelism. Before he became acting Archbishop of the Orthodox Church in East Africa, his missionary work took him to a distant part of western Kenya. His sad task one day was to bury a lovely twelve-year-old girl struck down by malaria.

That night as the rain pounded on the banana leaves and zinc roof of the little schoolhouse where he was trying to sleep, he agonized over the question: "What am I doing here?" He thought of education, civilization, development. Then suddenly a light seemed to flash in his mind.

> What our brothers and sisters in the isolated corners of Africa and Asia or in the outskirts of our large and rich cities long for, in their depression and loneliness, is not vague words of consolation, a few material goods or crumbs of civilization. They yearn, secretly or consciously, for human dignity, hope, to transcend death. In the end they are searching for the living Christ, the perfect God-man, the way, the truth and the life. All, of whatever age and class, rich or poor, obscure or famous, illiterate or learned, in their heart of hearts long to celebrate the Resurrection.[1]

Why do people circle the globe, defy disease and death, and experience heartbreak and agony to share the gospel with those who have not heard? Why do people make the equally long trek from suburb to inner city to tell the old, old story? Why do ordinary Christians brush aside inner hesitation and fear and explain their faith to neighbors next door and colleagues in the next office?

Not all the motives, of course, have been pure and good, and this has led some to question the validity of evangelism. They point to missionary "conquests" that were nothing more than efforts to exploit and control indigenous populations. Perhaps it would be better, they suggest, simply to encourage Hindus to be better Hindus and animists to be better animists. Furthermore, many ask, is it not the height of arrogance to claim that my faith is better than another person's beliefs?

These, however, were not Anastasios' conclusions, nor were they St. Paul's. In this chapter I want to examine the central biblical reasons for doing evangelism.

God's Love for the World

The most important reason for evangelism is God's astounding, overflowing love for a lost and broken world. The mission is not primarily ours. It is God's. It is because God so loved the world that we follow in the divine steps seeking to share that love.

When Karl Barth traveled to the United States, someone asked him to summarize the gospel. This brilliant theologian did not respond with a typical, complex, half-page German sentence. He simply said: "Jesus loves me. This I know, for the Bible tells me so." The simplicity of John 3:16 is as profound as the simple words of the children's song Barth cited. "For God so loved the world that he gave his one and only Son, that whoever believes in him shall not perish but have eternal life. For God did not send his Son into the world to condemn the world, but to save the world through him" (John 3:16–17). We share the gospel to spread this message of God's love.

Throughout the Scriptures we see God yearning, longing, eagerly seeking to bring us to himself (Jer. 31:20–21). At the cross, we do not see an angry God crushing a human victim. We see God the Father suffering in the agony of his only Son. "God demonstrates his own love for us in this: While we were still sinners, Christ died for us" (Rom. 5:8). In evangelism, we join the loving mission of the triune God who so loves the world that he does not want anyone to perish (2 Peter 3:9).[2]

If one has been sought and embraced by transforming love, how can one fail to lead others to that same embrace?

The Uniqueness of Christ

Anastasios pointed to a second, extremely important reason for evangelism—Jesus himself. Christians believe that the carpenter from Nazareth is more than a great ethical teacher, more than a radical prophet of justice. He is the eternal Word, Lord of the universe, true God as well as true man.

> Long ago God spoke to our ancestors in many and various ways by the prophets, but in these last days he has spoken to us by a Son, whom he appointed heir of all things, through whom he also created the worlds. He is the reflection of God's glory and the exact imprint of God's very being, and he sustains all things by his powerful word.
>
> Hebrews 1:1–3 NRSV

The wandering teacher from Nazareth is he in whom "God was pleased to have all his fullness dwell" (Col. 1:19). The Galilean champion of marginalized women and lepers was the eternal Word who in the beginning "was with God and was God" (John 1:1). The alleged criminal hanging limp on the middle cross is the one to whom every knee shall bow whether in heaven or on earth (Phil. 2:5–11).

Many modern intellectuals, some modern church members, even some modern theologians and missiologists can no longer make this confession.[3] If Jesus is only one of many wise teachers, then spreading his story becomes far less important.

Over the centuries, however, Christians have claimed that Jesus of Nazareth is true God as well as prophetic social critic. If that is genuine truth rather than tragic delusion, then Christians have no choice. In amazed awe and astounded joy we must tell the whole world the Good News that the Creator of the galaxies once trod the dusty paths of our little planet to bring us God's salvation.

If one believes this central confession about Christ made by Christians through the centuries, how can one fail to tell others?

The Only Way to Salvation

However unpopular in a relativistic age, however offensive to secular social activists and devotees of other religions, the New Testament clearly teaches that Jesus is the final revelation of God and the only way to salvation.[4] "I am the way and the truth and the life," Jesus declares. "No one comes to the Father except through me" (John 14:6; cf. 3:36). To the astonishment of the religious leadership in Jerusalem, Peter dared to insist almost immediately after the crucifixion that salvation was available only through the crucified and risen Nazarene: "There is salvation in no one else, for there is no other name under heaven given among mortals by which we must be saved" (Acts 4:12 NRSV).

Because the Incarnate One was the eternal Word, he alone provides an adequate revelation of God. "No one knows the Father except the Son and those to whom the Son chooses to reveal him" (Matt. 11:27). "No one has ever seen God. It is God the only Son, who is close to the Father's heart, who has made him known" (John 1:18 NRSV).

Because Christians have been given this precious treasure of God's divine revelation, we *must* evangelize.[5] We cannot keep this truth to ourselves.

The supreme revealer of God is also the only mediator of salvation. "There is one God; there is also one mediator between God and humankind, Christ Jesus, himself human, who gave himself a ransom for all" (1 Tim. 2:5–6 NRSV; also 1 Cor. 8:5–6).

This unique revealer and mediator is not some mystical notion or philosophical concept. He is precisely the one who became flesh in the womb of a startled Jewish maiden two thousand years ago. He is precisely the one who challenged the status quo, taught the way of shalom, and died on a Roman cross. That specific, historical person is the one of whom we confess that "God was pleased to have all his fullness dwell in him, and through him to reconcile to himself all things, whether things on earth or things in heaven, by making peace through his blood, shed on the cross" (Col. 1:19–20).

Jesus of Nazareth, the Word become flesh, is the only way to salvation. That is the historic Christian claim. Roman Catholic and evangelical leaders alike confess their common belief in "the absolute uniqueness of Jesus Christ . . . the only Savior."[6]

If you believe this truth confessed by the church universal through the centuries, how can you neglect evangelism?

Obedience to His Command

Christians also spread the gospel because our Lord gave the command.[7] His final words, according to Matthew, issued a powerful missionary mandate.

All authority in heaven and on earth has been given to me. Therefore go and make disciples of all nations, baptizing them in the
name of the Father and of the Son and of the Holy Spirit, and
teaching them to obey everything I have commanded.

MATTHEW 28:18–20; CF. ALSO LUKE 24:45–49;
JOHN 20:21–23; ACTS 1:6–8

Jesus grounds his command in his unique authority. If he were
just a wise teacher, a brilliant philosopher, or a shrewd social activist,
we might debate the wisdom of his summons. But if we believe
that he is Lord of heaven and earth, then we can only accept it with
joyful obedience.

Paul and the early church did just that. Everywhere they went,
they told the story.[8] Many if not all shared Paul's sense of com-
pulsion to evangelize. "Woe to me if I do not preach the gospel!"
(1 Cor. 9:16).

For too long, too many Christians ignored the Lord's command. Some relegated the assignment to a special group of Christians. Some claimed the missionary mandate applied only to the
apostolic age. Most of us simply fill our days with other things. We
need to recover what William Carey, the great British missionary
pioneer, understood so clearly. The evangelistic mandate is a divine
imperative.[9] The risen Lord commands us—all of us—to spread
his saving story.

If we know who he is, dare we despise his last command?

Love for Neighbor

Knowing Jesus Christ is the most wonderful thing that has happened in my life. Meaning, wholeness, hope, and joy have all flowed
in abundance from this living relationship with God in Christ.
From my own experience as well as the promise of Christ, I believe
that there is absolutely nothing I could share with those I love that
would bring anywhere nearly as much joy and blessing as the living knowledge of my Lord. If I love my neighbors, I will eagerly
tell them about the best treasure I have.

The full biblical Christ meets the longings of the whole person. Christ brings meaning and purpose in life as one discovers how we fit into and play a role in God's breathtaking, cosmic plan to bring the entire created order to wholeness in Christ. Christ brings forgiveness and a liberating freedom from guilt as we learn that God welcomes and embraces sinners who trust in the One on the cross. Christ brings an ever growing personal transformation of the ornery, cussed persons we all are. Christ brings a loving, redeemed community of believing sisters and brothers who now begin to live a common life in which the social and economic brokenness of the world is being overcome. Christ brings a new power, standard, and community for seeking justice in the larger society.[10] Christ brings an answer to that terrifying question mark, death itself. And Christ brings a wondrously empowering hope that sustains us when social justice wanes and the flesh fails.

I don't mean to overstate the case. My faith is sometimes weak, my sanctification dreadfully partial, and the church scandalously unfaithful. But again and again, in spite of failures, Christ has brought joy and fullness of life in cascading abundance. Knowing the only true God and Jesus whom he sent is indeed life eternal (John 17:3). This abundant life begins now as we believe. And it continues forever. I cannot imagine a more wonderful way to live now and through all eternity than walking in daily relationship with this friend, Savior, and Lord.

Can you love your neighbor and not share this joyful treasure?

Lost without Christ

I wish I could stop with these glorious, *positive* reasons for evangelism. But the New Testament also teaches that people are lost without Christ. And Jesus himself, the apostle of love, says more about eternal separation from God than anyone else in the New Testament. These are not popular claims in our pluralistic world. But we cannot ignore them if the Scriptures are our guide and Jesus is our Lord.

Paul pointedly asserts that before their conversion, the educated, religious Ephesians were ignorant of God and without hope.

"Remember that at that time you were separate from Christ, excluded from citizenship in Israel and foreigners to the covenants of the promise, without hope and without God in the world" (Eph. 2:12). When the Thessalonians accepted Christ, they turned from idols to the true and living God and were rescued from coming wrath (1 Thess. 1:9). Paul assured the Colossian Christians that God "has rescued us from the dominion of darkness and brought us into the kingdom of the Son" (Col. 1:13).

The lostness and hopelessness outside Christ extends to every area of life. Guilt or shame burden and crush those who have never heard of God's incredible mercy. Women, minorities, and the poor are oppressed. The well-off are bored, and their lives lack meaning and purpose. All of us puzzle over the mystery of life, wondering if the short, fleeting days of our moment on planet earth are a meaningless flicker in the billions of years of time on billions of randomly spinning galaxies. Even apart from the question of God's wrath toward sin, people are lost without Christ.

Knowing they are lost, how can I fail to share the most hopeful, healing reality I have ever encountered?

The Wages of Sin Are Death—Eternal Death

Everywhere in the New Testament—whether in Jesus or the Epistles—there is a clear consistent warning. The holy Creator hates sin (but not sinners). A day of judgment is coming. Those whose sins are not forgiven must face God's terrible wrath.[11] "We must all appear before the judgment seat of Christ." It is precisely because Paul knew this and had a holy fear of the Lord that he sought eagerly to persuade people to accept Christ (2 Cor. 5:10–11).

The basic argument of Romans 1–3 is that all people are sinners standing under God's holy condemnation. "The wrath of God is being revealed from heaven against all the godlessness and wickedness" (Rom. 1:18). Both Jews who have the special revelation of the law and Gentiles who have general revelation in creation fail to live up to all the truth they have. "All have sinned and fall short of the glory of God" (Rom. 3:23; cf. 3:10–18).

All parts of the New Testament warn about a coming day of judgment. That was one of the reasons Paul urged the educated, religious Athenians to repent: "Now [God] commands all people everywhere to repent. For he has set a day when he will judge the world with justice by the man he has appointed" (Acts 17:30–31; also 2 Cor. 5:10–11). Jesus gave the same warning: "A time is coming when all who are in their graves will hear his voice and come out— those who have done good will rise to live, and those who have done evil will rise to be condemned" (John 5:28–29; cf. Matt. 16:27). Revelation 20 paints an awesome picture of a final judgment before the great throne of God. Those whose names are not in the book of life depart from the presence of the God of love (vv. 11–15).

Discussion of eternal separation from God is undoubtedly the most difficult of all biblical teachings. Many would rather ignore or reinterpret this hard truth. But it is part of God's Word. Paul warns that those who live in sin—whether adultery or greed—"will not inherit the kingdom of God" (Gal. 5:21; 1 Cor. 6:9–10). Jesus is equally blunt. In fact, it is precisely Jesus himself, the ultimate expression of God's overwhelming love for sinners, who says the most about this dread topic.

Jesus' parable of the sheep and the goats clearly teaches that everyone will appear before him at the final judgment. The righteous enjoy eternal life in the presence of God. The wicked can only wait fearfully for the terrible words, "Depart from me, you who are cursed, into the eternal fire prepared for the devil and his angels" (Matt. 25:41). When Jesus explains the parable of the wheat and the weeds, he again speaks of a final judgment. The Son of Man (Jesus' preferred title for himself) will throw all who cause sin and do evil "into the fiery furnace, where there will be weeping and gnashing of teeth" (Matt. 13:41–42; cf. also 13:49–50).

It is not entirely clear what Jesus means in Mark 3:28–29 by the "unforgivable" sin. But whatever it is, it clearly involves eternal separation from God. So terrible is the reality of eternal absence from the living God that Jesus recommends chopping off a hand or foot rather than living in sinful disobedience. "It is better for you to enter life maimed or crippled than to have two hands or two feet and be thrown into eternal fire" (Matt. 18:8).[12]

One measure of biblical faithfulness in our time will be whether we dare to declare the warning about coming judgment and the possibility of eternal separation from God as clearly as Jesus did. Certainly it will not be our dominant note. We will begin and end as Jesus did, with God's astounding, overflowing mercy. But we will also, as he did, issue the warning. If we do not, we will be like the watchman in Ezekiel. Because he failed to announce the warning, God held the watchman accountable for the people's destruction (Ezek. 3:16–19).

These texts raise many hard questions. Do the wicked burn literally in everlasting fire? Does God's wrath continue forever in never-ending punishment? And what about the billions who die without ever hearing of Christ?

I doubt that the literal imagery is the essential point. C. S. Lewis thinks that the essence of God's punishment of sinners is to accept forever their free choice of sinful rebellion against the only source of goodness and love. As a result they choose to depart forever from the One in whom alone they can find joy, fulfillment, and life.[13] Obviously Lewis's interpretation is only that. It has no biblical authority. But he is at least correct in underlining the fact that the essence of the biblical teaching on eternal death is eternal separation from the only source of love and goodness in the universe.

Does punishment last forever? Devout Christians thoroughly committed to the full authority of the Scriptures disagree on the answer. Some say yes.[14] Others, after a careful study of the key words, have concluded that the biblical texts speak of total destruction of the wicked, not eternal conscious torment. Those who think this second view is the most faithful exegesis of the biblical texts include John Stott, key drafter of the Lausanne Covenant, and evangelist Michael Green.[15] This issue received considerable discussion at the Consultation on Evangelical Affirmations (May 1989), an important gathering called by Carl Henry and Kenneth Kantzer to reaffirm essential evangelical perspectives. In the final declaration, the participants voted not to exclude the position of John Stott and Michael Green.[16]

Whichever way one exegetes the texts, the result is something so terrible that we should all be driven to our knees interceding with burning zeal for those who turn from Christ. For they "will be punished with everlasting destruction and shut out from the presence of the Lord" (2 Thess. 1:9). What can be more awful than to depart forever from the loving presence of the living God?

Is that the fate of billions today and through the centuries who die without ever hearing the gospel of Christ? Is it only those who consciously confess Christ in this life who will be saved? Again Christians committed to biblical authority are divided.[17] Some say yes. Others believe we should not exclude the possibility that somehow whether before or after death, Christ will reveal himself to those who truly seek God even though they have never heard the gospel while on earth. How biblical is this second position?

Some things are clear, I believe. Universalism (the belief that all will eventually be saved) is wrong. It simply contradicts the texts that we have just examined. Some people reject Christ and depart eternally from God. Nor are all religions possible means of salvation. Jesus Christ, the God-man, is the only way to the Father—all who are saved are saved through him.

Equally clear and very important is the wonderful truth that God eagerly desires the salvation of everyone. The Lord is patient, "not wanting anyone to perish, but everyone to come to repentance" (2 Peter 3:9). God our Savior "desires everyone to be saved and to come to the knowledge of the truth" (1 Tim. 2:4 NRSV). God is like the good shepherd who leaves the ninety-nine sheep who are safe to search for the one lost lamb. "Your Father in heaven is not willing that any of these little ones should be lost" (Matt. 18:14).

But what of the billions who never hear the gospel? The Bible has no explicit discussion of that question. What it does teach clearly is that God holds people accountable for what they know, not what they do not know. At Athens, Paul referred to the many stone images of Greek gods and goddesses and then said that "in the past God overlooked such ignorance" (Acts 17:29–30; cf. also Acts 14:16–17). Speaking of the time before the giving of the law to Israel, Paul acknowledges that sin was present but adds that "sin is not taken into account when there is no law" (Rom. 5:13).

Earlier, in the long argument about the sinful rebellion of both Jew and Gentile, Paul says that creation reveals God sufficiently to leave us without excuse (Rom. 1:18–20). But people are judged only on the basis of what they know: "All who sin apart from the law will also perish apart from the law, and all who sin under the law will be judged by the law" (Rom. 2:12). Then, however, Paul adds a very intriguing comment. Even though the Gentiles do not have Israel's law, nevertheless "the requirements of the law are written on their hearts, their consciences also bearing witness, and their thoughts now accusing, now even defending them" on the day of final judgment (Rom. 2:15). Are some who have never known God's special revelation during this life "defended" ("excused") because of their response to what they did know?

In John's Gospel, Jesus also relates responsibility to knowledge.

> If I had not come and spoken to them, they would not be guilty of sin. Now, however, they have no excuse for their sin. . . . If I had not done among them what no one else did, they would not be guilty of sin.
>
> JOHN 15:22–24

Earlier, in a discussion of spiritual blindness, the Pharisees angrily ask if Jesus thinks they are also blind. Jesus responds: "If you were blind, you would not be guilty of sin; but now that you claim you can see, your guilt remains" (John 9:41).

God is fair as well as merciful and holy (Rom. 2:6–10). God judges us on the basis of what we know, not what we do not know.

Some conclude that since (1) God wants all to be saved; (2) God judges people on the basis of their knowledge; and (3) Christ is the only way to salvation, therefore we should conclude that after death some people encounter Christ and respond in faith.[18] However attractive that may be, there is no clear biblical basis for teaching it.[19] Therefore, as a Christian who seeks to submit all my thinking to the authority of God's Word, I dare not teach that or hold out that assurance.

At the same time, no clear biblical teaching excludes that possibility either. I know of no biblical text that explicitly says that those who die without hearing the gospel will never have a chance. If God chooses to grant them an encounter with Christ the only Savior, I certainly do not object! But I cannot teach that will happen because there is no clear biblical basis for it.

What we do know *for sure* is that now in this life God offers salvation to those who believe and repent. "Now is the day of salvation" (2 Cor. 6:2). So we must proceed as fast as possible with the glorious mission of sharing the gospel with those who have never heard.

Finally, I must confess that I simply do not know about those who die without hearing the gospel. I know that God is fair. I know that God longs for the salvation of all. I leave this mystery in the hands of my loving Savior whose cross is the ultimate combination of love and justice.

That may seem like a timid cop-out.[20] I would argue, on the other hand, that it represents proper theological modesty rather than timidity. Again and again throughout church history, confusion has arisen and heresies have threatened precisely because people went beyond the clear teaching of Scripture. The Bible leaves many intriguing and important questions unanswered. Cautious speculation is certainly legitimate, but we dare not teach what is not clearly biblical. What the Scriptures do tell us is more than sufficient to live as faithful people now. We should concentrate on that, get on with the tasks and teachings that are clear, and be humble enough to remain uncertain where Scripture has not clearly spoken. That means leaving the future of those who die without hearing the gospel in the hands of our God who at the cross perfectly combines justice and mercy.

This position does not lead to a loss of passion for evangelism. Because we know that sinners stand under the wrath of God, because we know that judgment day is coming, because we know that God allows people to reject his merciful love and depart eternally from him, because the Bible teaches all that clearly, we return with renewed zeal to the awesome task of imploring people to confess Christ. With St. Paul we confess that all of us must appear before the judgment seat of Christ, so that each may receive recompense for what has been done in the body, whether good or evil. "Therefore, knowing the fear of the Lord, we try to persuade others" (2 Cor. 5:11 NRSV).

Knowing that I have been sent as a watchman to warn those who are perishing, how dare I fail to shout with fear and trembling: Please dear son, daughter, neighbor, turn from the way of death to my loving Savior who seeks you with arms outstretched!

Our Eschatological Hope

We evangelize because in Jesus' life and resurrection, God has drawn back the curtain and shown us a glimpse of the future.[21] We know that it is God's intention that God's will be done on earth as it is in heaven. God fought the decisive battle with evil on the cross. The resurrection demonstrates that Christ's kingdom will finally prevail throughout the universe. The kingdoms of this world will indeed become the kingdom of our Lord (Rev. 11:15). In God's time, at Christ's return, human civilization, even the groaning creation, will experience God's cosmic salvation.

Incredibly, God uses our evangelistic efforts to move history toward that goal (Rom. 10:14–21). In fact Jesus said this glorious, final victory over evil will not happen until the gospel of the kingdom is preached to the whole world (Matt. 24:14). Overwhelmed by the agony of our world, filled with longing for the day when God will wipe all tears from our eyes, we return to the evangelistic task, confident yet amazed that it is through the foolishness of preaching that we help move the world toward the coming kingdom.[22]

Knowing God's grand design, how can I fail to invite people to enjoy its splendor?

The Glory of God

We share the gospel so that the whole world may be full of God's glory.[23] Paul longed for the day when every tongue would "confess that Jesus Christ is Lord, to the glory of God the Father" (Phil. 2:11). He begged others to pray for his evangelistic work so that the message would spread quickly in order that God would be honored (2 Thess. 3:1). At the cross, the Son glorified the Father (John 12:20–36). When God uses our evangelistic work to bring others into right relationship with himself through the cross, we bring glory to the Creator.

Having tasted the sweet, awesome splendor of God's glory, how can I not eagerly play my small part in spreading it throughout the universe?

As I confessed at the beginning of this chapter, I wish I had spent more time on evangelism in the last thirty years. I am sure that my special calling has been to be an evangelical social activist. Others have the special calling of evangelist. But God invites and summons every Christian to spread this fantastic gospel. I intend, by God's grace, to do better in the future.

During the International Charismatic Consultation on World Evangelization (Brighton, 1991), I attended a workshop led by a friend, Anglican leader James Wong, from Singapore. He shared a simple device that his congregation has found effective in increasing everyone's evangelistic work. They call it the 5-3-1 method. At the beginning of each year, every member of his congregation asks God to guide him or her to think of five people who do not yet know Christ. Then they pray regularly that in the course of the year they will have the opportunity to share the gospel story with at least three of them and the joy of leading at least one of them to Christ.

I have decided to do that in my own life. I now share this simple approach with my seminary students. With eager expectation, I anticipate the repeated joy of introducing more people to my Lord in the next three decades than in the past three.

The reasons for doing evangelism are many and powerful. Evangelism is grounded in the abounding love of the Creator of the galaxies. In evangelism, we share the story of the Eternal Word who became flesh in the Nazarene carpenter to provide the only way of salvation for the whole world. This dying, risen Savior commands us to spread his Good News. And we know he is right as we discover again and again that the most loving thing we can do for our neighbors is lead them to our dearest treasure. As we see their lost, broken agony and remember Christ's warning that sin leads to eternal death, our eagerness to share this loving Redeemer takes on deeper urgency. And the biblical hope reminds us that all who believe will one day sing and dance in a renewed creation to the glory of our God of love.

Knowing all that, how can I not be more faithful in the coming years in telling the old, old story to those who have never heard?

8

WHY DO SOCIAL ACTION?

> There is no greater menace in the church than a born-again
> Christian without a social conscience.
>
> METHODIST EVANGELIST ALAN WALKER,
> SPEAKING IN SOUTH AFRICA IN 1980[1]

August 13, 1987, was one of the more exciting days of my life.
During a long ride across Kenya in the back seat of Bishop Gitari's
car, I discussed evangelism, politics, and mission with Bishop Gitari
and Reverend Frank Chikane.

Reverend Frank Chikane is a black, South African, Pentecostal
minister who was tortured by a white deacon from his own church.
Chikane became the General Secretary of the South Africa Council
of Churches. The Reverend David Gitari is now Archbishop of
Kenya, where his challenge to undemocratic government has led to
repeated verbal attacks by the president of Kenya and eventually an
attempt on his life. Over the last fifteen years, Gitari's emphasis on
evangelism has produced massive church growth in his diocese.

The experiences shared by Chikane and Gitari during that
absorbing discussion and since then raise the question of social
concern and political engagement in a fascinating way. Both the
black political leadership of Kenya and the white apartheid lead-

ership in South Africa advised Gitari and Chikane to stick to preaching. Both refused.

Bishop Gitari has emphasized both evangelism and community development since he organized the diocese of Mt. Kenya East. The result has been fantastic church growth. The number of new Christians has grown much faster than the population in this diocese that (until divided recently) covered two-fifths of Kenya. For years, Bishop Gitari opened one (and sometimes two) new churches each month.[2]

Bishop Gitari's pastoral work, however, has led him into political controversy. He has publicly condemned political assassination, economic injustice, and undemocratic politics. He dared to challenge the voting practice of "queueing"—having to stand in line behind the candidate you wanted to vote for! After several years of struggle, the president of Kenya finally announced a return to the secret ballot in December 1990.

Bishop Gitari's courageous challenge regularly infuriated top politicians who warned him to "keep politics out of the church." His refusal resulted in several feature stories in the *Kenya Weekly Review* (Kenya's equivalent of *Time*)—and eventually an attempt to murder him. One midnight in April 1989, a large gang raided his house, intending to kill him. Gitari scrambled up on his roof and began to shout. His outcry quickly summoned a large crowd of supportive neighbors, and the attackers fled.

Was Bishop Gitari right to challenge political injustice? Or should he have remained preoccupied with evangelism? Some evangelical churches apparently thought the latter course would have been better. They withdrew from the National Council of Churches of Kenya when Bishop Gitari led the battle against queueing.[3]

White leaders in South Africa had a similar message for Frank Chikane. In my interview with him, Reverend Chikane explained that the white leadership of his church cut off all funds for his congregation because he was "involved in politics."

Chikane grew up as an evangelical and became the pastor of a Pentecostal church. Already active in evangelism during university years, Chikane started two other congregations while pastoring his own church. Pastoral duties, however, got him into trouble. Reverend Chikane was not a part of any political organization, he told me, but he did feel obligated to visit the families of church members who were in prison. The result was prison and torture for himself. During one ghastly six-week ordeal, he was tortured in terribly bloody ways. And a white deacon from his own Pentecostal denomination supervised the torture.[4] Fortunately, Reverend Chikane escaped death. After being pushed out of the pastorate, Chikane became involved in the struggle against apartheid. When I interviewed him in 1987, he had recently been named General Secretary of the South African Council of Churches. Since then, he has played a visible, crucial role in the dismantling of apartheid.

Were Gitari and Chikane right or wrong? Should they have stayed with evangelism and church planting? Or at least avoided politics? This chapter seeks for answers to these questions by exploring the biblical basis for social concern.

Three Types of Social Concern

It is helpful to distinguish relief, development, and structural change. The categories are not airtight. At the edges, they flow together. Usually, however, it is possible and helpful to distinguish these three different types of social concern.

In relief, we minister to victims of natural or social disaster, seeking to provide immediate handouts of food, shelter, and other necessities so people survive. Food and clothing distribution to inner-city residents, and disaster relief after a flood, earthquake, or famine are all examples of relief.

In development we seek to help individuals, families, and communities obtain appropriate tools, skills, and knowledge so they can care for themselves. Offering better agricultural seeds and tools, digging wells, and providing loans to those who want to start small businesses are all examples of development.

It has often been said that when you give a person a fish, you feed that person for a day, but when you teach a person to fish, you feed that person for a lifetime. Relief prevents starvation today. Development brings self-sufficiency. At least in principle—in an ideal world.

But we live in the real world where many of the fishponds are owned or controlled by small groups of powerful, wealthy persons. Slavery, apartheid, and the dictatorship of the Marxist party in communist societies are all examples of this kind of abusive power. Such elites sometimes are very upset when poor people (who often are occasional laborers on their large holdings) learn new skills, acquire new tools, and move toward self-sufficiency. Equally problematic, the elites often own most of the productive resources such as land in an agricultural society. Any suggestion of sharing power and the basic productive resources with those who have none frequently meets intense hostility. But that must happen somehow through structural change.[5] If one is to fish for a lifetime, one must have a share in the fishpond.

Structural change happens at the macro level of law, politics, and economic life. Politics is one of the important ways to change the basic societal structures to create greater freedom, democracy, economic justice, and environmental sustainability.

Is there biblical warrant for doing relief, development, and structural change? The answer is yes. Virtually every major biblical teaching undergirds and demands social concern and helps shape its character.[6]

Key Theological Doctrines and Social Concern

God

The first article of the Christian creed issues a ringing call to social concern. The Bible tells us that the holy, loving God we worship has a special concern for the poor, weak, and destitute. Anyone who wants to love and obey this biblical God must share the same concern.

There are literally hundreds of verses. *For They Shall Be Fed* is a two-hundred-page book that I edited, filled almost exclusively with biblical texts about God's concern for the poor.[7] The psalmist celebrates Yahweh as both the creator and defender of the oppressed (Ps. 146:6–9). In chapter four, we saw that tender compassion for the poor and marginalized was a central concern of Jesus and evidence that he was the Messiah.[8] God destroyed first Israel and then Judah because of their oppression of the poor.[9] Jeremiah teaches that we do not know God properly if we do not seek justice for the poor (Jer. 22:13–16). Repeatedly the prophets warn that God abominates religious ritual separated from concern for justice.[10] Jesus said bluntly that if we fail to feed the hungry and clothe the naked we go to hell

(Matt. 25). The Bible says more about God's concern for the poor than it does about prayer or the atonement or Jesus' resurrection.

Nor is it merely an ethical teaching. It is first of all a theological truth, a central doctrine of the creed, a constantly repeated biblical teaching about the God we worship. The biblical insistence on God's concern for the poor is first of all a theological statement about the Creator and Sovereign of the universe.

In light of this extensive biblical teaching, it is simply incredible that so many modern Christians, especially evangelicals, have largely ignored this central truth about God. I remember talking to a prominent evangelical leader about fifteen years ago. He had just discovered the hundreds of biblical verses on God's concern for the poor. How, he asked me, was it possible for him to study at an evangelical college, take his theological degree at an evangelical seminary, and become a faculty member at an evangelical school and never learn about God's special concern for the poor?

It is difficult to overstate the importance of this biblical teaching about the poor—but it can be done! Some liberation theologians[11] and some statements from the World Council of Churches[12] make it *the* central biblical truth, *the* criterion of biblical faithfulness and evangelism. That, too, is wrong.

That is to overstate a crucial point. Concern for the poor is not the *only* important aspect of Christian social concern or mission. We dare not become so preoccupied with it that everything else becomes secondary.

Nor dare our concern for the poor become a secondary matter that we remember only if we have spare time and money. God's concern for the poor is central to God's character. We do not know God properly if we fail to share that concern for the poor. As the WCC's *Mission and Evangelism* rightly insists, proclamation of the gospel to the poor is "*a* priority criterion by which to judge the validity of our missionary engagement today."[13] The second Lausanne Congress on World Evangelization also placed great emphasis on God's concern for the poor. The final manifesto insisted that "the law, the prophets, and the wisdom books, and the teachings and ministry of Jesus all stress God's concern for the materially poor and our consequent duty to defend and care for them."[14] The Christian doctrine of God provides our first foundation for biblical social concern.

Creation

The Creator has chosen to create and declared the result very good. Even when people rebel against God, God still continues to provide the created gifts of sun and rain on good and evil alike (Matt. 5:45). The created good of whole, joyful human life is so good that Jesus did not withdraw the gift of healing from those who declined to become his followers.

Equally amazing is the biblical teaching that persons have been made in the image of God and have been given stewardship over the earth (Gen. 1:27–30). We are also called to care for and watch over each other. Persons have a creation mandate to care for the earth (Gen. 2:15) and to nurture societies where people can realize more of the wholeness intended by the Creator.

Grounding our social concern in creation means that social concern is not merely pre-evangelism. It is true that partnership with the poor in the struggle for development and justice often has a powerful evangelistic impact. And we rejoice when that happens (as long as we avoid problems such as psychological manipulation and hypocritical "rice Christians"). But social concern need not be pre-evangelism to be legitimate. Our doctrine of creation tells us that it is good for all people to enjoy the bounty of the Creator during their three score years and ten. Certainly we want them also to know and love our Lord. But if God continues to shower the good gifts of creation on all, regardless of their faith or unbelief, then Christians too should work for physical, social, economic, and political well-being for all. Simply on the basis of creation, those tasks have validity and importance.

A Biblical View of Persons

Each person, John Stott says, is "a body-soul-in-community."[15] Persons are not merely bodies or merely souls. Nor are we lone rangers.

Any view of persons that reduces us primarily or exclusively to mere bodies or mere souls is fundamentally wrong. Since we are not merely material beings, nothing in the material world can finally satisfy us. Material wealth, sex, political power are all finally inadequate. We are made for relationship with God and invited to live forever in God's presence. Therefore, any solution to the human problem that focuses primarily on economic development or structural change via politics is bound to fail.

On the other hand, our bodies are not a mere accident. The Creator made us body-soul unities. Even when St. Paul longed to leave the body and be with the Lord, he insisted that God's final plan for us is *bodily* resurrection—that wholeness of body-soul unity intended by the Creator (1 Cor. 15:35ff.; 2 Cor. 5:1–4). If the body is so good that the Creator became flesh, rose bodily, and promises to restore the whole created order including our bodies, then any approach to human need that ignores or neglects physical needs is flatly heretical.

Black evangelist/social activist John Perkins underlines this point. As he ministered in the midst of white racism, whites often said, "John, I love your soul." They wanted to lead him to Christ without struggling against racial (and related economic) oppression. Perkins's answer is profoundly biblical: "My soul is in a black body. And if you really want to get to my soul, you're first going to have to deal with this body."[16]

Nor are we created to live as isolated hermits. Made in the image of the triune God who is a community of Father, Son, and Holy Spirit, persons are created so that only in community do we become what the Creator intended. We need family, community, society to become all we are meant to be. And where the structures of community oppress and destroy rather than nurture and support, then the biblical understanding of persons summons us to change oppressive systems. Whether through immediate relief, long-term development, or structural change, we seek to enable all persons to live as interdependent partners in a supportive community of neighbors.

Sin

Our proud rebellion against the Creator has both destroyed an open relationship with God and devastated the created order. The biblical doctrine of sin tells us that our total being, not just our body, is fallen. Our corrupt minds produce brilliant rationalizations for our self-interest—whether racism, sexism, or economic exploitation. Unfortunately, but inevitably since we are persons-in-community, human sin has permeated our social structures and institutions to such a degree that they are always a tragic mixture of good and evil.

Christians are not preoccupied with sin, however. We know that God is now about the business of defeating Satan and rolling back his satanic inroads into the good creation. Therefore, Christians join in that battle to correct all the evil results of sin. Christians are called to expose the "deeds of darkness" (Eph. 5:11). Since we know that we are persons-in-community, we will never suppose that we can solve all the problems merely by changing individuals. Exposing and correcting evil social systems is important. Equally important, since we know the root of the problem is our continuing rebellion against God, we will never suppose that merely modifying the environment can create entirely new, whole persons. Divine, transforming grace is imperative. And since we know that sin will persist until Christ's return, we will reject utopian dreams of perfect persons, families, and societies in the present even as we struggle hard now to erect signs of that coming wholeness. Only at the end will Christ wipe away all tears and conquer all evil.

Christology

The biblical teaching on the person and work of Christ also summons us to vigorous social concern.

In chapter four we saw how Jesus challenged what was evil in the status quo. He exposed the deeds of darkness, challenging society where it was evil. Identifying with the poor, marginalized, and outcast, he summoned the whole Jewish people to live now the values of his dawning kingdom. Anyone familiar with Jesus feels a powerful call to challenge every injustice in society. Matthew's summary of Jesus' work shows that Jesus ministered to the whole person: "Jesus went through all the towns and villages, teaching in their synagogues, preaching the good news of the kingdom and healing every disease and sickness. When he saw the crowds, he had compassion on them, because they were harassed and helpless" (Matt. 9:35–36; so, too, almost exactly, Matt. 4:23). Preaching and ministering to physical needs were both central in Jesus' life and work. He preached and healed. He satisfied both sick hearts and sick bodies. A vast amount of space in the Gospels is devoted to accounts of Jesus taking care of people's physical needs. God-in-the-flesh thought he could spare—or rather ought to spare—a great deal of his potential preaching time and devote it to meeting the physical needs of people. Should we not follow in his steps?

Nor did Jesus heal merely as a sign of his deity or as evidence that the messianic kingdom was arriving. To be sure, that was *one* important reason for his miracles (cf. John 20:30–31). Again and again, however, the Gospel texts show that Jesus met physical needs because he had compassion and pity on those who were suffering.[17] Matthew 14:14 reads: "When Jesus landed and saw a large crowd, he had compassion on them and healed their sick."[18] Luke 7:13 speaks of Jesus' compassion for the widow who had lost her only son: "When the Lord saw her, his heart went out to her and he said, 'Don't cry.'" Helping men and women enjoy a happy, fulfilled human life for their three score years and ten mattered a great deal to Jesus.

For the disciple who confesses that Jesus is her sovereign Lord, Jesus' example is crucial. In fact, Jesus is the Christian's *only* perfect model and example. What the early church did is interesting, and we should study their attempts to follow Jesus with the deepest respect. But the practice and example of the early church—*unlike* the canonical writings produced by the early church—are not normative for the Christian. The early church undoubtedly made mistakes. It may even have been one-sided in its emphasis. But Jesus' example is perfect because he was both true man and true God.

Jesus' teaching is as clear as his life. When he announced his mission in the synagogue at Nazareth, it had a powerful component of social action. He had been sent, he said, to heal the blind, release the captives, and liberate the oppressed (Luke 4:18–19). He warned his disciples that religious hypocrites who make a pretense of public piety and at the same time devour the houses of widows will suffer great condemnation (Mark 12:38–40).

Jesus' teaching in the parable of the last judgment in Matthew 25 is frighteningly clear. He warned that failure to help the needy neighbor involves not just unfaithfulness but also damnation. This parable demonstrates the Christocentrism of Christian social concern. Jesus reminds us that when we aid the "least of these," we are ministering to him.[19] Behind the sorrowing Indian mother whose heart is crushed as she tenderly rocks her starving child stands our

Lord. Behind the black man whose ego and initiative have been destroyed by a dreary, unending series of low-paying jobs and a thousand racial slurs stands our Lord. Christ identifies very closely with the poor, the mistreated, and the oppressed. Hence, we meet our Lord when we minister to the needy neighbor.

But that is not all! It is precisely because the risen Lord now lives in us and regenerates us that we have the spiritual energy to give ourselves for others. Christ in us impels us to move outside our comfortable rural or suburban communities to stand and cry and labor with him among the mistreated masses yearning to be free. Regeneration links justification by faith alone and involvement in social righteousness. When we help change institutions that oppress the poor, we minister to him who atoned for our sins. Wherever we look we see Christ. Christ forgives us. Christ lives in us. And Christ confronts us in the faces of the oppressed.

Doctrine of Salvation

In chapters four and five, we saw how a fully biblical understanding cannot separate salvation and social concern. To be sure, if we reduce salvation to forgiveness of sins and eternal life in a platonic heaven, then there is little connection between salvation and social concern. But that is a distorted reduction of the biblical view of salvation.

The New Testament understanding of the atonement includes Christ as example and conqueror of the powers of evil as well as Christ the substitute for our sins. The salvation we enjoy now includes that redeemed community of transformed disciples challenging fallen status quos in the name of their risen conquering Lord. And even when the raging powers of darkness gain temporary victories, we know that the day of cosmic salvation will surely come when the kingdoms of this world will become the kingdom of our Lord and even the groaning creation will be at peace. With such a hope ablaze in our hearts, how can we fail to erect signs of that coming salvation throughout the created order?

Today almost all Christians agree that biblical faith summons us to minister to the physical, material needs of people—at least through relief and development. But what about structural change via politics?

Jesus did not organize Evangelicals for Social Action to lobby the Roman senate. So does that mean that we should not?

Should We Be Political?

There are at least three *practical* reasons for trying to fight evil by changing structures instead of relying totally on individual, personal charity.

Effectiveness

I'll never forget a story I heard from an Indian bishop in Bangalore in 1980.

There used to be a mental institution in India, he said, that had a fascinating way of deciding whether inmates were well enough to go home. They would take a person over to a water tap, place a large water bucket under the tap, and fill the bucket with water. Then, leaving the tap on, they would give the person a spoon and say, "Please empty the bucket." If the person started dipping the water out one spoonful at a time and never turned the tap off, they knew he was still crazy!

The Indian bishop then made the point that Christians so often approach social problems in an individualistic way—one spoonful at a time—and overlook complex social systems. Structural change, he argued, would be more effective.

Sri Lanka used to have a dreadful problem with malaria. Millions died. Then they decided to spray the marshes where the mosquitoes bred, since the mosquitoes were spreading the malaria. In three years this structural approach of preventive medicine reduced the death rate by as much as Western Europe had cut the mortality rate in three hundred years.[20] Was that not only more effective but also more Christian than praying for the sick one by one or building more hospitals for individual victims?[21]

Dignity

Structural change is often not only more effective but also morally better. It nurtures dignity. Personal charity and philanthropy still permit the rich donor to feel superior. And it frequently makes the recipient feel inferior and dependent. Institutional changes, on the other hand, give the poor and marginalized new opportunities to shape their own future. Belonging to a union is much better than being a very well treated slave—better both for the worker's self-respect and for the employer's attitude toward the worker.

Less Haphazard

Furthermore, structural change is often less arbitrary. Personal charity is too haphazard. It depends on the whim and feelings of the well-off. Many needy people fail to meet those who can help. Proper institutional change, on the other hand, automatically benefits a whole group of people.

Structural change is often more effective, morally better, and less arbitrary. "But those are not biblical arguments," someone may object. Is there a biblical case for structural change?

Does the Bible grapple with the notion of "social sin"? With the reality of unjust structures and oppressive systems? The answer is clearly yes—in both the Old Testament and the New.[22]

Society and Anthropology

Before looking at those texts, however, it is necessary to ponder an important implication of the biblical view of persons. God made us finite social beings. Finite persons created for community and given stewardship over God's garden inevitably create social systems and institutions. Since we are social beings who reach fulfillment only in community with others, we necessarily design patterns of relationship and values that guide those social patterns and relationships. Since we are called to be coworkers with God in carefully nurturing God's gorgeous garden, we necessarily develop tools and cooperative patterns for shaping the earth. And since we are finite, living here only for a few short years, we necessarily design systems of education and communication for passing on to future generations what we have learned.

The resulting social systems (of family, economics, politics, and the ethico-religious ideas that undergird them) take on a life of their own. Persons, of course, create these social systems, but the social systems are older than any currently existing individuals. We all frequently adopt and follow our society's accepted systems and values without conscious individual decision.[23] To the extent that the social system and supporting values are good (e.g., when they encourage lifelong marriage covenants), they nudge us toward wholeness. To the extent that they are evil (e.g., when they promote ethical relativism, sexual promiscuity, and legal structures and economic patterns that work against keeping one's marriage covenant), the systems themselves are evil.

Since we are social beings created for community, we simply cannot be all God wants us to be if we live in evil social systems. That is not to forget that even the most oppressed person can accept Christ and be on the way to eternal life. But the slave, oppressed laborer, or malnourished woman cannot fully enjoy the dignity, freedom, and wholeness intended by the Creator.

One need only remember the history of modern slavery to remember how powerful and oppressive evil social structures can be. Over the years, untold millions of "pagan" Africans died from rape, starvation, torture, and sharks on the way to the brave new world of "Christians." The "lucky" five to ten million who survived the journey had to endure being whipped, being bred like animals, and the systematic destruction of almost all ancestral traditions.[24] All this was legal. Most slaveholders were Christians who accepted without much thought the rationalizations of this systemic oppression. Even those who tried to be kind to individual slaves found it exceedingly difficult to escape the attitudes and assumptions of white superiority. The system molded, corrupted, and twisted both slave and master. Its enormous power finally yielded only after incredible agony, struggle, and bloodshed.

The social sciences of our time help us understand the complexity and power of social systems, but people understood the reality of social systems long before modern sociology came on the scene. The Bible is very clear that the social structures that shape our lives are very important. And it is equally clear that those structures are, on the one hand, necessary and good, and on the other, fallen and oppressive.

The Old Testament and Social Sin

The prophets regularly denounced social sin as well as personal sin. Amos 2:6–7 is a classic example.

> They sell the righteous for silver,
>   and the needy for a pair of sandals.

> They trample on the heads of the poor
>> as upon the dust of the ground
>> and deny justice to the oppressed.
> Father and son use the same girl
>> and so profane my holy name.

Most of this text denounces economic oppression. Scholars point out that the "righteous" person who is sold for silver or sandals is a poor person with a good legal case,[25] but the rich and powerful bribe the judges and win. Corrupt legal systems result in gross economic injustice. But then the last two lines condemn sexual misconduct (perhaps cult prostitution). God abhors both sexual sin and economic oppression.[26]

Chapter 5:10–12 continues Amos's attack against unfair structures—in this case an oppressive legal system supporting oppressive economic structures:

> You hate the one who reproves in court
>> and despise him who tells the truth.
> You trample on the poor
>> and force him to give you grain. . . .
> You oppress the righteous and take bribes
>> and you deprive the poor of justice in the courts.

Isaiah fulminates against legislators and bureaucrats who write and implement oppressive laws (Isa. 10:1–4). And the psalmist insists that God will wipe out those who "frame mischief by statute" (Ps. 94:20 RSV).[27]

Amos 4:1–2 shows that we sin against God and neighbor when we choose to participate in unjust systems.[28] Amos denounced the wealthy women of his day because they encouraged and participated in the oppressive economic and judicial structures that brought them wealth.

> Hear this word, you cows of Bashan on Mount Samaria,
>> you women who oppress the poor and crush the needy
>> and say to your husbands, "Bring us some drinks!"
> The Sovereign LORD has sworn by his holiness:
>> "The time will surely come

when you will be taken away with hooks,
the last of you with fishhooks."

Amos predicted that a foreign nation would conquer Israel, tear down the cities, and drag the wealthy women away by the nose. Because they chose to participate in and benefit from oppressive structures, God brought terrible punishment on these affluent women.

Social Evil in the New Testament

In the New Testament, the word *cosmos* (world) often conveys the idea of structural evil.[29] In Greek thought, the word *cosmos* referred to the structures of civilized life, especially the patterns of the Greek city state that were viewed as essentially good.[30] But the biblical writers knew that sin had invaded and distorted the structures and values of society.

Frequently, therefore, the New Testament uses the word *cosmos* to refer, in C. H. Dodd's words, "to human society in so far as it is organized on wrong principles."[31] "When Paul spoke of 'the world' in a moral sense, he was thinking of the totality of people, social systems, values, and traditions in terms of its opposition to God and his redemptive purposes."[32] Before conversion, Christians followed the values and patterns of a fallen social order: "You were dead in your transgressions and sins, in which you used to live when you followed the ways of the world" (Eph. 2:1–2). Paul and John urge Christians not to conform to this world's pattern of evil systems and ideas (Rom. 12:1–2).

> Do not love the world or the things in the world. The love of the Father is not in those who love the world; for all that is in the world—the desire of the flesh, the desire of the eyes, the pride in riches—comes not from the Father but from the world. And the world and its desire are passing away, but those who do the will of God live forever.
>
> 1 John 2:15–17 nrsv

Behind the distorted social structures of our world, according to St. Paul, are fallen supernatural powers under the control of Satan himself. When Paul says that before their conversion the

Ephesians had "followed the ways of this world," he adds: "and of the ruler of the kingdom of the air, the spirit who is now at work in those who are disobedient" (Eph. 2:2). Paul warns that "our struggle is not against flesh and blood, but against the rulers, against the authorities, against the powers of this dark world and against the spiritual forces of evil in the heavenly realms" (Eph. 6:12).

Both Jews and Greeks in Paul's day believed that both good and evil supernatural beings stand behind and powerfully influence social and political structures.[33] Modern secular folk may find that hard to believe. But when I look at the demonic evil of social systems like Naziism, apartheid, and communism, or even the complex mixture of racism, lack of jobs, sexual promiscuity, drugs, and police brutality in American inner cities, I have no trouble at all believing that Satan and his gang are hard at work fostering oppressive structures and thus doing their best to destroy God's good creation.[34]

These fallen supernatural powers work to twist and distort the social systems that we as social beings need in order to be whole. By seducing us into many wrong choices that create evil systems, by working against attempts to overcome oppressive structures and sometimes by enticing politicians and other powerful leaders to use the occult,[35] these demonic powers shape our world. Evil is far more complex than the wrong choices of individuals. It also lies outside us both in powerfully oppressive social systems and in demonic powers that delight in defying God by corrupting the social systems that God's human image-bearers need.

Pope John Paul II has rightly insisted that evil social structures are "rooted in personal sin." Social evil results from our rebellion against God and our consequent selfishness towards our neighbors. But the "accumulation and concentration of many *personal sins*" create evil social structures that are both "oppressive and difficult to change."[36] When we choose to participate in and benefit from evil social systems, we sin, as did the affluent women of Amos's time, against God and neighbor.

The Sinned-Against

When we genuinely understand the nature of social sin, then we see that the oppressed are the "sinned-against."[37] Raymond Fung has insisted that when we seek to work with those oppressed by unjust economic and political structures, it is crucial to see them as victims—as the sinned against. Approaching them with this understanding helps us empathize with their oppression. It also encourages us to challenge the oppressors and work to correct the injustice.

At the same time, we must be careful to avoid several possible mistakes. We dare not forget that the oppressed are also sinners who need to repent of *their* sins, even though those sins are often different from those of the oppressors. Furthermore, we dare not attack the oppressors as those who sin against the oppressed in such a way that we deny the humanity of the oppressors. Unlike Marxism that calls for the elimination of oppressors, Christianity sees oppressors as sinful persons whom God loves so much that God wants to free them from their oppression.

It is especially important to be very clear that both oppressor and oppressed need more than new and improved social structures. Sin is deeper than even very evil social systems. Therefore people need both better social systems and also a new living relationship with Christ that creates transformation at the core of their personalities.[38]

Jesus and Politics

The Scriptures condemn social sin. Evil social systems maim and destroy people. Structural change is often better and more effective than individual acts of charity.

But all that does not answer the question of Jesus and politics. Earlier I noted that Jesus did not organize Evangelicals for Social Action to lobby the Roman senate. Does that mean that we should not? It is crucial to understand Jesus' particular political setting. He was a member of an oppressed colony ruled by a totalitarian, imperialistic Roman dictatorship.[39] He had no Roman political rights.

Even in Palestine, the three standard political options of his time were all unfaithful to the values of Jesus' dawning kingdom. The Herodians and Sadducees collaborated with the oppressive Romans to protect and extend their privileged, unjust lives. That political option never tempted Jesus. The Essenes withdrew to the desert to form a separatist community, waiting passively for the coming of the

Messiah. Quietistic withdrawal was not Jesus' way either. The third political option chosen by Jesus' contemporaries was that of the revolutionary Zealots who took up the sword to drive out the Roman oppressors. Jesus said his followers would love their enemies, even oppressive Romans.

In Jesus' setting, there was only one "political" option left. That was to summon the entire society to change and then form a new community living at the heart of the society for all those ready to challenge the status quo. So that is what Jesus did. That was a "political" option; indeed, the only faithful one in that context.

I think there is another point that requires emphasis: Jesus was sent by God to the Jewish nation, not the entire Roman empire. Jesus came as the Jewish Messiah summoning the entire Jewish community to accept and follow its Messiah. We have seen that he did not limit his message only to religious leaders or to "inner, spiritual" themes. Challenging wrong economic practices and social bias against the poor and marginalized was just as much a part of his kingdom teaching as was his instruction on prayer and worship. To say that Jesus' messianic mission to the Jewish nation was not "political" is to spiritualize and misunderstand his whole gospel of the kingdom.

To be sure, it was not exclusively or primarily political. The wonderful proclamation of God's free grace was right at the heart of his message. He declined the role of judge. He vigorously rejected the invitation to accept the popular messianic conception of a conquering military hero who would lead the violent revolution against Rome.

But he declared that God's messianic reign was breaking into history in his person and work. He summoned the whole Jewish community to adopt his kingdom values on economics, marriage, women, leadership, enemies—in short, everything. All those who accepted the invitation became a part, after his death and resurrection, of God's movement for spreading the messianic salvation, accomplished by a Jew in Jerusalem, to the whole world.

In his lifetime, however, Jesus' mission was to the Jewish people. God did not call him to go to Athens or Rome. It is true that he did not organize a political group to lobby the Roman senate, but neither did he organize a "foreign missionary" society to evangelize the Romans. He was sent to the Jews. If the fact that Jesus did not organize a political movement to shape imperial politics means that we should not, then neither should we evangelize other nations since Jesus did not do that either.

After his resurrection, he sent his disciples out to lead people to faith and teach them everything he had taught. That meant making disciples who would submit every corner of their lives to Jesus. That includes economics just as much as worship, one's political life just as much as one's prayer life.

Even in Palestine, of course, Jesus did not do precisely what we most commonly associate with politics. He did not join Herod's cabinet or organize a narrowly political movement. As we have seen, the three popular, narrowly political options for Jesus in his own time were all incompatible with kingdom values. Modeling a new social order appeared to be the only faithful political option in the Jewish colony of an undemocratic empire during the time of Jesus.

Not all political contexts in our time, however, are like that of the first century, although some in fact are strikingly similar. Christians under Soviet and Chinese communism probably had less freedom for political activity than did Jewish colonials in the Roman Empire. Where the situation is similar, a similar response is appropriate.

Often, however, we have many political opportunities to work for justice, peace, democratic process, and freedom. The fact that Jesus could not use radio and television does not mean we should not. Similarly, the fact that his political options were fewer than ours does not mean we should not use the political process to work for structural change whenever that is possible.

Biblical faith summons believers to active social concern. In some circumstances, we will engage in immediate relief to prevent disaster. In others, we will do long-term community development. And in still others, we will work politically to improve socioeconomic and political structures. Always, our goal will be to obey and glorify the God revealed in Scripture as the One who seeks wholeness for all.

In chapter seven, we saw how strongly the Bible calls Christians to the task of evangelism. This chapter has shown that hundreds of texts summon Christians to a vigorous social concern. The next two chapters will offer a new model on how to relate these two biblical commands.

PART 5

INCARNATIONAL
KINGDOM
CHRISTIANITY

9

Distinguishing Evangelism from Social Action

What good is it for a man to gain the whole world, yet forfeit his soul?

MARK 8:36

Even over the telephone, Raleigh Washington's voice danced with joy. I had called to see if he could join the Board of Directors of Evangelicals for Social Action. (He did.) But first he wanted to tell me about 225 people that his church had led to Christ the previous week.

Raleigh Washington is now a prominent African-American leader of Promisekeepers, but for more than ten years he was the pastor of Rock of Our Salvation Church (Evangelical Free)—an inner-city, interracial congregation on the west side of Chicago. Intimately connected with the church is Circle Urban Ministries, a wholistic community center led by Glen Kehrein, a white farm boy from Wisconsin. Circle has a medical clinic with seven full-time doctors, a legal clinic with two full-time lawyers, a low-income housing program that has renovated millions of dollars of housing for the poor, and job-creation programs to build an economic base in the inner city.

That week of stunning evangelistic success did not happen in a vacuum. Hurting inner-city residents knew that the people inviting them to Jesus were the same folk who provided essential health care, housing for the homeless, and help in finding a job or finishing high school. And the community center staff knew that unless they could offer more than excellent medical or legal help, they would never get to the heart of the problems and produce lasting change.

For a time, in fact, Circle Urban Ministries did lose much of its evangelistic zeal. Theoretically, they believed in both evangelism and social action, but the second got most of their attention. When Raleigh Washington started planting a church in the heart of the community center in 1983, a wholistic balance was reestablished. Now when they sense a spiritual need, doctors and lawyers feel free to speak of Christ— or encourage the person to arrange a visit to one of the three chaplains who now work both in the community center and the church. The result has been a rapidly growing inner-city congregation with over three hundred members.

That is the kind of wholistic mission that is both biblical and effective. It is also the kind of ministry that illustrates a fifth model of the relationship between evangelism and social concern.

In chapter two I outlined four dominant models. All had major weaknesses. Now that I have explored the gospel of the kingdom, salvation, and conversion and developed biblical reasons for doing evangelism and social action, I am ready to develop a fifth model. This model, I believe, is fully grounded in the preceding biblical study. It also combines the strengths and avoids the weaknesses of the other four models.

Defining Evangelism and Mission

What is evangelism? The New Testament word *evangelize* is simply the verb form of the noun *gospel*. To evangelize, therefore, is to share the gospel. When a different verb is used with *gospel* in the New Testament, that verb is most often the word *preach*. And in most of the examples of preaching in the New Testament, according to C. H. Dodd, the preaching is directed to non-Christians.[1] Verbal proclamation of the gospel to non-Christians with the intention and hope that they will repent, accept Christ, and join his new kingdom community is therefore central to evangelism.

It is important to see that verbal proclamation is one essential component of evangelism but also that it is not the only way we share the gospel. Jesus, surely, is the best illustration of how to communicate the Good News. If anything is clear in Jesus, it is that he announces the kingdom by word and deed. God Incarnate (the perfect combination of logos and action) shared the Good News by verbal proclamation and visible demonstration.

That, of course, raises an important question. If we evangelize by word and deed, does that mean that social action is part of evangelism? Is digging wells in a Hindu society or working politically to end injustice evangelism? And if so, can we evangelize social structures, multi-national corporations, and nations?

Many contemporary Christians think that the answer to these last two questions is yes. In *Mission and Evangelism,* the World Council of Churches insists that the call to conversion is "addressed to nations, groups, and families."[2] David Lowes Watson claims that "communities, cities, nations, conglomerates must not only be analyzed as sinful but must be called to repentance, and can be expected to repent. Their salvation, along with that of individuals, is to be nurtured."[3]

How should we evaluate this claim?

I certainly believe that we should work politically to change unjust structures. But it is confusing and misleading to call that work evangelism. Several weighty reasons indicate that we should define evangelism in a way that makes it distinct from (although certainly *not* unrelated to) social action.

First of all, it is confusing nonsense to talk about repentance and conversion in the case of nations and corporations. Corporate structures can change their policies (and even issue statements acknowledging wrongdoing), but General Motors and the U.S. government cannot accept Jesus Christ as personal Lord and Savior, undergo baptism (even if they only sprinkle!), become an active member of a local church, take communion, experience daily personal fellowship with the Holy Spirit, and look forward to personal bodily resurrection at the return of Jesus Christ. Only *persons* can do that. As M. M. Thomas said at the WCC's Fifth General Assembly in

Nairobi, "Only people can be addressed and only people can respond."[4]

That is not to deny what Donald McGavran calls "people movements"[5] and David Gitari "community evangelism."[6] In more communal, less individualistic societies, a whole village may deliberate together and decide together to accept Christ. Vinay Samuel insists rightly that frequently in evangelism we should address the whole person in community, not isolated individuals.[7] But if repentance and conversion are genuine in "community evangelism," each person makes a *personal* decision and enters into a *personal* (as well as a corporate) relationship with the living God. At the core of biblical faith is the radical truth that God calls each person to respond to Christ's invitation.[8] In evangelism, we address only persons, not social structures, because only persons can become disciples of Christ.[9]

A second reason for insisting that evangelism and social action are distinct is that they have different outcomes. Social action may lead to cleaner water, more democracy, or greater economic justice, but having these valuable goods is simply not the same thing as knowing that your sins are forgiven, rejoicing in a personal relationship with Jesus Christ, and knowing that you are on the way to living forever in the presence of the risen Lord. Enjoying these latter treasures is possible only if you learn about the gospel and accept Jesus Christ. In fact, you could enjoy everything that the best social action can produce in terms of material well-being and just social structures and still be in active rebellion against God and on your way to eternal separation from God. Conversely, a malnourished, oppressed person dying of starvation can experience a living relationship with Christ and be on her way to life eternal in the Savior's presence.

This second point does not mean that there is no connection between evangelism and social action. In chapter ten, we will see how in fact they are inseparably interrelated in numerous ways. But they are not identical, in part, because crucial aspects of the results of evangelism on the one hand and the results of social action on the other are significantly different.

The story of my friend James in South Africa illustrates this point. I could have joined James and worked with him for years to change the unjust structures of apartheid. That surely would have been a Bible-believing, born-again kind of thing to do! But even if the two of us had succeeded in making a decisive contribution to the dismantling of apartheid after a decade of Herculean effort, the result of that labor would not necessarily have included the personal conversion of James. He might still have been in rebellion against God. Only when James accepted Christ's offer of grace did he become a disciple of Jesus Christ on the way to living forever with the Lord.

Third, just as the outcome of evangelism differs from the outcome of social action, so, too, do the intentions of the persons doing each. In evangelism, the central intention is to lead non-Christians to become disciples of Jesus Christ. In social action, the central intention is to improve the socioeconomic or psychological well-being of people for their life here on earth.

Fourth, we should distinguish between evangelism and social action in order to protect the integrity of social action! In chapter eight, I argued that simply on the basis of creation, Christians have an adequate theological reason for improving human well-being in society. Social action does not need to be pre-evangelism and be done with an evangelistic purpose in order to be legitimate. Feeding the starving, ending slavery, and promoting political freedom and economic justice have their own biblical justification whether or not those who benefit ever accept Christ. If, however, evangelism and social action are identical, then every act of social concern is evangelism, which means that verbal proclamation and the intention of leading non-Christians to Christ must be central components of social responsibility.

Fifth, equating evangelism and social action endangers the integrity and practice of evangelism. If everything that Christians are sent into the world to do is evangelism, then the special task of communicating the gospel to non-Christians with the hope that they will accept Christ gets lost easily. And that is precisely what has happened in many circles that equate evangelism and social action. Almost all the emphasis (time, energy, and money) falls on social action in which the goal is improving humanity's socioeconomic well-being. Little and sometimes no attention is given to verbal proclamation and other activity intended to invite non-Christians to accept Jesus.

Furthermore, since social action is equated with evangelism, one cannot even talk about this terrible neglect. You cannot charge people with neglecting evangelism even if they never invite anyone to accept Christ if social action is evangelism and they are engaged in social action. Therefore you cannot even ask if time, money, and personnel are being allocated properly between evangelism and social action. Given the terminology, one can claim that one's church or mission agency is completely involved in evangelism even if one never spends a dime or a minute on leading persons to Christ.

Refusing to distinguish between evangelism and social action is doubly dangerous. It frequently leads to neglecting a central part of what the New Testament means by evangelism. And then the very terminology makes it impossible to call attention to this one-sided, heretical neglect.

Sixth, evangelism and social action are distinct because one can do the latter but not the former without any verbal proclamation. One can do valid social action without ever speaking of Jesus and his dawning kingdom. Devout Christians can work with Muslims, Hindus, secular humanists, and New Agers to lobby government to protect the environment, and on occasion, it will be entirely proper for them to work at and accomplish this goal without any explicit word about Jesus' kingdom, death, and resurrection. It is, of course, true that if these colleagues in social action know that you are a Christian and are protecting the environment because you love the Creator, then your actions will also be a witness to Christ. But unless somewhere the word about Christ has been communicated, your social action by itself cannot witness to anything beyond yourself and your honorable concerns.

Unlike social action, evangelism is totally impossible unless the gospel word is proclaimed at some point and people are invited to believe. As Michael Nazir-Ali says, "Evangelism is not about how good we are or even how good the Church is, it is about how good God is."[10] Unlike social action, evangelism is impossible unless the gospel message is announced.

Evangelism and social action are not identical. They are distinct, albeit closely related, activities.[11]

162

To insist on a distinction between evangelism and social action is *not*, however, to draw that distinction exclusively at the point of verbal proclamation versus visible demonstration.[12] Both Jesus' actions and his words were central to his announcement of the kingdom. Paul explicitly says that he led the Gentiles to faith "by word and deed" (Rom. 15:18–20). A wealthy, uncaring church that shares only words with the starving will rightly fail because its very life denies its message. As John Stott said in his plenary at Lausanne, "We can evangelize by word of mouth, . . . by print, picture and screen, by drama. . . , by good works of love, by a Christ-centered home, by a transformed life."[13] Word and deed belong together.

The proper way to distinguish evangelism and social action is in terms of intention. Evangelism is that set of activities whose primary intention is inviting non-Christians to embrace the gospel of the kingdom, to believe in Jesus Christ as personal Savior and Lord, and join his new redeemed community.[14]

Social action is that set of activities whose primary goal is improving the physical, socioeconomic, and political well-being of people through relief, development, and structural change.

In real life, of course, these two sets of activities are seldom if ever neatly and tightly separated. People who are known to love Jesus do social action—often explicitly in his name. Frequently, the same people in the same programs both offer relief and development and also invite non-Christians to accept Christ. Furthermore, as I shall argue below, this close interrelationship is usually highly desirable, but the fact that evangelism and social action are tightly interrelated does not mean that they are identical.

It is helpful to distinguish the primary *intention* from other related *dimensions* of the same activity. In his last work published after his death, Orlando Costas argued persuasively that there is an evangelistic *dimension* to every task the church does.[15] The primary intention of worship is to praise God. But worship, as the Orthodox especially insist, can have a powerful evangelistic dimension.[16] The basic intention of sharing within the body of Christ is simply to be Jesus' new redeemed community. But mutual love and caring in the church frequently have a significant evangelistic dimension as the beauty and goodness of genuine Christian community attracts a broken world.

Similarly, the primary intention of social action is preventing starvation, empowering the poor, and improving social structures so that persons created in God's image can enjoy more of the wholeness the Creator intended during their three score years and ten. Even if they never confess Christ, this improved material wholeness is a good desired by the Creator. It has its own integrity and worth quite apart from any evangelistic dimension. At the same time, the Christian who knows that the Creator also longs to live in eternal communion with every person will also rejoice in the fact that social action done by Christians in the name of Christ will often have a clear evangelistic dimension even though that is not the first (or only valid) reason for offering bread or justice.

Orlando Costas, I believe, is right:

> Not everything that the church does is evangelization. The church is called to undertake several missional tasks. However, everything that the church *is* and everything that the church has been sent to *do* has an evangelistic dimension. . . . One ought not to confuse evangelization with the multiple missional tasks of the church. Nevertheless, we ought to recognize the evangelistic potential of all these tasks.[17]

Costas, in fact, is using precisely the same distinctions as those used in the report from the Consultation on the Relationship between Evangelism and Social Responsibility (CRESR) in Grand Rapids in June 1982 sponsored by the WEF and the Lausanne Committee for World Evangelization: "Evangelism, even when it does not have a primarily social *intention,* nevertheless has a social *dimension,* while social responsibility, even when it does not have a primarily evangelistic *intention,* nevertheless has an evangelistic *dimension.*"[18]

Since evangelism is not identical with social action but Christians are called to do both, we need a broader term when we want to speak of both of them. I agree with John Stott that the word *mission* is perhaps the most helpful.

Mission does not refer to everything that God does or even everything that the church does. God the Creator sustains the world in a way that we do not. That divine activity is not part of the mission of the church. The church also has many crucial internal tasks such as worship, Christian education, and nurturing the Christian community. They are all important, and they all have a significant dimension that relates to both evangelism and social action. But the primary intention of each relates to the inner life of the church, not to mission in the world.

Mission refers to "everything the church is sent into the world to do."[19] Jesus says in John 20:21: "As the Father has sent me, I am sending you."[20] If anything is clear, it is that Jesus both preached and healed. Jesus explicitly said that he came both to proclaim the gospel and to serve (Mark 10:45).[21] If we are sent in the same way as Jesus, then our mission in the world includes both evangelism and social responsibility.[22]

But which is more important?

In What Sense Is Evangelism Primary?

Both the Lausanne Covenant (1974) and the CRESR report (1982) insist that although evangelism and social concern are both important aspects of Christian mission, evangelism nonetheless is primary. In what sense, if any, is that true?

It was during the exciting days of vigorous debate at Grand Rapids in 1982 that I first saw clearly that this question of "primacy" really consists of at least five sub-questions: (1) A logical question: Can you have Christian social responsibility without first having Christians? (2) An ontological question: Is anything (or indeed everything) in this world as important as a living relationship with God that leads to eternal life? (3) A vocational question: Are not different Christians gifted with different callings and do they not therefore properly allocate their time very differently? (4) A temporal question: Does not the immediate circumstance (e.g., a devastating flood) influence what in particular situations one does first? (5) A resources question: How do we allocate scarce resources of time, personnel, and money? To think carefully about the question of the primacy of evangelism, we must examine each of these questions.

The Logical Question

Can you have Christian social responsibility without first having Christians? This is a point so simple and obvious that it appears almost trivial once stated. But surely it is the case that if we are to have *Christian* social responsibility, then we must first have evangelism, which is God's means to produce Christians. In that sense, therefore, the evangelizing of a person is both logically and temporally prior to that same person's acts of *Christian* social action.[23]

The Ontological Question

Is anything in the world, indeed even everything in the world, as important as eternal life? This is the heart of the question of primacy.

To answer no, to say that it would be better to lose the whole world than lose eternal life, is not to say that the soul is good and the body evil. It is not to ignore the fantastic importance, according to the Creator, of health, food, and justice in history. But it is to say what the Christian martyrs of all ages have confessed with their very lives. Obeying God and living forever with the living God is more important than enjoying food, health, even life itself for three score years and ten.

That is surely what Jesus meant to teach us in the important saying in Mark 8:34–38:

> If any want to become my followers, let them deny themselves and take up their cross and follow me. For those who want to save their life will lose it, and those who lose their life for my sake, and for the sake of the gospel, will save it. For what will it profit them to gain the whole world and forfeit their life? Indeed, what can they give in return for their life? Those who are ashamed of me and of my words in this adulterous and sinful generation, of them the Son of Man will also be ashamed when he comes in the glory of his Father with the holy angels (NRSV).

Jesus warns us not to forsake him and his gospel in order to acquire the things of this world—whether money, fame, or power. "Do not be afraid," Jesus said, "of those who kill the body but cannot kill the soul. Rather, be afraid of the One who can destroy both soul and body in hell" (Matt. 10:28). Even if we gained everything in the world but turned our backs on Christ, it would be the height of folly, because at the final judgment, Jesus as the Son of Man would turn his back on us.

Nothing in this world is as important as eternal life. I would rather die of starvation or torture than depart eternally from God, the only source of love and goodness in the universe (2 Cor. 4:16–18). I know that is relatively easy for well-fed, comfortable Western folk to say. Every time we say it, we must renew our commitment to work sacrificially to end starvation and injustice. But the statement is still true and important. Social action, no matter how good or extensive, cannot by itself set people on the path to eternal life. Only evangelism, in which we share the gospel and invite people to accept Christ, can do that.

To be sure, there is some meaningful sense in which social action has eternal consequences.[24] Matthew 25 warns that if we fail to feed the hungry, we go to hell. But few suppose that Jesus meant to teach a crass works-righteousness in which good social action toward the poor automatically earns eternal life. We can demonstrate our faith with our actions, but eternal life is a gift that comes as we trust in Christ, not something we earn by any amount of superb social action.[25]

The Vocational Question

How much time should each Christian spend on evangelism and social action? Christians have many different callings—doctor, politician, pastor, educator, homemaker, business person, evangelist. Not every person in every calling is obligated to spend the same amount of time on everything. Specialization is legitimate. That does not mean that any Christian should suppose that he or she should only do evangelism or only do social action. Every Christian should do some of both. But the New Testament teaching on spiritual gifts encourages specialization (Eph. 4:11–12).[26] Those who have the spiritual gift of administration should concentrate there, and those with the spiritual gift of evangelism rightly spend most of their time in that area.[27]

It is crucial, however, that everyone affirms the importance of the others' vocations. When the evangelist or the social activist claims that his calling is more important, it is divisive and destructive.[28] When both stress the importance of the other's work, the church is blessed and united.

The Temporal Question

Must we always present the gospel before we meet pressing material need? I know of no one who would argue that today. In times of emergency, it is entirely proper to feed the starving and clothe the naked without speaking of Christ. At other times, it will be just as appropriate to invite people to accept our Lord before any social action is undertaken. It all depends on the circumstances.[29]

The Question of Resources

If evangelism and social action are not identical, then we have to decide how to divide our limited time, money, and personnel. Should evangelism or social action receive more?

Some have argued that we do not have to make this choice because we can do both: "Seldom if ever should we have to choose between satisfying physical hunger and spiritual hunger, or between healing bodies and saving souls, since an authentic love for our neighbor will lead us to serve him or her as a whole person."[30] Unfortunately, that is an easy answer that does not work. Only if we had unlimited resources, or if every program deserving support perfectly combined evangelism and social action, would that easy answer work.

In fact, many very good evangelistic programs (student evangelism, for example, or Billy Graham crusades) contain very little direct social action. Similarly, many very good programs of social action (e.g., Bread for the World's excellent political work for the poor) have very little direct evangelistic intent. These programs are not wrong because they are not doing both. But since they are not, we have to make choices. And our resources, alas, are very limited. The last time I checked, my family budget and my church's budget were definitely finite. So I have to choose between giving a very small amount of dollars all to student evangelism, all to lobbying for legislation that empowers the poor, or some to each.

How do I decide? Some would argue that since God uses evangelism to bring people to faith in Christ that leads to eternal life whereas social action only improves life on this earth, evangelism must receive most of our limited resources. Nothing, absolutely nothing is as important as living forever with God for all eternity. Therefore, they argue, most of our time, money, and personnel should go to evangelism.

But just when that argument begins to sound convincing, I think of Jesus. Surely he understood the importance of life eternal better than we do, and yet he chose to devote vast amounts of his potential preaching time to healing sick bodies that he knew would soon degenerate, decay, and rot in one, ten, or fifty years. If you look at the space in the Gospels devoted to Jesus' preaching and healing, there is certainly no indication whatsoever that Jesus thought that most of our time and other resources should be devoted to evangelism and only the little that is left over should be available to meet physical human needs.

Jesus cared for the whole person. He offered God's forgiveness and physical healing in equal abundance. Clearly, Jesus taught that gaining eternal life is more important than gaining everything in this world. But neither his words nor his example ever hint at the suggestion that therefore the task of inviting people into the kingdom should receive most of our resources and that attending to people's material needs is a secondary task to be done with spare time and money. Jesus clearly devoted large amounts of time and energy to both. And Jesus is our only perfect model. If God Incarnate thought he could—no, *must*—devote large amounts of potential preaching time to the healing of sick bodies, then surely we are unfaithful disciples if we fail to follow in his steps.

Perhaps the closest Jesus came to addressing the question of priority was when a scribe asked him which is the greatest commandment (Matt. 22:34–40; Mark 12:28–34). The first commandment, Jesus replied, is to love God with all one's heart. And the second is to love one's neighbor. "There is no commandment greater *than these*" (Mark 12:31). Jesus did not mean that a right relationship with God is so important that love for neighbor can be neglected. In fact, in Matthew's account Jesus says that the second command is like the first *(homoios)*, i.e., equal to the first in importance.[31] Jesus knew from the Old Testament that love for God is inseparable from love for neighbor. So Jesus' response to the question about the greatest commandment is that the double, interrelated command of love for God and neighbor stand above all other commands. "All the Law and the Prophets hang on these two commandments" (Matt. 22:40).

When it comes to resources of time, personnel, and money, I believe the example of Jesus points us toward devoting approximately equal amounts to both evangelism and social action. That is not some ironclad rule to be applied rigidly. Particular circumstances call for special responses.[32] But over an extended period of time, congregations and denominations that want to follow the example of Jesus will devote large amounts of resources to both evangelism and social action.[33] If some feel called to do a little more of the one than the other, I certainly will not object—as long as they are doing a lot of both rather than just maintaining the church building! But following Jesus' example will certainly mean repenting and forsaking the tragic one-sidedness of recent decades in which some groups focused almost exclusively on evangelism and others were preoccupied largely with social action.

It will also mean rejecting church growth leader Donald McGavran's suggestion that we should adjust the proportion of social concern and evangelism "so that maximum finding occurs."[34] Jesus is the norm, not some calculation of how to maximize short-term church growth. It may be that in the short run more white racists would, in some circumstances, flock to the church if we failed to say and show that racism is sin. It may be that more Brahmins in India might accept Christ in the short run if the evangelist neglected to teach and demonstrate that God has a special concern for marginalized untouchables. Indeed, Jesus might have enjoyed larger crowds if he had stated the cost of discipleship less harshly. Instead, precisely when his popularity was growing, he insisted that anyone who wants to become his disciple must be ready to forsake everything (Luke 14:25–28).

Furthermore, short-term success that produces superficial Christian disciples will lead to long-term disaster. Faithfulness to biblical teaching and the example of God Incarnate, not some calculation of short-term church growth, should determine our balance of evangelism and social concern.

Evangelism has a logical priority for Christian social action. Far more important, its outcome—eternal life—is so momentous that nothing in the world can compare with it. But that does not mean that everyone, regardless of vocation, should devote at least 51 percent of his or her time to direct evangelism. Nor does it mean that we must invite the starving to accept Christ before we feed them. But if we truly follow Jesus, then Christian congregations and denominations will enthusiastically devote large amounts of resources to both evangelism and social action.

10

An Inseparable Partnership

Good News and good works are inseparable.

Manila Manifesto

Getting to know John and Vera Mae Perkins has been one of the special blessings in my life. They have lived the kind of incarnational kingdom Christianity that I am pleading for in this book.[1]

John Perkins fled the racism of rural Mississippi as a young man, but after his conversion John and Vera Mae moved back to the small, segregated town of Mendenhall to live and preach the gospel. First they did evangelistic Bible clubs in the high schools. Then when they saw how much the black students needed special help, they started a tutoring program. The same attention to the needs of those with whom they were sharing the gospel led to housing programs, medical clinics, and cooperative businesses—even political engagement.

Through everything, John and Vera Mae kept leading people to Christ, discipling a new generation of converted leaders and building the church. For them, evangelism and social concern are inseparable partners.

Evangelism and social action are far more closely related both conceptually and in real life than I was able to say in the last chapter. To insist that evangelism is not identical with social action, I stressed the ways in which they are distinct.

Now I want to show how inseparably intertwined they are. In real life, they are frequently very closely interrelated as in the wholistic work of John and Vera Mae Perkins and of Rock/Circle Ministries in Chicago. And even when specific organizations properly focus largely on one or the other, there are numerous interrelationships. "Good News and good works," says the *Manila Manifesto,* "are inseparable."[2]

I want to explore five specific areas of interrelationship.

The Theological Framework of Biblical Evangelism

Genuinely biblical evangelism provides a theological framework that shows that evangelism is inseparable from social action. This is true as the evangelist explains sin, invites people to accept Christ as Lord, and does both—using the *contextual incarnational* model of Jesus.

Biblical evangelism calls on people to repent of sin—all sin, not just some privatized list of personal sins. A biblically faithful evangelist will call on people to repent of involvement in unjust social structures in the way that evangelist Charles Finney insisted that converts forsake the social sin of slavery.[3] Racism, sexism, and economic oppression are an affront to God.[4] Therefore simply by doing biblically faithful, evangelistic preaching about sin, the evangelist challenges unjust structures. By paying equal attention to repentance of both personal and social sin, the evangelist already forges a powerful link to social action.

Similarly, the evangelist who calls on people to accept Jesus Christ as Lord as well as Savior again establishes a framework where social action can flourish. Jesus' lordship is part of the gospel (2 Cor. 4:3–5).[5] Accepting him as Lord means surrendering every corner of one's life, not just Sunday morning and family life. A biblical evangelist will explain that coming to Jesus means letting him be Lord of the boardroom as well as the bedroom.

Further, genuine evangelism will be an incarnational, contextual evangelism that applies the gospel to the whole context of the persons addressed. Jesus did not throw words at sinners from afar.

173

He lived among them and modeled how the Good News of the kingdom brings radical transformation of the status quo. The evangelist is a harmless peddler, not a faithful proclaimer of the gospel, as Vinay Samuel and Chris Sugden insist, unless she shows how the gospel challenges men and women "within the whole context in which they live."[6] Is it not astonishing that during the International Year of the Child, twenty-one foreign-sponsored mission agencies did child evangelism in India without discussing the evil of child labor oppressing forty million Indian children?[7]

Evangelism Promotes Social Action

Second, biblical evangelism both results in and aims at social action.[8] Social action is the result of evangelism in the very specific sense that again and again history has shown that new Christians born again by the power of the Spirit are powerfully transformed and consequently change history.[9] From the individual examples of my good friend James Dennis to the hundreds of thousands changed in the Wesleyan revivals to the millions of fatalistic untouchables transformed by the gospel into confident participants in modern India, the evidence is clear.[10] The gospel creates new persons whose transformed character and action change the world.

Ultimately, the problems of our world are rooted in sinful rebellion against God. When drug abusers or sexually irresponsible sinners are converted, society improves. When oppressors repent of racism and economic injustice, society improves. New persons create better societies.

None of this, unfortunately, is automatic. Unless Christians are taught about the social implications of the gospel, they will have little positive impact on society. It is naive nonsense to suggest that new converts automatically start correcting social evils. Southern Baptist evangelist Delos Miles describes a church where one prominent member ran the bank that refused to make loans to poor folk.[11] Another prominent church member operated a loan office that did make loans to poor folk—at extravagant rates! I wonder if these "born again" church pillars blamed the poor for being lazy and shiftless. Both men may have said they cared about the poor. They did not recognize their actions as oppressive. The biblical evangelist will insist that being a Christian includes living a converted lifestyle and engaging in converted business practices.

Tragically, missionaries have too often failed to share the full biblical truth with new converts. I once had an exceedingly lively debate with a person from Wycliffe Bible Translators when I suggested that we have sometimes translated Romans without also translating Amos.[12] If we teach new converts among the poor the truth about justice as well as justification, they will quickly see how to apply that to their oppressive social structures. Nothing is more liberating to poor, oppressed folk than the full biblical message that the One who died for their sins is the God of the poor who abhors unjust structures. When done in a fully biblical way, evangelism creates new persons who turn from sin, live new lives, experience new dignity and worth, and consequently challenge structures of oppression in the name of the biblical God who, they know now, lives in their hearts and reigns in the world. Social action results from evangelism.

Social action is also one goal of evangelism. Christ redeemed us in part to create a people "zealous for good deeds" (Titus 2:14 NRSV). We have been "created in Christ Jesus to do good works" (Eph. 2:10). Evangelism both results in and aims at social action.

The Common Life of the Church Shapes Society

When the church truly models what it preaches—when it genuinely breaks through the sinful barriers of racism, class prejudice, and oppression—its very existence has a powerful influence on the larger society.[13] According to H. Richard Niebuhr, the church is a "social pioneer." As it engages in social action, it expresses "the highest form of social responsibility."[14]

The inner life of the church is also an "enfleshed evangelistic word."[15] In his plenary address at Lausanne, Michael Green underlined the astonishing evangelistic impact of the common life of the early church:

These Christians embraced all the colors, all the classes, and all the untouchables of ancient society. . . . Their caring for each other in need became proverbial in antiquity. When people saw how these Christians loved one another, . . . they listened to the message of Jesus. . . . Unless the fellowship in the Christian assembly is far superior to that which can be found anywhere else in society, then the Christians can talk about the transforming love and power of Jesus until they are hoarse, but people are not going to listen.[16]

Ephesians 3:1–7 provides the theological foundation for this practical truth. According to Ephesians 3:6, the church is part of the gospel! Ephesians 2:11ff. shows how the cross of Christ overcame the worst ethnic hatred of the ancient world and created one new body of Christ wherein the wall of hostility between Jew and Gentile was overcome. Since God accepted both on exactly the same basis, namely faith in Christ's atonement, they were now one. Period.

Then in chapter three, Paul goes on to describe the gospel that he preaches as a "mystery." What is this mystery? Verse 6 defines this mystery. It is the multi-ethnic body of believers! "This mystery is that through the gospel the Gentiles are heirs together with Israel, members together of one body, and sharers together in the promise in Christ Jesus. I became a servant of *this gospel*" (Eph. 3:6–7). The new interracial church is part of the gospel.[17] The fact that by God's grace there is now a new redeemed community whose common life is visible proof that the messianic kingdom has burst into history is part of the Good News we share.[18]

When the church is a visible demonstration of the gospel it preaches, then its own fellowship has strong evangelistic dimensions. The quality of its common life attracts non-Christians to the Lord of the church.

Similarly, when the church dares to be the church, when the church models a new reality that transcends the brokenness of surrounding society, it leavens the whole social order.[19] Hospitals and orphanages started among Christians who cared about the needy. Sunday schools began as places to teach reading, writing, and arithmetic to illiterate kids caught in the oppression of child labor. Sunday was their only free day. Slowly, the larger society saw that access to hospitals and universal education were good things that everyone should enjoy. Living a model that challenges the sinful neglect or oppression of the larger society often brings social change.[20]

A church that fully implemented New Testament teaching would offer a powerfully attractive alternative to our world so broken by greed, corruption, selfishness, and racism. Think of what would have happened in 1980 if all the Christians in South Africa or Northern Ireland—or, for that matter, Greater Philadelphia—had truly begun to care for each other and share their time, their money, and their lives with each other across racial and economic lines in the way that the early church did. Think of how a worldwide church, fully implementing Paul's guidelines (2 Cor. 8:8–15) for economic sharing in the body of believers would challenge our world so tragically divided between rich and poor. Quite apart from any direct political activity, the impact would be enormous. Nothing would be more revolutionary than simply living out day by day the full biblical teaching that in Christ there is neither Jew nor Greek, black nor white, because we are all one in Christ.

We have no business asking government to change unless our churches lead the way. The church, understood as Jesus' new messianic community, has been a missing link in much recent Christian social action. I applaud the tremendous concern for racial equality and peace that mainline churches expressed in the sixties. And I confess sadly that evangelical leaders and churches were at best largely silent when Martin Luther King's ringing words and daring acts moved the United States a little closer to justice.

But there was, at least in the white mainline churches, a missing link as white clergy marched and protested for justice and peace. To a tragic degree they were asking Washington to legislate what Christians—even their laity—refused to live. Consequently, they were generals without troops.

One evening in the late sixties, a group of pastors gathered together in a Chicago suburb to work against racism. They felt terrible that their all-white suburb refused to admit African-Americans. And they knew that the economic and political leaders were behind this systematic exclusion. So they met together to develop a strategy for bringing political pressure on the politicians and business leaders to force them to accept nonwhite residents.

After a long, intense discussion, one participant got up and asked a different question of the assembled pastors: "Are not the mayor, the top business leaders, and bank presidents members of your churches?" Everyone else was puzzled. No one saw any connection between that fact and their political strategizing. It didn't even occur to them that the first step should be to work within the body of Christ to model there a radical alternative to society's racism.

When Christian leaders go to government to call for sweeping structural change, we have more integrity and power when we can say: "We are part of Christian communities that are already beginning to live out what we are calling you to legislate." Our call for costly changes in foreign policy toward the Two-Thirds World designed to implement greater global economic justice has integrity only if we are a part of Christian congregations that are already beginning to incarnate a more simple lifestyle that points toward a more just, ecologically sustainable planet. Our call for nuclear disarmament and international peace has integrity only if there is growing peace and wholeness in our families and churches.

If I am not doing everything in my power to allow the Holy Spirit to bring healing between my wife and me, and wholeness among the members of my congregation, then it is sheer arrogance and stupidity for me to call on senators or presidents and tell them how to bring peace in the international community. It is only as the people of God begin truly and visibly to be Jesus' new alternative society, it is only as we genuinely start to incarnate the radical values of Jesus' new kingdom that we can powerfully impact the unjust structures of society. But when the church truly models Jesus' new values, the mysterious new reality of the church has an explosive impact on the larger community.

The last two points make it clear how evangelism impacts society as redeemed persons and the redeemed community of believers influence the total social order. Sometimes, people refer to this impact loosely as the "spill-over" effect of Christian faith in the world, but that image is not adequate. Too easily it can lead to the notion of two quite unrelated realities of church and world. Certainly they are distinct and dare not be confused. But when the church is faithful to Jesus, it penetrates the world far more profoundly than the image of "spill-over" suggests.

Jesus' own images of salt, yeast, and light are more dynamic and powerful.[21] Each of Jesus' images indicates that the church penetrates deeply into the world. The light shines throughout the darkness. The salt soaks into all the meat. The yeast leavens the whole dough. Quite apart from their direct political engagement, redeemed people who truly model the gospel of the kingdom penetrate and transform society.

Social Action's Evangelistic Dimension

Fourth, social concern also fosters evangelism.[22] Conversely, the church's silence on injustice undermines evangelism.[23] Samuel Escobar tells the story of a missionary society working in Bolivia in the early twentieth century. When they bought land in Huatajata, 250 serfs came with the land. Repeated efforts to evangelize the serfs (Aymaras) failed. Then in 1942, the missionaries abolished serfdom and gave the land to the serfs. The church began to grow. Ten years later, a national program of land reform cited the successful Huatajata mission experiment to support the larger program of land reform. After that, church growth among the Aymaras increased even more.[24]

Every Christian who ministers with sensitivity and love among the poor has experienced the same result. When we care for people in Jesus' name, our acts of mercy open hearts to the gospel. When we stand with the poor to challenge the way they are treated, they are more likely to accept our invitation to turn to Christ.

There is, to be sure, potential danger here. Our social concern dare not be a gimmick designed to bribe people to become Christians. Social action has its own independent validity. We do it because the Creator wants everyone to enjoy the good creation. At the same time, when our genuine compassion also has an evangelistic dimension, we rejoice. Again and again, that is exactly what happens when we truly care for the needy and stand with the oppressed who seek justice.[25]

We must, however, face a hard reality. Sometimes, in the short run, challenging unjust structures slows down church growth. If the mainstream German church in the 1930s had clearly and strongly opposed Nazism, there would have been severe persecution and probably a short-term decline in church attendance. In the long term, however, that prophetic faithfulness would probably have helped restore the credibility of Christian faith for secular

179

Europeans who have continued to forsake Christianity in droves since the end of World War II.[26]

Discipleship and the Environment

Fifth, social action can help protect the fruits of evangelism.[27] If inner-city converts must return to a social setting where all the legitimate jobs have moved to the suburbs and drug running seems to be the only way to make a decent living, the temptation to sin is enormous. One could say similar things about many other social problems. William Booth, the founder of the Salvation Army, condemned environments where "vice has an enormous advantage over virtue." Such a setting, he protested, is "atheism made easy."[28] Social action that creates good jobs in the inner city and gets rid of drug operations will make it easier for new converts to be faithful disciples of Jesus.

Evangelism and social action are inseparably interrelated. Each leads to the other. They mutually support each other. In practice, they are often so intertwined that it would be silly and fruitless, indeed destructive, to pull them apart.[29] Evangelism and social action are distinct, equally deserving of resources, and inseparably interrelated.

This fifth model—wholistic mission as incarnational kingdom Christianity—includes the strengths and avoids the weaknesses of the first three models outlined in chapter two.[30] It also provides a better framework for solving problems that arise.

Incarnational kingdom Christianity addresses all the deepest concerns of those who focus primarily on individual soul-winning. It agrees that nothing is more urgent than sharing the wonderful news of the one Mediator, Jesus Christ, who reconciles lost sinners with a holy God. Utopian social schemes that forget that sin is deeper than mere social structures will fail. Similarly, the radical Anabaptist model's emphasis on the church as Jesus' new redeemed community is central to wholistic mission. The same is true for the dominant ecumenical model's concern for peace, justice, and the integrity of creation. Christians who ignore the biblical truth that the Creator is God of the poor and fail to seek justice for the oppressed are disobedient and heretical. Furthermore, the biblical view of persons, sin, and salvation is far more wholistic than most post-Enlightenment, individualistic Western Christians imagine. Only the central concerns of the fourth model, which abandons fundamental truths of historic Christian orthodoxy, fail to find a place in model five.

The wholistic approach of model five solves problems better than other approaches. I mention two: the decline of mainline churches and the problem of "redemptive lift."[31]

The disastrous decline of mainline Protestant churches in the past thirty years is common knowledge. To be sure, some people have left for the *wrong* reasons. Some parishioners resented their church's courageous stand for racial and economic justice and therefore switched to one-sided evangelical congregations where these "uncomfortable" social topics did not come up. But the major reason for decline has been the loss of a passion for evangelism grounded in loss of certainty about the central theological truths of historic Christian orthodoxy. If one is not sure if Jesus is truly God incarnate, if one is not sure Christ is the only Mediator, then evangelism becomes less urgent or even irrelevant.

Mainline churches should *not* abandon their courageous stand against racism, economic injustice, and oppression, but they do need to ground their social action in solid biblical orthodoxy. And they need to become as enthusiastic about leading lost sinners to Christ as they are about liberating the oppressed of the earth.

Donald McGavran focused on a different problem in his classic book, *Understanding Church Growth*. McGavran was troubled by a problem similar to what John Wesley had observed in the eighteenth-century revivals. Wesley lamented the fact that new converts experienced sweeping transformation, became industrious and eventually well-off economically, and then they (or their children) lost their faith.

McGavran observed the same fairly rapid increase in wealth among poor folk who became Christians. One result was that their new economic status seemed to cut their connections with their larger circle of non-Christian neighbors. They were now "different" and therefore far less effective in evangelizing those neighbors. McGavran's primary solution was to insist on the primacy of evangelism and church growth and therefore make sure that evangelism received a majority of the resources.[32]

Incarnational kingdom Christianity offers a better solution. A central key is to teach new converts the full truth about God's concern for the poor and oppressed. Then as new Christians become transformed persons freed from destructive habits and begin to enjoy growing material abundance, they will reach out in wholistic mission to their poor neighbors. Discipled to have an equal passion for evangelism and social change, they will model Christ's incarnational identification with the poor. Rather than moving away from the poor in the slums or rural communities, they will remain there, modeling new possibilities, sharing economic resources, and inviting everyone to Christ.

A friend of mine, Judge Nelson Diaz of Philadelphia, is a wonderful example. Nelson grew up in Harlem, raised by a poor single-parent Puerto Rican woman. Fortunately, faith in Christ kept him from the destruction of gangs and drugs. Instead, he got a good education, became a successful lawyer, and eventually a judge of the Court of Common Pleas of The First Judicial District of Pennsylvania. In June 1992, he co-chaired The Billy Graham Crusade in Philadelphia.

I was a counselor for that Crusade and was there the night Judge Diaz shared his testimony. The audience was deeply moved as he shared his rise from poverty to great success. He also described the racism he faced in law school and the way he organized Hispanic and African-American students to demand change. What impressed me most, however, was the reminder of where he lives and worships. He and his family live in a very poor section of North Philadelphia. The inter-racial congregation of African-Americans, whites, and Hispanics of whom he is a leader is right in the middle of one of the dreadfully poor and dangerous parts of the inner city. He lives there and worships there because he knows that poor community desperately needs his presence, example, and leadership. Because he trusts Jesus, he dares to stay.

I started this section on incarnational kingdom Christianity with a conversation with Raleigh Washington, the pastor of Rock/Circle in Chicago. A story of one of their recent converts provides a good summary of my thesis that evangelism and social action are distinct, approximately equally deserving of resources, and inseparably interrelated. Not so long ago, Cassandra Holmes Franklin came to Rock/Circle's medical clinic, seeking a doctor's help. She got that, but they also told her about Jesus. Soon she came to Christ, joined Rock Church, and started singing in the choir. A little later she married Showen, the father of her two children, who also soon came to personal faith. Now her husband has a job as a partner in an economic development venture of Circle Ministries starting a small business.[33]

That is incarnational kingdom Christianity. Rock Church could do the evangelism and hope that someone else would provide health care and jobs. Circle Ministries could provide housing and employment and hope that someone else would lead people to Christ who transforms persons, bringing new values, dignity, initiative, and honesty, which, in turn, make the job-creation programs work better. But Christian mission works best when evangelism and social concern come together in the name and power of Jesus.

11

Our Historic Moment

As the third millennium of the redemption draws near, God is preparing a great springtime for Christianity.

JOHN PAUL II[1]

Christians privileged to live in the last decade before the year 2000 face a historic opportunity.

The number of Christians worldwide is growing at unprecedented rates. A shrinking global village and new technology make it easier to get the message of Christ to those who have never heard. Growing agreement on both the urgency of evangelism and the importance of a wholistic approach encourages optimism. And historic political changes have opened more doors to the gospel. The last decade of the second Christian millennium is a breathtaking time to be a disciple of Jesus Christ.

Reasons for Hope

Global Christianity is on the move. Considerably more people have become Christians in the twentieth century than in any previous century. In 1900, there were about 558 million Christians. In 1992, there were 1,833 million. Experts predict that in eight years—by the year 2000—there will probably be 2,130 million.[2]

One must quickly add that this explosive expansion is almost exactly parallel to the total global population growth. There are also vastly more non-Christians today. In 1900, Christians represented 34.4 percent of the global population. Christian statistician David Barrett estimates that Christians will be 34.1 percent in 2000 A.D. There is still much to do.

The ratio of committed Christians to non-Christians, however, offers real hope. Barrett estimates that the number of committed, "Great Commission" Christians is growing at 6.9 percent a year—more than twice as fast as the total world population.[3] Precise statistics are not available, so one must be careful.[4] But Ralph Winter probably correctly identifies a significant trend when he suggests that in 1950, there were approximately twenty-one non-Christians for every "Bible-believing" Christian. By 1980, he says, there were only eleven non-Christians for every "Bible-believing" Christian. And by 1992, the ratio was less than 7–1.[5]

Pentecostals and charismatics today are the most successful at evangelism, and their numbers are growing at explosive rates. In 1970 there were seventy-two million. Twenty-two years later (1992), they had increased more than 500 percent to 410 million. Barrett estimates that by the year 2000, Pentecostal and charismatic Christians alone will number 560 million.[6]

The tremendous growth of the church in the Third World is another reason for joy and hope. In 1900 at least 75 percent of all Christians were white folk living in places like Europe, North America, and Russia. By 2000, 56 percent of all Christians will be Third World Christians living outside those traditionally "Christian" countries. The number of Christians in Africa, Asia, and Latin America will have increased 1300 percent in one hundred years to almost 1.2 billion people.[7]

It is extremely significant that the number of Third World missionaries is increasing at an astonishing rate. By 1990, there were 49,000 Third World missionaries spreading the gospel in countries other than their own.[8] By the year 2000, there will probably be 100,000.[9] When one remembers that in 1900, the total number of all foreign missionaries was only 62,000, one can see the magnitude of the huge body of Third World missionaries.[10]

The wonderful privilege of sharing the gospel cross-culturally with people of a different language and history is no longer a "Western" or "White European" activity. Africans are coming to evangelize in Europe and North America. Native American Navajo Christians are sending missionaries to European Laplanders, and European Gypsies are spreading the gospel in the African country of Madagascar!

Another reason for hope is the growing agreement in many parts of the church that evangelism and social concern must go hand in hand. Evangelicals in the Lausanne movement and the World Evangelical Fellowship have increasingly affirmed the importance of social concern.[11] And ecumenical Protestants and Roman Catholics have recently made strong statements about the importance of evangelism.[12]

It is not just evangelicals and charismatics who are stressing evangelism in the last decade of the twentieth century. At Lambeth '88, the worldwide Anglican communion called the 1990s the "Decade of Evangelism," passing a resolution "recognizing that evangelism is the primary task of the Church."[13] John Paul II has called 1990–2000 the "Universal Decade of Evangelism." His 1991 *Redemptoris Missio* is a ringing call to Roman Catholics for renewed attention to sharing the gospel with those who do not know Christ. "The poor are hungry for God, not just for bread and freedom. Missionary activity must first of all bear witness to and proclaim salvation in Christ and establish local churches which then become means of liberation in every sense."[14]

Finally, the breathtaking political changes unleashed by Mikhail Gorbachev and Boris Yeltsin have thrown open new doors to the gospel. Atheism is no longer the official religion of Eastern Europe and the countries of the former Soviet Union. The church has survived and conquered one of history's most brutal, most sustained attempts to stamp it out. Millions of people in former communist countries are eagerly exploring Christianity, hoping that it will provide the foundation they desperately seek for rebuilding their societies.

The collapse of communism means more than a new opportunity for spreading the gospel openly in Eastern Europe and the old Soviet Union—although that in itself is momentous and wonderful. The victory over communism has come in the name of freedom and democracy. The "virus" of freedom is spreading everywhere around the globe and will slowly but surely open new opportunities for the gospel in China, North Korea, and even closed Muslim societies.

The end of the cold war offers the possibility of a period of greater peace, justice, and freedom. Human selfishness will undoubtedly cooperate with Satan to slam shut many of these opening doors. But the 1990s offer the world's people a historic opportunity to cooperate rather than fight. If rich nations would share more to empower the poor, and everyone would work together to preserve the environment, our children could begin the first century of the third millennium A.D. with a reasonable prospect that it can be safer and freer than the last century of the second millennium. In such a world, Christians would be more free to spread the gospel and apply biblical faith to every area of life.

The Problems

Our optimism, however, must be guarded. Satan has not been converted. Human sin continues its stupid, destructive rampage. There are many reasons for deep concern.

Among the most serious problems is the fact that modern secularism has seduced hundreds of millions in Europe and North America. In Europe, the heartland of Christianity for more than a thousand years, only a tiny percent of the people are practicing Christians. Only about 5 percent of the people attend church every Sunday in countries like Germany, France, and England. Seventy-five percent of France is nominally Catholic, but only 6 percent are practicing Catholics.[15]

For two hundred years now since the Enlightenment, Western intellectuals have turned aside from biblical revelation. They have worshiped the false god of "scientism," blindly believing that nature is all that exists and that science is the only path to truth.

Modern science is a wonderful tool made possible by the designing hand of a good and wise Creator. But Western secularism has made it a false god. Tragically, the intellectual elite of the West and increasingly, too, of the rest of the world have bowed the knee to this pseudoscientific secularism. Unless contemporary Christians learn better how to combat modern secularism, Christianity will continue to lose ground in the West and among the globe's intellectuals.[16]

In part, at least, the United States has escaped some of the impact of modern secularism. Over the last decade, 44 percent of adults in the United States attended church every Sunday. Market researcher George Barna reports that in 1992, weekly church attendance was up to 49 percent.[17]

Attending church, however, is not the same thing as following Jesus. So much of North American Christianity is social fluff. People attend church but don't make Jesus and his dawning kingdom the center of their lives. Secular values effectively shape large areas of their thinking and living. North American Christians are not successfully resisting Hollywood's sensuality, Wall Street's materialism, or the general culture's individualistic relativism.[18] Their political views are more a reflection of their history and geography rather than Jesus and the Bible.

Kenneth Kantzer, former editor of *Christianity Today,* says materialism is one of the most serious problems for North American Christians.[19] U.S. evangelicals have roughly $800 billion in after-taxes income. We spend $8 billion on weight-reduction programs and only one fourth as much (a mere $2 billion) on missions.[20]

The worldwide pattern of Christian consumption is similar. Global Christianity is wealthy. Christians make up only one-third (33 percent) of the world's people, but we receive about two-thirds (62 percent) of the world's total income each year.[21] Tragically, we spend about 97 percent of this vast wealth on ourselves! One percent goes to secular charities. A mere 2 percent goes to all Christian work.[22] But even that tiny 2 percent we give to Christian causes is largely spent on ourselves—i.e., in our home congregations and in our home countries. In 1992, Christians worldwide had a total income of $9,696 billion. We gave only $169 billion (1.74 percent) to all Christian work. And only $9.2 billion of that—a mere 5.4 percent—went to foreign missions.[23]

While most Christians live in affluence or at least comfort, one-quarter of our world suffers grinding poverty. Each day, over 100,000 people die of starvation and malnutrition. Each day, too, 55,000 people die without even having heard about Jesus.

One of four people (1.4 billion) in our hurting world live in near absolute poverty.[24] Starvation and malnourishment torment and deform their bodies and dreams. Many are starving or malnourished. One of four people in our broken world also live and die without ever being told about the gospel.[25] They enter eternity without hearing even once about God's incredible love in Christ.

And the two groups largely overlap. Most of the desperately poor are unevangelized. Does that matter? Is that important to people who are followers of the One who said that he came to bring good news to the poor and offer eternal life to the perishing? It should! René Padilla is certainly right that according to biblical faith, "there is no place for statistics on how many souls die without Christ every minute, if they do not take into account how many of those who die, die victims of hunger."[26]

It is both biblically heretical and strategically stupid for rich Christians to neglect the world's poor. With the collapse of communism, one of the greatest threats to global peace will come from North-South hostility grounded in the growing gap between rich and poor. Ethnic hostility, racial prejudice, and environmental destruction will also pose terrible dangers for our children and grandchildren.

As we cast probing, expectant eyes toward the twenty-first century, Christians have many reasons for optimism and many reasons for concern. Wholistic mission, a faithful biblical combination of the things we so often divide, offers the best hope for reducing the dangers and maximizing the opportunities.

Incarnational Kingdom Christianity for the Third Millennium

Our world desperately needs committed Christians who do both evangelism and social concern—who both think and strategize vigorously as well as pray increasingly for the renewal, presence, and power of the Holy Spirit—who both build the church and transform society. Our world desperately needs incarnational kingdom disciples committed to wholistic mission.

Think of the impact if wholistic mission became central to every institution of the church. Our Christian schools and colleges would send forth a steady stream of talented Christian leaders equipped to change the world by building the church and transforming society. Our evangelistic and church planting programs and structures would nurture a concern for social transformation. Our organizations devoted to relief, development, and structural change would integrate prayer, the work of the Holy Spirit, and evangelism into their social agendas. Our seminaries would train pastors eager and able to lead wholistic congregations that have an equal concern for inward nurture in the local congregation and outward action in the world for evangelism and social transformation. More and more local congregations would become powerful demonstration projects of the coming kingdom.

I cannot develop all of the implications of wholistic mission, but I want to sketch out very briefly a few ideas for wholistic revivals, wholistic apologetics, wholistic political engagement, and wholistic congregations. We can transcend one-sided Christianity!

What would happen if Christians most identified with evangelism would join with Christians most engaged in social action and Christians most concerned with renewal in the power of the Holy Spirit in city-wide crusades? We could call the meetings shalom revivals.[27] The Old Testament word *shalom,* as we saw earlier, means wholeness in every way—right relationship with God, neighbor, and earth.

Shalom revivals would include the clear evangelistic invitation to accept Christ of the typical Billy Graham Crusade. But shalom revivals would also feature a vigorous call to Christians to share with the poor and seek justice for the oppressed. Equally central would be an invitation to all Christians to deepen their walk with the Lord by opening themselves unconditionally to the fullness of the Holy Spirit. During the invitation, those who do not know Christ would be invited to come forward to accept him. Lukewarm Christians would be encouraged to come forward to surrender their lives fully to God and receive the fullness of the Holy Spirit's fruits and gifts. Christians would be urged to come forward if they sensed God calling them to make new concrete commitments for Christian service—whether in new evangelistic efforts or a new engagement to solve the tragedies of world hunger, broken inner cities, and a devastated environment; whether in new programs of Christian renewal, or concrete political engagement.

190

Perhaps Billy Graham could begin shalom revivals. Graham has increasingly included a significant social component (Love in Action) in his crusades. What would happen if Graham would invite South Africa's Desmond Tutu as the representative of Christian social activists and Thailand's Kriengsak Chareongwongsak as the representative of charismatic Christians to join him in a major city-wide shalom revival?[28] Christian agencies involved in evangelism, social action, and renewal in the power of the Spirit would all participate. Christians who come forward to dedicate their lives to new service would be linked to organizations involved in evangelism, social action, and church renewal.

Wholistic apologetics would fit well with wholistic revivals. Earlier I talked about the problem of Western secularism, which pervades the intellectual world—especially our universities, which are overwhelmingly non-Christian. Enlightenment secularism is one reason for the loss of faith among educated people, but another crucial reason is Christian failure. We have not lived what we preached. In disgust, many intellectuals have turned away from our hypocritical Christianity.

What would happen if wholistic churches among the poor like Raleigh Washington's Rock of Our Salvation in Chicago launched a movement of apologetics and evangelism at places like the University of Chicago? They would certainly need sharp minds to counter the intellectual doubts of secular university folk. But they would also offer a daring challenge: "Come and investigate our interracial church of black and white, rich and poor worshiping and working together to solve the desperate problems of our inner-city community. Secular social workers, humanist educators, and politicians seem powerless to reverse the collapse of our inner cities. But it is happening here by the power of God at Rock/Circle ministries because we know people need both justification and justice. Christianity is true and therefore it works. If you still have intellectual doubts, we will gladly discuss further the historical evidence for Jesus' resurrection, or your questions about God's existence. But we also invite you to visit our interracial, multi-class congregation and witness the power of God overcoming the racial and economic divisions that are tearing our world apart."

191

I wonder how the secular intellectual community would respond to that kind of apologetics and evangelism.[29] Some, of course, would still prefer the immediate pleasures of relativistic, individualistic secularism. But more and more people in the universities realize that Enlightenment secularism, like its offspring atheistic Marxism, has failed. Tragically, however, these people often turn to Eastern religion rather than to Christianity—in part because they think that Christianity does not help us solve the terrible problems of global hunger, economic injustice, racial oppression, militarism, and ecological destruction. So they turn to the old monistic gods marketed under a modern, New-Age label. Full-orbed biblical Christianity is what they need. And the best way to help them to see that is by wholistic discipleship and wholistic apologetics.

A biblically grounded Christian movement of wholistic political engagement could help authenticate that kind of wholistic apologetic. Everybody knows, at least to some degree, that we must solve desperate problems like the collapsing family, devastated inner cities, a billion plus hungry neighbors, and ecological devastation. But solutions grounded in secular assumptions will continue to fail.

Worldwide, we need widespread political engagement by committed Christians grounded in thoroughly biblical assumptions.[30] Such a movement would know that politics is important but limited in what it can do. Only God through transforming grace can create new persons, although wholesome social structures can encourage good and discourage evil. Intermediate institutions like churches, schools, the media, and businesses are crucial to prevent the growth of despotic, all-powerful governments. Such a movement would renounce political ideologies of left and right and seek to develop concrete political proposals that are thoroughly grounded in biblical ethical principles and careful factual analysis. Because it was shaped by God's agenda, such a movement would be concerned with strengthening the family and empowering the poor, with both peace and freedom, with both the sanctity of human life and the preservation of the environment. Such a movement would offer the world an alternative social vision.

Such a movement would also challenge the tragic materialism and selfishness of contemporary Christians.[31] Nominal "Christians" control about two-thirds of the world's wealth. They control the politically dominant nations in Europe and North America. Tragically, precisely this "Christian" world refuses to make the costly sacrifices that would help poor nations both to solve their environmental problems and nurture a decent life for all their people.

I believe that the basic notions of freedom and democracy that are sweeping our globe are rooted in biblical truth. But the poor of the earth will not long espouse freedom and democracy if the nations who promote it turn their backs on their plea for food and justice.

We face a historic opportunity on planet earth. Full peace and justice, of course, will come only at Christ's return. But we have been able to end slavery and expand the boundaries of freedom and democracy. In the next few decades we could move further. The rich could share in dramatic new ways with the poor to reduce global poverty and renew the environment. In that kind of world of growing justice and ecological wholeness, there would be fewer international conflicts. The important tasks of defending human rights and expanding the boundaries of freedom and democracy would be more successful. Greater freedom would provide greater opportunity to share the gospel. Human societies would still be a messy mix of good and evil. But our children and grandchildren— indeed all God's children—could live in a less dangerous world.

That future, however, requires political decisions by today's dominant nations that enable all the world's people to share more equitably in the good earth's bounty. And that requires sacrifice today by affluent nations in which the majority of voters are nominal "Christians." Is it too much to hope that a sustained worldwide political movement by biblical Christians working for justice, life, peace, and freedom could persuade selfish, materialistic voters to make the necessary sacrifices? If that happened, the next century would be safer. The Creator would be honored. And non-Christians around the world would be more open to the faith that produced that kind of unselfish concern for others.

I hope that the last few paragraphs (and earlier chapters) have convinced you that Christians should seek to shape political life. But it would be incredibly silly to think that politics is the only way we change the structures of society.

We also need wholistic Christians in every realm of society—business, media, education, law, as well as government. Christian leaders who think through and implement the implications of genuinely biblical principles for the economy, law, medicine, education, and the media are engaged in social transformation just as much as persons in government.

Nor should leaders in medicine or law neglect their evangelistic opportunities. As they live by different norms and call for surprising changes, people will wonder why. In response, they can tell people about Christ as they continue shaping their particular area of society according to biblical principles.

Finally, I work and pray for wholistic congregations—thousands and thousands of congregations across the globe so in love with Jesus that they cannot stop inviting non-Christians to come to Christ and so compassionately concerned for needy neighbors that they cannot stop feeding the hungry and empowering the oppressed.

When I speak to pastors' conferences, I sometimes ask them how many congregations they know that are both leading people to Christ every year and also immersed in social action. Tragically, most pastors cannot think of even one! A few know one or two somewhere in the world. A handful know several. Then when I ask them what Jesus would think about what they have just told me, they smile sadly. What a terrible, almost unbelievable tragedy.

Network 9:35, sponsored by Evangelicals for Social Action, seeks to correct that tragedy. Grounded in Jesus' example of ministering to the whole person (Matt. 9:35), Network 9:35 works with local congregations who want to strengthen both their evangelism and their social ministry and link them tightly together. Network 9:35 offers conferences, seminars, tools, consultation, congregation-to-congregation mentoring, and a web site on the Internet with wholistic models, chat rooms, and up-to-date information on wholistic ministry. Via the 9:35 web site, persons can network with others engaged in wholistic ministry in other parts of the country and world.[32]

If Jesus spoke the truth, if the Bible is God's Word, then every Christian congregation should be wholistic. Every Christian congregation should be equipping its people for the work of evangelism, praying constantly for the salvation of sinners, and regularly—month by month—experiencing the joy of welcoming new believers into the circle of Jesus' redeemed community. Every Christian congregation should also be immersed in service to the hurting and broken in their own community and around the world. That kind of church would end the scandal of one-sided Christianity.

That kind of church might sometimes encounter angry resentment at its uncovering of evil, but more often it would experience respect and awe at the visible presence of God's transforming power. That kind of church would grow. That kind of church would help feed the hungry and restore the environment. That kind of church would set people on the path of life eternal where, with unspeakable joy, believers will dance forever in a restored creation in the presence of the One who is both Creator and Redeemer.

Appendix

Is Social Justice Part of Salvation?

Should we use the word *salvation* in a narrower way to refer only to what happens when persons consciously confess Christ and enter his new community? Or, should we adopt the broader usage of ecumenical Christians (model three in chapter two) and use salvation language to apply both to the above and also to growing freedom and justice in society as a whole?

It is important to listen with an open mind to the best case to be made for the broader usage. Nor dare we forget the fear of people like Gustavo Gutiérrez, that those who adopt the narrower language do so "to protect their interests." "It is those who by trying to 'save' the work of Christ will 'lose' it."[1]

It is also extremely important to avoid unfair stereotypes. The CRESR[2] moved well beyond the individualistic understanding of salvation of model one. Salvation is personal and social (within the body of believers) and will be cosmic at Christ's return.[3] Nor should one distort the broader usage and suggest that advocates of model three want to reduce salvation merely to what results from horizontal social change via politics (model four).

The real debate is between those who believe we should use salvation language only to refer to the full range of redeemed relationships between God and believers and among believers that results when persons come to living faith in Jesus Christ. That includes forgiveness of sins, personal sanctification, and transformed relationships within the church. It also includes the cosmic restoration that Christ will bring at his return when every knee will bow. But salvation language, in this view, should not be used to talk about the growth of freedom and justice in human society beyond the church when Christians and non-Christians alike create more free, just social systems. To be sure, people who adopt the narrower view of salvation insist strongly that Christians should combat social sin and change unjust structures. They believe that Christian faith has a powerful "spill-over" effect in the larger society. But we should call the result justice, freedom, and environmental wholeness, not salvation.

The broader view, advocated by the conservative subtype of model three, prefers to use salvation language to refer to all of the above. Salvation includes both what happens when people consciously accept Christ and join the church and also what happens when whole societies become more just and free. Many of the people who use this broader language have a solidly orthodox theology and an evangelistic zeal to lead non-Christians to a living faith in Jesus Christ.[4] But salvation refers to God's total saving plan to correct Satan's distortion of the created order. That happens most clearly in the church, but it also happens when whole societies reduce institutional racism like apartheid, or economic oppression, or child labor.

The debate about whether or not it is correct to speak of the coming of the kingdom in the larger society is directly parallel to the debate over how broad salvation is. Jesus prayed that the kingdom would come "on earth as in heaven." David Bosch argues that "the kingdom comes wherever Jesus overcomes the Evil One. This happens (or ought to happen) in fullest measure in the church. But it also happens in society."[5] Therefore we should speak of the coming of the kingdom and the presence of salvation when society enjoys growing freedom and justice.

Which of these two views is more faithful to the Scriptures? Which will better help Christians today to accomplish all that the Lord of the church desires? A careful examination of the strongest arguments for each position should help us decide.

Toward a Broader Definition

A Wholistic Image of Persons

Some people reject the broad use of salvation language because they operate with a highly individualistic view of persons, including a strong body-soul dualism. They see only the personal and not the social aspects of sin. And they forget that since persons are created for community, we cannot enjoy all the wholeness God intends unless evil social systems are transformed.

Carl Braaten suggests that an unbiblical body-soul dualism accounts for much evangelical rejection of the broader use of salvation language. He argues: "There is no such thing as the salvation of souls apart from the body. . . . We play out the drama of God's salvation in our bodies and nowhere else."[6]

Such a claim is obviously too sweeping. As Mortimer Arias points out, the thief on the cross, precisely as he was leaving this body in death, received Jesus' comforting promise that "today" he would be with him in paradise.[7] Braaten himself goes on to observe that one could, in principle, be living in a perfect social system and still stand guilty before God.[8] Conversely, one could be dying of hunger and still also be rejoicing in the Lord and confident of life eternal. (Christians, to be sure, who tolerate such tragedy in the body of Christ are guilty of damnable sin.)

Braaten's basic point, however, is correct. There are people who see salvation primarily or exclusively as the saving of individual souls. Coming to Christ means receiving forgiveness and a ticket to heaven with little impact on life on this earth. Such folk grossly distort the biblical view of persons as body-soul unities. They overlook the central way, as we saw in chapter five, that salvation language in both testaments refers to God's healing of broken bodies and the restoration of wholeness between persons. They forget that the transformed relationships in Jesus' new redeemed community are part of what the New Testament means by salvation.

But we can say all of that (and thus reject an unbiblical body-soul dualism) and still insist that the limited improvement in society outside the church should be called justice, rather than salvation.

Social Sin and Structural Change

Does recognizing the reality of social sin require the broader usage? Many have argued that since sin is both personal and social, therefore salvation is both individual and structural in the sense that systemic improvements outside the church should be included in salvation.[9] It is certainly true that the fall resulted in broken relationships not just with God but also with neighbor. The Bible pointedly condemns evil social systems.[10] It also insists that a right relationship with God demands right relationships with neighbor.[11]

God created us social beings. Therefore, as Orlando Costas insists, it is both unbiblical and naive to work with an individualistic sociology that views church and society as merely the "sum total of individuals."[12] We dare never suppose that the *only* way to change the world is to convert individuals. Personal conversion does impact society—in fact far more than secular social activists dream or imagine.[13] But it is simplistic to ignore the profound way that social systems impact people's behavior. A strictly enforced speed limit changes how fast we drive. Welfare systems that reward irresponsibility and pregnancy outside marriage encourage immoral behavior. We cannot create new, unselfish persons or perfect social systems through political change. But the recent spread of democratic institutions shows that the systems of society can be changed. And those institutions certainly shape us in powerful ways.

In fact, since persons are social beings made for community, we simply cannot enjoy full humanization apart from changed social structures. Even as a slave, to be sure, one can be forgiven and destined for eternal life. But one cannot enjoy the dignity, freedom, and wholeness intended by the Creator as a slave, an oppressed laborer, or a malnourished woman. Conversely Vinay Samuel and Chris Sugden are correct to insist that when social systems that dehumanize women or the poor are changed and treat them with greater dignity, the new sense of self-worth in the poor is a significant (albeit not total) overcoming of the brokenness of the fall.[14]

But again, none of the above arguments require the broader definition of salvation. The fact that we are persons-in-community means that there must be a powerful social element to salvation. But that is precisely what adherents of model two assert in their vigorous emphasis on redeemed relationships in the church.

It is clearly very important to change unjust social structures both because the Bible teaches that they displease our holy God and also because they dehumanize persons. But many Christians today place a high priority on political action designed to improve social systems without calling the results salvation.

The salvation that Christians enjoy and the kingdom that Christ initiated certainly have a "spill-over"[15] effect in the world when Christians change the larger society in the name of Jesus as an obedient witness to his kingdom values. God has certainly used Christians (and Hindus) in India to change an oppressive caste system in significant ways. The educated, prosperous Hindu woman from an untouchable caste certainly enjoys a new dignity and wholeness. She does not need to confess Christ to enjoy these benefits of Christ's kingdom, but is it precise to say she shares "in God's saving work"? Is it precise to say this action of (partially) eliminating the caste system is "part of God's work of breaking down the dividing wall of hostility between separated groups, of creating in himself one new humanity in Christ"?[16] Ephesians 2:14–15 clearly refers to people who have personally accepted Jesus Christ and therefore enjoy Jesus' new community where dividing walls of race and class are being broken down. To use this language and speak of salvation in reference to someone who explicitly chooses to remain a practicing Hindu seems contradictory. Is it not more faithful to biblical language and more respectful of her religious choice to speak, instead, of justice and human rights? With reference to the struggle against caste, Vinay Samuel and Chris Sugden rightly conclude that the resulting social "transformation is not salvation. . . . Those who do not confess Christ are not saved by the kingdom in this world; only obedience to and faith in the King can provide salvation."[17] We should describe the "benefits" or "spill-over" effects that non-Christians enjoy because of the obedient sociopolitical action of Christians with words other than salvation.

Cosmic Salvation

We saw in chapter five that God's plan of salvation will eventually extend not only to individuals but also to society and creation itself. The kings of the earth, Revelation 21 promises, will bring their glory into the New Jerusalem. Even the groaning creation will experience Christ's saving power at the second coming (Rom. 8). Furthermore, both these passages suggest significant continuity between nature and history as we know it and the coming kingdom. Certainly there is radical discontinuity. Because of sin, we cannot create the perfect kingdom through political engagement. Christ will do that at his return. But there is also continuity. Wherever justice, freedom, peace, and wholeness emerge in society we can surely say both that Jesus Christ the Lord of history is at work tugging history toward that perfection that will come at his return and also that the limited goodness and beauty that societies experience now as they move in that direction will be purged and taken up into the future kingdom in some mysterious yet substantial fashion.

Does that mean that salvation language should be applied to that limited goodness now? Nowhere does the New Testament do that.

Romans 8:18ff. is instructive. Both persons and the whole created order groan in anticipation of the final redemption of all things. But there is an important difference in the present between believers and creation. Paul says that Christians already have the "firstfruits" of the Spirit and indeed "have been saved" in the hope of the final eschaton (vv. 23–24). But he does not say either of these things about creation. There is no hint that the created order apart from persons has already in some partial sense been so redeemed or saved. Paul merely says that it will be fully redeemed at the eschatological revealing of God's glory and that meantime it stands on tiptoe in eager anticipation of that eschatological deliverance. Romans 8:18ff., then, offers no support at all for using salvation language today to refer to environmental or socioeconomic improvements in the larger society beyond the church. Nor does the rest of the New Testament.

Christ's Present Lordship over the World

Repeatedly, the New Testament makes the astounding claim that the crucified and risen carpenter from Nazareth is *now* Lord of the world as well as the church (Eph. 1:22; Col. 1:15–20). In the Great Commission, Jesus declares, "All authority in heaven and on earth has been given to me" (Matt. 28:18). And Revelation 1:5 says Jesus is *now* "ruler of the kings of the earth." Does that mean that Christ's reign and salvation are present in the world as well as the church?

Obviously, as we saw in the last section, some of the benefits of the work of salvation are present among those who do not confess Christ. But the New Testament (except for two possible exceptions) always uses salvation language to apply only to what happens when persons accept Jesus Christ as Lord and Savior and enter his new redeemed community. Similarly *absolutely none* of the scores of New Testament texts on the kingdom of God speak of the presence of the kingdom apart from conscious confession of Jesus Christ.

Unless one is a universalist and believes all are already saved (although they do not know it), one must make some distinction between Christ's saving and sustaining activity, presence and lordship. As Creator and Sustainer of all things, Christ is now Lord *de jure* (by right) of the whole world. But as Savior, he is Lord *de facto* (in fact) only of those who acknowledge him.[18]

201

Rejecting the Distinction between Creation/Redemption

According to this widely used theological distinction, God's work in creating and sustaining the world is not identical with his work in redeeming it. Everywhere, by general grace God works to sustain creation, preserve order, and create justice for all, including those who continue to reject Christ. Only in the history of Israel and the atoning life, death, and resurrection of Jesus Christ, however, has God offered saving grace. Today it is only when persons confess Christ and join his redeemed community that we can speak of salvation as a present reality.

What are the major objections to the creation/redemption distinction?[19]

First, it is argued that such an approach ignores the eschatological dimension of Christian faith. It neglects the significance of the fact that Jesus' kingdom has already broken into history in saving action and will continue the battle with evil until Christ returns to complete his victory over sin in the whole created order. Because of this neglect, the traditional categories tend to relegate God's action in society to sustaining order rather than correcting oppression. Thus Christians become conservative allies of the status quo, rather than the vanguard of social critique and change.[20]

Second, a dualism easily develops where the "spiritual" realm of the individual believer and the church becomes far more important than the "secular" realm of nations and societal systems. Christian energies become focused largely or exclusively on the inner spiritual life, evangelism, and the church. Justice in society is neglected.[21]

Third, if the redemptive work of Christ is limited to where there is conscious confession of Christ, then, according to Vinay Samuel and Chris Sugden, "this means that any true change toward God's purpose for man in society, arising out of the death and resurrection of Christ, can take place only within the confines of the church."[22] This is the source of evangelical confusion about the relationship between evangelism and social concern: "Since the acknowledgment of Christ is always required for any true social change, evangelism always has a priority."[23] Instead Samuel and Sugden want to insist that God works redemptively outside the church to conform the world to his plan of redemption.[24] Samuel and Sugden argue that "whenever God works in the world, that work is based on the victory Christ won over sin and evil on the cross."[25] To think otherwise is tri-theism. It is to believe in three gods rather than one Trinitarian God, because it separates God's providential action from his redeeming activity in Christ in a way that wrongly suggests that God acts in two fundamentally different ways.[26]

There is no necessary reason why the creation/redemption schemes must lead to neglecting or minimizing the importance of the dawning messianic kingdom and its radical critique of the status quo. To be sure, if one argues that the ethical values of Jesus' kingdom pertain only to some private, personal sphere and not to all life and society generally, then one radically weakens the social impact of Jesus' dawning kingdom.[27] Sinners, of course, cannot follow Jesus' ethic very well. But they should. Their failure to do so is a crucial measure of their rebellion and brokenness.

Kingdom people will insist on measuring every fallen society by the norms of the kingdom that Jesus inaugurated and will return to complete. Because the resurrection confirmed Jesus' announcement of the kingdom, Christians know which direction history is going. Therefore they will also work vigorously to prod society to move, however imperfectly, in that direction. The fact that they call the limited results "justice" rather than "salvation" need not in any way lessen their commitment, because they remember that some day the Lord will return and complete their work. Then, with gratitude for their modest victories in the work of justice, they will shout with joy: "The kingdom of the world has become the kingdom of our Lord" (Rev. 11:15). If Christians become allies of an oppressive, conservative status quo, it is not because they distinguish between creation and redemption.

Second, does the creation/redemption dualism necessarily lead to other misconceived and damaging dualisms? It is true that some people who distinguish creation and redemption also operate with a platonic body-soul dualism in which redemption pertains only to the soul and eternal life in an immaterial heaven. That, as we have seen, is not the biblical view. Some also operate with a spiritual-secular dualism where only personal faith and the church are "spiritual." But such thinking flows from modern secularization, not biblical faith. The Bible insists that God is Lord of all—both the inner life and the life of politics and business. Working in business or politics in obedience to Christ is just as "spiritual" as being a pastor, or a "foreign missionary." Neither of these misconceived dualisms, however, has any necessary connection with the proper distinction between creation and redemption.

What of the third argument? I cannot see how it is accurate to say that if one speaks of the presence of salvation only where there is conscious confession of Christ, then all social change in the direction of God's purposes for society must happen in the church. The transformed lives of Christians have a "spill-over" effect in the larger society in many ways. Their proclamation of biblical revelation about truth and ethics is persuasive for some who are not Christians. Their transformed, Spirit-filled lives and redeemed communities provide attractive role models even for non-Christians. Their vigorous challenge of social injustice and successful political engagement transform structures and social mores in a way that enriches the lives of everyone. In all of these cases, we must say that the redemptive work of Christ among Christians produces enormous change both in the church and in the world. The fact that we call the limited change in the larger society justice and freedom rather than salvation in no way changes the fact that it flows from God's saving action in Christ.

What of the charge of tri-theism? One does not fall into tri-theism simply by distinguishing various activities of God, unless those activities are contradictory. Everywhere the Scriptures distinguish between God's holiness and love, justice and mercy. The same God both punishes and forgives. God's condemnation of sinners is compatible but not identical with his pardoning of sinners. One cannot say that Christ on the cross reveals the totality of what we know about how God deals with us. God's action of condemning some to eternal separation from the living God at the last judgment (Matt. 25) is also a clear part of what the Scriptures tell us about God's activity. It is not contradictory to what God in Christ does on the cross but it is surely distinct.

As Carl Braaten says, "God has both law and Gospel ways of acting in the world."[28] God's work in giving the law is not identical with God's action in giving the gospel. The two are interrelated but they are not identical.

Similarly, God's work in creation and redemption are closely interrelated but not identical. God creates an order of nature and history in which persons are invited to respond in obedience to the divine Partner. When human sin produces devastation throughout the created order, God acts both to sustain that order and also to develop a plan of redemption that will, when completed at Christ's return, restore that created order to wholeness. But until that time of consummation, God continues to invite persons to accept his gracious offer of salvation and begin to experience now some of the fullness of that ultimate salvation. Many, however, refuse, and God wills to allow them the freedom to decline his saving invitation to join the redeemed community. Unless one maintains the distinction between creation and redemption, it becomes difficult and perhaps impossible to understand or maintain the important New Testament distinction between those who accept God's offer in Christ and join the church and those who do not. Without this distinction, as Carl Braaten points out, we would simply merge Christianity and civilization in the disastrous way that American civil religion often has.[29]

Colossians 2:15 is often cited to argue that there is biblical precedent for using salvation language to apply to structural change. Paul says of Christ's victory on the cross: "And having disarmed the powers and authorities, he made a public spectacle of them, triumphing over them by the cross." What does this text mean?

By "powers and authorities" *(archai kai exousiai),* Paul refers both to the structures and social mores of society and also to supernatural, fallen beings who lie behind and work through these structures.[30] Exactly what happens to these powers and authorities at the cross? The language comes from Roman military history. A successful Roman general forced the rulers of a conquered nation to march barefoot behind the Roman general's chariot.[31]

Paul therefore means that at the cross, Christ won a decisive victory over the powers and authorities. He broke their power and humiliated them. Presumably their ability to hinder Christ's purposes have been significantly weakened.

Paul, of course, hardly means that their evil power is totally broken. Frequently he talks about the way that Christians continue to do battle with these same powers (e.g., Eph. 6:12).

Probably Jesus' conflict with Satan and his evil forces is instructive. Jesus said explicitly that he saw Satan fall like lightning. He saw himself as binding the evil strongman.[32] But he never supposed that those evil powers were totally defeated. Nor did he ever say they were redeemed.

Similarly, in Colossians 2:15, there is no reference at all to the *redemption* of the powers and authorities at the cross. The text talks of unwilling submission, not voluntary acceptance of Christ. Their power is broken, but any transformation that has occurred is far too incomplete to speak of redemption.

But does not Colossians 1:19–20 use salvation language in a parallel situation? This passage says that "God was pleased [aorist] . . . to reconcile [aorist infinitive] to himself all things, whether things on earth or things in heaven, by making peace [aorist participle] through his blood shed on the cross." In verse 16, Paul had talked of the fact that all things in heaven and earth had been created through Christ. And he explicitly included the powers and authorities. Now he uses the past tense (aorist) to say that all things *have been* reconciled through Christ's cross. In the context of this discussion of God's cosmic plan of salvation, surely we must take "all things" to refer to much more than just persons. Every part of the created order has both been created by and reconciled in Christ. (Of course that does not mean that every single person will be saved. Paul was not a universalist. But it does mean that every area of creation has been affected by the cross.)

The word *reconciliation* is one of the important terms in Paul's salvation word group. Since this text places this act of reconciliation in the past tense, there may be some legitimacy for speaking of reconciliation and therefore salvation having already begun to impact all things in heaven and earth. Perhaps this text offers some warrant for using salvation language for the partial emergence of shalom in the larger society.

But again, important questions arise. Paul says all things have been reconciled to God. Obviously, however, he does not even mean that all persons have already been reconciled.[33] In other places, he urgently begs nonbelievers to be reconciled to God (2 Cor. 5:20) precisely because he believes that apart from faith in Christ they are lost and without hope in the world (Eph. 2:12). Therefore, the meaning of Colossians 1:20 must be that at the cross, Christ won the decisive victory that makes it possible for people to be reconciled to God when they hear and accept the gospel. The aorist tense, then, does not tell us *when* they are actually reconciled. It rather tells us that God's decisive action that makes that reconciliation possible has already occurred.[34]

The same reasoning applies to the cosmic redemption of all things. The cross was surely the decisive victory that makes that possible, but one must go to other texts to discover when that redemption occurs. As we have seen, *nowhere* else in Paul or the rest of the New Testament is there any use of salvation language to apply to creation or the structures of society before Christ's return in glory. Therefore, we ought to interpret Colossians 1:20 in a way consistent with the rest of Paul and the New Testament.

That means that the impact of Christ's life, death, and resurrection has already broken the power of evil throughout the entire created order in some significant way. At least two crucial things follow. First, Satan cannot prevent the growth of Christ's redeemed community. Second, greater progress in correcting some of the evils in society is possible. The latter is in some significant sense a result of the victory at the cross over the invisible powers of evil. And, it takes flesh as Christians who know the power of salvation influence and change social systems. But if we want to stay with New Testament usage, we will not call change outside the redeemed community of believers "salvation."

I do not find convincing the arguments for abandoning the creation/redemption distinction. In fact, Paul uses it clearly precisely in Colossians 1:15–20. Christ is both Creator and Sustainer of all things (vv. 15–17) and Redeemer of all things (vv. 18–20). The two activities are wonderfully and marvelously interrelated and complementary. But they are not identical.

Toward a Narrower Definition

None of the arguments in favor of the broader usage are convincing.[35] And strong arguments support the alternative.

Virtually all New Testament usage supports the narrower definition. Nowhere does the New Testament speak of the presence of the kingdom proclaimed by Jesus except where Jesus himself is physically present or where people consciously confess him as Messiah, Savior, and Lord. Nowhere does the New Testament unambiguously use salvation language for what happens outside the church except when it talks about the cosmic transformation of all things at Christ's return (at which point, church and world will be the same!). Biblical usage simply does not support calling the growing justice and freedom we produce in society today "salvation."

The broader terminology poses a problem for one's doctrine of the church. Surely the church is normally present where people experience salvation. Therefore if Vietnam was, in some sense, saved when the war ended, one would suppose that the people of Vietnam were also in some sense in the church. As Carl Braaten says, unless we maintain some basic distinction between creation and redemption, Christianity merges with civilization. The basic New Testament distinction between the church and world becomes difficult or impossible.

The same kind of argument applies to the issue of eternal salvation. Unless one is a universalist (and some, but not all, who use the broader language are), one must distinguish between those who by God's grace have experienced that acceptance with God that leads to eternal life and those who reject Christ's offer of salvation. If everybody in society is "saved" because social justice has increased, then again this distinction becomes difficult.

One way that many people who use the broader terminology solve these last two problems is by distinguishing different kinds of salvation. Samuel and Sugden argue, as we have seen, that the world outside the church experiences some kind of "salvation" through Christ. But they clearly insist just as vigorously (because they are *not* universalists) that "conscious acknowledgment of that victory [of Christ on the cross] takes place in the church, and salvation in its full sense is linked with that conscious acknowledgment."[36] In a similar way, liberation theologian Gustavo Gutiérrez insists that socioeconomic liberation is salvation. But it is not the fullness of salvation.[37] Liberation or salvation therefore has several distinct levels. Socioeconomic liberation now is not the same as complete salvation that includes a right relationship with God and eternal life.

But does not this process of distinguishing various levels of salvation end up introducing the same kind of distinctions that the earlier categories, justice and salvation, were intended to signify? So we cannot avoid "dualism" if that means distinction. Is it not more helpful therefore to stick with biblical categories?

Many—probably most—of the things advocates of the broad usage want to protect can be affirmed just as well by advocates of the narrower language. Christ is now Lord of the world as well as the church, and works in the world to increase peace and justice. That means moving history now in the direction of the coming kingdom that provides the criteria for judging historical changes now. Christ uses non-Christians as well as Christians to accomplish his will in the world.[38] The impact of salvation in Christ has a powerful effect in the world as well as the church.[39] God's ultimate intention is a cosmic salvation that transforms persons, societies, and the whole groaning creation. All that and more can and should be affirmed enthusiastically by advocates of the narrower language.

One could collect statements from many times and places in support of the narrower usage. "We cannot," René Padilla says, "accept the equation of salvation with the satisfaction of bodily needs, social amelioration, or political liberation."[40] John Calvin said that "the Kingdom of God is set up and flourishes only when Christ the Mediator unites men to the Father, both pardoned by the free remission of sins and born again to righteousness."[41]

The Lausanne Covenant repented of evangelical neglect of social action and affirmed its importance. But it refused to equate justice and salvation: "Although reconciliation with man is not reconciliation with God nor is social action evangelism, nor is political liberation salvation, nevertheless we affirm that evangelism and socio-political involvement are both part of our Christian duty" (sect. 5).

I conclude that the church today would be wise to use the language of salvation to refer only to what happens when persons accept Christ and join the redeemed community and what will happen when Christ returns to bring a cosmic restoration of the whole created order. That means that even now salvation is personal and social (in the church). And it will be cosmic and total.

Changing oppressive social structures to bring dignity, health, freedom, and economic well-being to people is enormously important. But it is social justice, not salvation. That usage is both more biblical and better able to protect the church today from serious theological error.[42]

Notes

Preface

1. Walter Rauschenbusch, *A Theology for the Social Gospel* (New York: Abingdon, 1945), 15.

2. No title works perfectly. I do not mean that we share the gospel only by our words. In fact, in this book I insist that we rightly share the Good News by both word and deed. The title *Good News and Good Works,* however, seeks to point to the integration of evangelism and social action that biblical faith demands.

3. Ronald J. Sider, *Cup of Water, Bread of Life* (Grand Rapids: Zondervan, 1994). This book is available from Evangelicals for Social Action, 10 E. Lancaster Avenue, Wynnewood, PA 19096 (800-650-6600).

Chapter 1

1. I have used a different name to protect his identity.

2. Interestingly, the prominent secular philosopher Anthony Flew recently said basically the same thing; see Anthony Flew and Gary Habermas, *Did Jesus Rise from the Dead?* (San Francisco: Harper, 1987), 3.

3. I have done a little work in this area. See, for example, my "A Case for Easter," *HIS* (April 1972): 27–31. For a more extensive discussion, see also my "The Historian, the Miraculous and Post-Newtonian Man," *Scottish Journal of Theology* 25 (1972): 309–19; "The Pauline Conception of the Resurrection Body in 1 Corinthians 15:35–54," *Novum Testamentum* 19 (1977): 1–18; and "Jesus' Resurrection and the Search for Peace and Justice," *Christian Century* (3 November 1982): 1103–8.

4. For the Declaration and the background, see Ronald J. Sider, ed., *The Chicago Declaration* (Carol Stream: Creation House, 1974).

5. "Evangelism, Salvation and Social Justice," *International Review of Mission* 54 (1975): 251–67.

6. Ronald J. Sider, "Reflections on Justice, Peace and the Integrity of Creation," *Transformation* (July–September 1990): 15–17.

7. See below, 136–37, for more details.

Chapter 2

1. David J. Bosch, *Transforming Mission* (Maryknoll: Orbis, 1991), 401.

2. H. Richard Niebuhr has pointed out that "a type is always something of a construct." No person or group fits perfectly into the four categories and several subcategories of my types or models. But they do help us understand the most important viewpoints of the modern debate. H. Richard Niebuhr, *Christ and Culture* (New York: Harper Torch Books, 1956), 43. Avery Dulles uses the word *model* in a similar way; *Models of the Church* (Garden City, N.Y.: Doubleday, 1978), 19–38. I have chosen a nonhistorical approach in this chapter. Obviously, a careful look at the historical development would be very illuminating (see, for example, Bosch's masterful *Transforming Mission*) but space and the purpose of this book preclude that approach.

3. Billy Graham, "Why Lausanne?" in J. D. Douglas, ed., *Let the Earth Hear His Voice* (Minneapolis: World Wide Publications, 1975), 31 (my emphasis).

4. Ibid., 29.

5. John Stott, "The Biblical Basis of Evangelism," in Douglas, ed., *Let the Earth Hear His Voice*, 65–78; John Stott, *Christian Mission in the Modern World* (Downers Grove, Ill.: InterVarsity, 1975).

6. Often reprinted, the Lausanne Covenant is in Douglas, ed., *Let the Earth Hear His Voice*, 3–9; see the similar position of C. Peter Wagner, *Church Growth and the Whole Gospel* (San Francisco: Harper, 1981), 87–91, 102–5.

7. Arthur Johnston, *Battle for World Evangelism* (Wheaton: Tyndale, 1978), 18.

8. Ibid., 18, 345.

9. Arthur P. Johnston, "The Kingdom in Relation to the Church and the World," in Bruce J. Nicholls, ed., *In Word and Deed: Evangelism and Social Responsibility* (Grand Rapids: Eerdmans, 1985), 111 (Johnston's emphasis).

10. See Donald A. McGavran, *Understanding Church Growth*, rev. ed. (Grand Rapids: Eerdmans, 1970), 26; and his more recent article, "Missiology Faces the Lion," *Missiology: An International Review* 17, no. 3 (July 1989): 337–40. Peter Wagner classifies McGavran's position in *Church Growth and the Whole Gospel*, 105–6. David J. Hesselgrave probably also belongs in this category; cf. *Today's Choices for Tomorrow's Mission* (Grand Rapids: Zondervan, Academic Books, 1988), 90.

11. Harold Lindsell, ed., *The Church's Worldwide Mission* (Dallas: Word, 1966), 234.

12. James A. Scherer, *Gospel, Church and Kingdom* (Minneapolis: Augsburg, 1987), 87–88 (emphasis added).

13. Donald G. Bloesch, *Essentials of Evangelical Theology*, vol. 2 (San Francisco: Harper, 1979), 156.

14. "Christianize the World? Forget It!" *Faith for the Family* (1981): 33 (a Bob Jones University publication), cited in Janel M. Curry-Roper, "Contemporary Christian Eschatologies and Their Relationship to Environmental Stewardship," *The Professional Geographer* 42, no. 2 (1990): 161.

15. Quoted in Bosch, *Transforming Mission*, 318.

16. The insistence of missiologists like Donald McGavran that whole villages or communities often come to Christ in "people movements" overcomes some of this individualism (see his *Understanding Church Growth,* 333–72).

17. See Michael Hill, "Paul and Social Ethics," in B. G. Webb, ed., *Christians in Society* (Homebush West, Australia: Lancer Books, 1988), 131–42.

18. Peter Kuzmic, "History and Eschatology: Evangelical Views," in Nicholls, ed., *In Word and Deed,* 153. On this and many other points, John Stott's position does not share the typical weaknesses of the first model.

19. See Bosch, *Transforming Mission,* 262–345; Samuel Escobar, "Has McGavran's Missiology Been Devoured by a Lion?" *Missiology* 17, no. 3 (July 1989): 150; Kuzmic, "History and Eschatology," in Nicholls, ed., *In Word and Deed,* 152–57.

20. Quoted in David J. Bosch, "Toward Evangelism in Context," in Vinay Samuel and Chris Sugden, eds., *The Church in Response to Human Need* (Grand Rapids: Eerdmans, 1987), 191.

21. For the Reformers' views, see Carl E. Braaten, *The Flaming Center: A Theology of the Christian Mission* (Philadelphia: Fortress, 1977), 15. For the Anabaptists', see Franklin H. Littell, *The Anabaptist View of the Church,* 2d ed. (Boston: Starr King Press, 1958), 109–26.

22. Yoder, *Politics of Jesus* (Grand Rapids: Eerdmans, 1972), 153–57. See also Jim Wallis, *Agenda for Biblical People* (New York: Harper, 1976), 129, 138. Neither Yoder nor Wallis, of course, fits perfectly into this second model.

23. See, for example, John Driver, "The Anabaptist Vision and Social Justice," in Samuel Escobar and John Driver, *Christian Mission and Social Justice* (Scottsdale, Penn.: Herald, 1978), 107.

24. Yoder, *Politics of Jesus,* 157.

25. Report from Section II, "Salvation and Social Justice"; *Bangkok Assembly 1973* (Geneva: World Council of Churches, n.d.), 90.

26. Section 10; The WCC's *Mission and Evangelism: An Ecumenical Affirmation* was approved by the Central Committee in July 1982.

27. Ibid., 5 (preface).

28. E.g., Leonardo and Clodovis Boff, *Salvation and Liberation,* trans. Robert R. Barr (Maryknoll: Orbis, 1988); and Gustavo Gutiérrez, *A Theology of Liberation,* trans. Caridad Inda and John Eagleson (Maryknoll: Orbis, 1973), 56ff., 145ff.

29. Bosch, *Transforming Mission,* 396.

30. *A Monthly Letter on Evangelism* (see no. 12, December 1986). The reports from the 1991 General Assembly in Canberra underline Fung's assessment. The official report from Canberra states: "There is an urgent need today for a new type of mission not into foreign lands but into foreign structures." (Section 46 of Section I; *Canberra 1991: Message, Report and Programme Policy Report of the WCC Seventh Assembly* [Geneva: WCC Publications, 1991]). A careful review of the official report of the Committee on Program Policy reveals the main agenda. The committee reports that all programs serve to confess Jesus Christ. But, after commenting on justice, peace, and the integrity of

creation, the committee says, "This has emerged as *the central* vision of the WCC" (*Canberra 1991,* 30 [emphasis added]). Section C on the "Wholeness of the Mission of the Church" mentions wholistic evangelism but devotes most of the space to justice and peace. Section IV lists four areas of program concentration for the years after Canberra: reconciliation in church and world; freedom and justice; right relationship with creation; full participation of women. Apparently evangelism is not important enough to merit even one special category out of four!

31. So Braaten, *Flaming Center,* 146.

32. Gustavo Gutiérrez, *The Power of the Poor in History,* trans. Robert R. Barr (Maryknoll: Orbis, 1983), 16–17. Gutiérrez does say the word also has a place, but "what basically counts is the deed" (p. 17). Vinay Samuel and Chris Sugden make the same point about M. M. Thomas; "Toward a Theology of Social Change," in Ronald J. Sider, ed., *Evangelicals and Development: Toward a Theology of Social Change* (Philadelphia: Westminster, 1981), 46.

33. *Salvation and Liberation* by Leonardo and Clodovis Boff provides a fascinating illustration. The Boff brothers affirm the transcendent side of salvation (including inner personal conversion and life after death). They also insist on distinguishing salvation and socioeconomic liberation. But the emphasis falls overwhelmingly on the latter, which is an authentic anticipation of the eternal kingdom (p. 62). The poor are *"the* eschatological criterion by which the salvation or perdition of every human being is determined" (p. 48, my emphasis). Salvation is appropriated by moral praxis—i.e., working for justice (p. 53). *"Only when* I follow the poor am I following Jesus" (p. 91, their emphasis). Conscious knowledge of Jesus Christ is not necessary to accept the kingdom and grace: "In the measure that human beings open themselves to justice and love, they are—even without knowing it—accepting and embracing the kingdom, grace and Jesus Christ" (p. 115). One dare not equate the kingdom with socioeconomic liberation, but "today it does turn out to be the main place" we experience the kingdom (p. 83). Salvation has many elements, but "there are certain dominant aspects today (the political aspect)" (p. 92).

34. Richard J. Mouw, *Political Evangelism* (Grand Rapids: Eerdmans, 1973), 13.

35. Ibid., 89 (Mouw's emphasis).

36. Orlando E. Costas, *The Church and Its Mission* (Wheaton: Tyndale, 1974), 69 (but see below, chap. 9, 164, for a change in his most recent book).

37. Vinay Samuel and Chris Sugden, "Evangelism and Social Responsibility: A Biblical Study on Priorities," in Nicholls, ed., *In Word and Deed,* 203.

38. See the discussion and citations in Chris Sugden's doctoral dissertation on Samuel's theology: "A Critical and Comparative Study . . ." (Ph.D. diss., Westminster College, Oxford, 1987), 264, 301–2.

39. Samuel and Sugden, "Evangelism and Social Responsibility," in Nicholls, ed., *In Word and Deed,* 210; Sugden, "Comparative Study," 273.

40. Samuel and Sugden, "God's Intention for the World," in Samuel and Sugden, eds., *The Church in Response to Human Need,* 142.

41. Papal encyclicals are often reprinted. They are always quickly available in *Origins: CNS Documentary Service.* Both the vast size of the Roman

Catholic Church and the unique sacramental ecclesiological emphasis in its evangelization might suggest a separate Roman Catholic model. In terms of the categories of this book, however, Roman Catholic thought does fit in model three. For a recent summary of Roman Catholic thought on evangelization, see Avery Dulles, "John Paul II and the New Evangelization," *America* 166, no. 3 (February 1, 1992): 52–72.

42. *EN,* 18. Subsequent citations in this section are all from *Evangelii Nuntiandi* (1975) except where otherwise indicated.

43. *Redemptor Hominis,* 14, quoted in Basil Meeking and John Stott, eds., *The Evangelical-Roman Catholic Dialogue on Mission 1977–1984: A Report* (Exeter: Paternoster, 1986), 45. See also *RM,* sect. 14 and *Gaudium et Spes,* sect. 22.

44. *Catechism of the Catholic Church* (New York: Image, 1995), 292.

45. See Scherer's pointed question in *Gospel, Church and Kingdom,* 230–31.

46. José Miranda, *Marx and the Bible,* trans. John Eagleson (Maryknoll: Orbis, 1974), 44.

47. Ibid., 48 (my emphasis).

48. Arend Th. Van Leeuwen, *Christianity in World History,* trans. H. H. Hoskins (New York: Scribner's Sons, 1964), especially 419–21.

49. *The Church for Others and the Church for the World* (Geneva: WCC, 1967), 15. (This statement comes from the European Group.)

50. Gibson Winter, *The New Creation As Metropolis* (New York: Macmillan, 1963), 60–61. See also Harvey Cox, *The Secular City* (New York: Macmillan, 1965), 256.

51. See Bosch, *Transforming Mission,* 326, 480.

52. Marian Bohen, "The Future of Mission in a Pluralistic World," *Theological Education* (autumn 1990): 31–43. For Hick and Knitter, see John Hick and Paul F. Knitter, eds., *The Myth of Christian Uniqueness* (Maryknoll: Orbis, 1987); Paul F. Knitter, *No Other Name?* (Maryknoll: Orbis, 1985).

Chapter 3

1. Brian Hathaway, *Beyond Renewal* (Milton Keynes: Word [UK], 1990). See also Hathaway's article, "The Spirit and Social Action—A Model," *Transformation* 5, no. 4 (October–December 1988): 40–43.

2. See the excellent discussion and citation of literature in Miroslav Volf, "Materiality of Salvation," *Journal of Ecumenical Studies* 26, no. 3 (summer 1989): 464–66. See also Brian Hathaway's unpublished speech at Brighton 1991.

3. The literature on the kingdom is vast. See, for example, George Eldon Ladd, *A Theology of the New Testament* (Grand Rapids: Eerdmans, 1974), 45–212 (especially the bibliography on 57–69); Norman Perrin, *Jesus and the Language of the Kingdom* (Philadelphia: Fortress, 1976); Bruce Chilton, ed., *The Kingdom of God in the Teaching of Jesus* (Philadelphia: Fortress, 1984) (a good history of the research); and the article *basileia* and related words in the *Theological Dictionary of the New Testament,* ed. Gerhard Kittel and Gerhard Friedrich, 10 vols. (Grand Rapids: Eerdmans, 1964–76), I, 564–94 (hereafter cited as *TDNT*).

4. Arthur Johnston, "The Kingdom in Relation to the Church and the World," in Nicholls, ed., *In Word and Deed,* 128. See also Madame Guyon's

classic comment on Luke 17:21 ("The Kingdom of God is within you"): "Thou becomest my King and my heart Thy Kingdom." *Madame Guyon: An Autobiography* (Chicago: Moody, n.d.), 73. Ken Gnanakan rightly rejects this exegesis; *Kingdom Concerns* (Bangalore: Theological Book Trust, 1989), 106.

5. For an introduction to dispensationalism, see C. Norman Kraus, *Dispensationalism in America: Its Rise and Development* (Richmond: John Knox, 1958); and Ernest R. Sandeen, *The Roots of Fundamentalism: British and American Millenarianism, 1800–1930* (Chicago: University of Chicago Press, 1970).

6. Mortimer Arias, *Evangelization and the Subversive Memory of Jesus: Announcing the Reign of God* (Philadelphia: Fortress, 1984), 8. Arias's book is one of the best popular treatments of the kingdom of God.

7. The language contains at least an allusion to Isaiah 29:18–19; 35:5–6.

8. Norman Perrin, *Rediscovering the Teaching of Jesus* (New York: Harper, 1967), 54.

9. See Ronald J. Sider, *Rich Christians in an Age of Hunger* (Dallas: Word, 1990), chap. 3; and Ronald J. Sider, ed., *Cry Justice: The Bible on Hunger and Poverty* (Downers Grove, Ill.: InterVarsity, 1980), 27–76.

10. See Gerhard von Rad's article on *eirene* in *TDNT*, II, 402–6 and Walter Brueggemann, *Living toward a Vision: Biblical Reflections on Shalom* (Philadelphia: United Church Press, 1976).

11. Many modern scholars have claimed otherwise. See the careful analysis of all the arguments and the extensive citation of the literature in Ladd, *Theology of the New Testament*, 135–92. See also Martin Hengel's vigorous rejection of a totally unmessianic Jesus in his *Victory over Violence* (London: SPCK, 1975), 81–112.

12. For the literature, see Ladd, *Theology of the New Testament*, 57–69.

13. Cf. also Luke 17:21. For the kingdom as present, see further, Arias, *Announcing the Reign of God,* 13–36.

14. See further, ibid., 28–30.

15. Ibid., 11.

16. Edward Schweizer, *The Good News according to Matthew* (Atlanta: John Knox, 1975), 132; and John Piper, *Love Your Enemies* (Cambridge: Cambridge University Press, 1979), 40–41.

17. Luke 15:1–2; Mark 2:15–17; Luke 7:36–50.

18. See chapter 6, 105–7, for fuller discussion.

19. Matthew 4:19; 8:22; 9:9; 10:38; 16:24; 19:21.

20. John Paul II, *Redemptoris Missio,* 18.

Chapter 4

1. On the Jubilee, see Sharon Ringe, *Jesus, Liberation and the Biblical Jubilee* (Philadelphia: Fortress, 1985); Robert Sloan, *The Acceptable Year of the Lord* (Austin: Scholar Press, 1977); and Donald W. Blosser, "Jesus and the Jubilee" (Ph.D. diss., University of St. Andrews, 1979).

2. For a discussion of Matthew's wording ("poor in spirit"—5:3), see Sider, *Rich Christians,* 99–100.

215

3. Emilio Castro, "Reflection after Melbourne," *Your Kingdom Come: Mission Perspectives* (Geneva: WCC, 1980), 228 (my emphasis). In recent correspondence, however, Emilio Castro says that he only means to say that "the relation of the church to the poor is *a* fundamental criterion of faithful mission" (Emilio Castro to Ronald J. Sider, May 25, 1992). With that I totally agree.

4. Boff and Boff, *Salvation and Liberation*, 48 (my emphasis).

5. See below, chap. 8, 139–40, for further discussion.

6. Peter Wagner seems to do that in *Church Growth and the Whole Gospel*, 17–18. But in recent personal correspondence (May 15, 1992), he says that "Thy kingdom come" involves eradication of racism, poverty, injustice, war, oppression, and discrimination—*literally.*"

7. John 12:6; 13:29.

8. Quoted in Joachim Jeremias, *New Testament Theology* (London: SCM, 1971), 175–76.

9. Marcus J. Borg, *Jesus: A New Vision* (San Francisco: HarperCollins, 1991), 92, 131.

10. Joachim Jeremias, *Jerusalem in the Time of Jesus* (Philadelphia: Fortress, 1975), 303–11.

11. See C. F. D. Moule, "The Significance of the Message of the Resurrection for Faith in Jesus Christ," in *Studies in Biblical Theology* no. 8 (London: SCM, 1968), 9.

12. Mishnah Sotah 3.4, quoted in Borg, *Jesus*, 146, n. 38.

13. Ibid., 133–34.

14. Quoted in W. Ward Gasque, "The Role of Women in the Church, in Society and in the Home," *Priscilla Papers* 2, no. 2 (spring 1988): 9.

15. See the recent book by Craig S. Keener, . . . *And Marries Another: Divorce and Remarriage in the Teaching of the New Testament* (Peabody, Mass.: Hendrickson Publishers, 1991), 21–45.

16. Arias, *Announcing the Reign of God*, 5.

17. Ibid., 6.

18. Ibid.

19. For a discussion of the "hard passages" in Paul, see appendix 2 of Gretchen Gaebelein Hull, *Equal to Serve* (Old Tappan, N.J.: Revell, 1987) and the literature cited in my *Completely Pro-Life*, 220, n. 34.

20. See Donald B. Kraybill, *The Upside-Down Kingdom* (Scottsdale, Penn.: Herald, 1978).

21. See H. W. Hoehner, *Herod Antipas* (Cambridge: Cambridge University Press, 1972), 220–21, 343–47.

22. See the literature cited in Borg, *Jesus*, 96, n. 23.

23. For the detailed references, for this and the following, see Ronald J. Sider and Richard Taylor, *Nuclear Holocaust and Christian Hope* (Downers Grove, Ill.: InterVarsity, 1982), 101–4.

24. Edward Schweizer, *The Good News According to Matthew* (Atlanta: John Knox, 1975), 132; and John Piper, *Love Your Enemies* (Cambridge: Cambridge University Press, 1979), 40–41.

25. Martin Hengel, *Victory over Violence* (London: SPCK, 1975), 58.

26. Piper, *Love Your Enemies,* 21–48; and the other literature cited in Sider and Taylor, *Nuclear Holocaust,* 335, n. 51.

27. See Vincent Taylor, *The Gospel according to Mark* (London: Macmillan, 1952), 452.

28. See the many references in G. H. C. MacGregor, *The New Testament Basis of Pacifism and the Relevance of an Impossible Ideal* (New York: Fellowship Publications, 1960), 48.

29. Nor is it surprising that Jesus' contemporaries viewed this radical disturber of the status quo as a prophet like Elijah or Jeremiah. See the references in C. René Padilla, "The Politics of the Kingdom of God . . ." in Vinay Samuel and Albrecht Hauser, eds., *Proclaiming Christ in Christ's Way* (Oxford: Regnum, 1989), 187.

30. Yoder, *Politics of Jesus,* 63. See also David Peterson, "Jesus and Social Ethics," in B. G. Webb, ed., *Christians in Society,* 88–91. Peterson challenges Yoder at some points but agrees with the basic thesis that Jesus posed a radical challenge to the status quo. See further, Vishal Mangalwadi, "Compassion and Social Reform: Jesus the Troublemaker," in Vinay Samuel and Chris Sugden, eds., *The Church in Response to Human Need* (Oxford: Regnum, 1987), 193–205.

31. See above, chap. 3, n. 11; and the studies by Borg, who reports that a majority of contemporary North American "Jesus scholars" believe that Jesus did *not* expect the end of the world in his lifetime (Borg, *Jesus,* 20, nn. 25, 26).

32. Wagner, *Church Growth,* 17–19.

33. See, for example, Christopher Sugden, "Evangelicals and Wholistic Evangelism," in Samuel and Hauser, eds., *Proclaiming Christ,* 47; and the two issues of *Transformation* that report on the ongoing international dialogue between Charismatics, Pentecostals, and evangelical social activists: *Transformation* 5, no. 4 (October–December 1988); and 7, no. 3 (July–September 1990): 1, 5–11.

34. See below, chap. 10, 175–79, for further discussion of this.

35. C. H. Dodd, *The Founder of Christianity* (New York: Macmillan, 1970), 90, 102.

36. For an emphasis on the contextual side, see Vinay Samuel and Chris Sugden, *Christian Mission in the Eighties: A Third World Perspective* (Bangalore: Partnership in Mission–Asia, 1981), 8–12.

37. Jürgen Moltmann, *The Crucified God* (New York: Harper, 1974), 132.

38. Leviticus 23:10–11, 15. See further, Murray J. Harris, *From Grace to Glory* (Grand Rapids: Zondervan, 1990), 220.

39. *TDNT,* I, 475.

40. It is often pointed out that Paul seldom uses the language of the kingdom to communicate the gospel. Actually, he uses the word *kingdom* fourteen times (Kirk, *New World Coming,* 55). Usually, however, he speaks of the gospel of salvation, or simply, the gospel of Jesus *Christ.* Paul, however, has not abandoned Jesus' central message. Jesus announced the messianic kingdom and identified himself as the Messiah. Paul's constant emphasis on the gospel of Jesus *Christ* (i.e., Jesus the Messiah) is his way of reaffirming that

Jesus the Messiah has indeed inaugurated the messianic kingdom. As a Jew, he could not have conceived of the coming of the Messiah without the coming of the messianic kingdom. "No kingdom, no Messiah!" (Kirk, *New World Coming,* 57).

41. That does *not* mean universalism. See below, 91–93, 128–33.

42. See, for instance, Chris Sugden and Oliver Barclay, *Kingdom and Creation in Social Ethics* (Bramcote, Nottingham: Grove Books, 1990), especially 19.

43. That does *not* mean that we should speak of the kingdom coming when justice emerges in secular society. See below, appendix, 196–209.

44. Howard Snyder, *Liberating the Church* (Downers Grove, Ill.: Inter-Varsity, 1983), 11. Also, Hathaway, *Beyond Renewal,* 161–62.

45. From the "Radical Discipleship" Statement; Douglas, ed., *Let the Earth Hear His Voice,* 1294.

Chapter 5

1. See Martin Luther's statement that justification by faith is "the principal article of all Christian doctrine." *Commentary on the Epistle to the Galatians* (James Clarke, 1953), 143. Also, the recent evangelical statement: "Justification by faith appears to us, as it does to all evangelicals, to be the heart and hub, the paradigm and essence, of the whole economy of God's saving grace. Like Atlas, it bears a world on its shoulders, the entire evangelical knowledge of God's love in Christ toward sinners." R. T. Beckwith, G. E. Duffield, and J. I. Packer, *Across the Divide* (Marcham Manor Press, 1977), 58. Precisely as an evangelical committed to the whole Bible, I consider that an exaggerated, one-sided statement.

2. For more detail, see Ronald J. Sider and James Parker III, "How Broad Is Salvation in Scripture?" in Nicholls, ed., *In Word and Deed,* 89–99, and the literature cited there. The chapter borrows freely from that earlier work.

3. E. M. B. Green, *The Meaning of Salvation* (London: Hodder and Stoughton, 1965), 16.

4. See further, Isaiah 51:4–5; 59:15–17.

5. Perry B. Yoder is correct in closely linking the Hebrew word *shalom* (peace, wholeness) to the OT understanding of salvation: *Shalom: The Bible's Word for Salvation, Justice, and Peace* (Newton, Kans.: Faith and Life Press, 1987), especially chapters 1, 2, 4.

6. See further, Green, *Salvation,* 102.

7. *Sozo* is used sixteen times to refer to healing. *Therapeuo* is used thirty-three times, and *laomai* is used fifteen times for healing: *TDNT,* VII, 990. Similarly, Acts 4:9; 14:9. In the Book of James, *sozo* is used to indicate both physical healing (5:15) and escape from divine punishment at the final judgment (5:19). Often the English translation obscures this fact. Mark 6:56 reads: "All who touched him were healed." But the word translated "healed" is *sozo,* the verb usually translated "save" (cf. also Matt. 14:36).

8. Some radical Pentecostals claim just that; see Miroslav Volf, "Materiality of Salvation: An Investigation in the Soteriologies of Liberation and Pen-

tecostal Theologies," *Journal of Ecumenical Studies* 26, no. 3 (summer 1989): 458, nn. 74–75. It is precisely this kind of claim that John Stott wants to reject (*Christian Mission*, 85–87). See also Robert Jackson, "Prosperity Theology and the Faith Movement," *Themelios* 15, no. 1 (October 1989): 16–24.

9. Miroslav Volf discusses a classical illustration in Martin Luther in "Materiality of Salvation," 450–51. Nor I think is John Stott right in saying "salvation . . . is moral not material." *Christian Mission*, 87 (see all of 84–101). Salvation includes both. But this does not mean that we should use the broad terminology of model three (see appendix 1, "How Broad Is Salvation?").

10. Jesus combined the tasks of the Suffering Servant (Isa. 53) with this heavenly Son of Man (Dan. 7) when he spoke of the necessity of his coming suffering (Mark 8:31; 9:31; 10:33, 45; 14:21) and return in glory (Mark 8:38; 13:26; 14:62). He came to serve and give his life a ransom *(lutron)* for many *(anti pollon)*. New Testament scholar Joachim Jeremias has shown that Jesus' words "body given" and "blood shed" in the institution of the Lord's Supper (Mark 14:21–24; Matt. 26:24–28; Luke 22:20; 1 Cor. 11:24) indicate a violent death—almost certainly a sacrifice that avails "for many" (*The Eucharistic Words of Jesus* [New York: Macmillan, 1955], 140ff.). The background is Isaiah 53 and this heightens the reference to the "new covenant" sealed with blood—his own blood that made possible the forgiveness of sins and established the new covenant for which the prophet Jeremiah had longed (Jer. 31:31–34). So the Son of Man sought and saved lost sinners.

11. Luke uses salvation language very frequently. See, for example, W. C. Van Unnik, "The Book of Acts, True Confirmation of the Gospel," in *Novum Testamentum* IV (1960); I. H. Marshall, *Luke: Historian and Theologian* (Exeter and Grand Rapids: Paternoster and Zondervan, 1971).

12. Green, *Salvation*, 126.

13. See John Stott's excellent discussion in *Christian Mission*, 103–14.

14. See below, appendix, 205, for a discussion of Colossians 2:15.

15. *Soteria* (salvation); *apolutrosis* (redemption); and *katallage* (reconciliation). John Stott has a careful discussion of *apolutrosis* and *katallage* in *The Cross of Christ* (Downers Grove, Ill.: InterVarsity, 1986), 175–82, 192–203.

16. See, for example, John Burnaby, *Amor Dei* (London, 1960), 220. Driver, *Understanding the Atonement*, 201–3, also puts most of the emphasis here.

17. See, for example, Gordon Rupp, *The Righteousness of God: Luther Studies* (London: Hodder and Stoughton, 1953).

18. The quotation from Psalm 32:1–2 in Romans 4:7–8 makes it abundantly clear that the meaning of *dikaiosune* in this passage is precisely that right relationship with God that results when God forgives and therefore does not count our sins against us. That is what Luther meant by forensic justification. But Paul also uses this same Greek word to refer to that genuine righteousness created in believers by the Holy Spirit. In Romans 6, Paul argues vigorously that believers dare not continue to let sin reign in their lives. Rather, they must offer themselves as "instruments of righteousness" (*dikaiosune*, v. 13). "You have been set free from sin and have become slaves to righteousness" *(dikaiosune)* (v. 18; cf. also v. 20). See, too, Ephesians 4:22–24.

The author of the article on this key word in the *Theological Dictionary of the New Testament* puts it well: "In Paul, therefore, *dikaiosune* can denote both the righteousness which acquits and the living power which breaks the bondage of sin" (II, 209–10).

19. Paul, of course, is simply drawing on the fullness of the great Hebrew words *shalom* and *sedaqa*.

20. Richard Longenecker shows how Paul's phrase "in Christ" incorporates all of this: *The Ministry and Message of Paul* (Grand Rapids: Zondervan, 1971), 98.

21. See the extensive discussion in Murray J. Harris, *From Grave to Glory* (Grand Rapids: Zondervan, 1990), 245–52.

22. See above chapter 3, 53–54, and Driver, *Understanding the Atonement*, 231–32.

23. Harris thinks that Philippians 3:21b refers to the same thing as Romans 8:18–23; *From Grave to Glory,* 246.

24. F. F. Bruce, *The Epistle of Paul to the Romans: An Introduction and Commentary* (Grand Rapids: Eerdmans, 1963), 170. A short statement by Jesus and another in Acts may also point to the restoration of creation expected by St. Paul. Jesus promised his twelve disciples that "at the renewal *[palingenesia]* of all things, when the Son of Man sits on his glorious throne, you who have followed me will also sit on twelve thrones, judging the twelve tribes of Israel" (Matt. 19:28). The crucial word *(palingenesia)* probably refers to the restoration of the universe to its original wholeness (Murray, *From Grave to Glory,* 249). Acts 3:21 says of Christ: "He must remain in heaven until the time comes for God to restore everything, as he promised long ago through his holy prophets." New Testament scholar Murray Harris thinks this passage also refers to the restoration of the "material world to this primeval purity and perfection" (ibid.).

25. See below, 205–7, for a discussion of *when* this happens.

26. Three verses earlier (v. 16; cf. also Eph. 1:10) Paul claimed that Christ was also the Creator of all things including the "principalities and powers." In chapter 8, 150–51, I argue that this language seems to refer both to the socioeconomic structures of our world and to powerful spiritual beings (who have fallen) that lie behind and impact those structures. Thus Paul's claim in Colossians 1 is that the social structures of our world and fallen spiritual forces behind them will eventually be restored to wholeness and right relationship to God.

27. See also Revelation 11:15. See further the discussion in Vinay Samuel and Chris Sugden, "Evangelism and Social Responsibility," in Nicholls, ed., *In Word and Deed,* 205–12.

28. John Stott's Lausanne address, "The Biblical Basis of Evangelism," in Douglas, ed., *Let the Earth Hear His Voice,* 76.

29. See below, 127–30.

30. John Courtney Murray, *We Hold These Truths: Catholic Reflections on the American Proposition* (Kansas City: Sheed and Ward, 1960), 186.

31. In his presidential address at the Evangelical Theological Society, H. Wayne House says with reference to 2 Peter 3:9–14 and Revelation 21:1: "We should understand these as statements of the passing of an old order or the purification of the physical world, not the obliteration of matter." "Creation and Redemption: A Study of Kingdom Interplay," *Journal of the Evangelical Theological Society* 35, no. 1 (March 1992): 9.

32. See my "Jesus' Resurrection and the Search for Peace and Justice," *Christian Century* (November 3, 1982): 1103–8.

33. See the vigorous debate on the question of continuity between Stephen Williams and Miroslav Volf in their articles on "Eschatology and Social Responsibility" in *Transformation* 7, no. 3 (July–September 1990): 24–31.

34. Harris, *From Grave to Glory,* 250–51. Far less convincing is Murray's claim that the "natural habitat" for Christ's resurrected body is "heaven" and that, similarly, the final home for Christians is heaven, not earth. He cites (p. 181) 1 Thessalonians 4:16–17 as support, but this text only says that believers will meet Christ in the air at his return. It says nothing about the location of their being forever with him. Similarly (p. 192) he refers to 1 Corinthians 15:44 and speaks of "a spiritual body" for us "in heaven." But again the text says nothing about heaven as the *location* for the "spiritual body." For a different view of the "spiritual body," see my "The Pauline Conception of the Resurrection Body in 1 Cor. 15:35–54," *New Testament Studies* 21 (1975): 428–39; and my "St. Paul's Understanding of the Nature and Significance of the Resurrection in 1 Cor. 15:1–19," *Novum Testamentum* 19 (1977): 1–18.

35. Orthodox Christianity also has a fourth model that I do not discuss here. In a very helpful discussion of these models, Gabriel Fackre suggests that it is useful to notice six aspects of each model: (1) the role of Jesus; (2) the problem to be solved; (3) the locus or place of the activity; (4) the focus of the model; (5) the action performed; and (6) the outcome that results. Gabriel Fackre, *The Christian Story* (Grand Rapids: Eerdmans, 1978), 111–27.

36. Especially identified with Peter Abelard (twelfth-century theologian) and modern liberalism.

37. See also John Stott's excellent discussion in *The Cross of Christ,* chap. 8.

38. Especially identified with Anselm (another twelfth-century theologian), Luther, and modern evangelicals.

39. *Cross of Christ,* 338. See all of chapters 4–6.

40. See Driver, *Understanding the Atonement,* 34, 249 (and elsewhere).

41. Webster, *A Passion for Christ,* 153.

42. Gustav Aulen, *Christus Victor,* trans. A. G. Hebert (New York: Macmillan, 1951). See also Stott, *Cross of Christ,* chap. 9.

43. René Padilla, "The Politics of the Kingdom of God and the Political Mission of the Church," in Samuel and Hauser, eds., *Proclaiming Christ in Christ's Way,* 191.

44. See John Sobrino, *Christology at the Crossroads* (Maryknoll: Orbis, 1979), 179, 184–86, 190, 227, 304. Driver, *Understanding the Atonement,* does this to some extent (e.g., 57, 249). But see the balance in *Mission and Evangelism,* sect. 7.

45. I am indebted to Yoder, *Shalom,* 63ff., for this idea. I wish, however, that he had a stronger emphasis on the substitutionary model and grounded the approach more clearly in Chalcedonian Christology.

46. See the great statement at the WCC's San Antonio meeting (May 1989), by Orthodox theologian Anastasios of Androussa, "Address by the Moderator," in Frederick R. Wilson, *The San Antonio Report* (Geneva: WCC, 1990), 107.

47. See Driver, *Understanding the Atonement,* 247. Unfortunately, Driver overstates this crucial point when he says that restoration of community is "the central thrust of God's saving activity." It is *one* central aspect.

48. See also Stott, *Cross of Christ,* chap. 10.

Chapter 6

1. Jim Wallis, *The Call to Conversion* (New York: Harper, 1981), 8.

2. Wallis, *Conversion,* xiv–xv. Jim Wallis, *Revive Us Again: A Sojourner's Story* (Nashville: Abingdon, 1983), 35–51.

3. See the article "Conversion" in Colin Brown, ed., *The New International Dictionary of the New Testament,* 3 vols. (Grand Rapids: Zondervan, 1975–78), I, 354 (hereafter *NIDNT*).

4. *TDNT,* IV, 984–86.

5. Brown, ed., *NIDNT,* I, 355.

6. *TDNT,* IV, 976. See also Verkuyl's excellent definition in *Contemporary Missiology,* 200.

7. *TDNT,* IV, 1000–1006.

8. Ibid., 1002–3.

9. Brown, ed., *NIDNT,* I, 356.

10. "Repentance, faith, and discipleship are different aspects of the same thing." Ibid., 358. See also Gabriel Fackre's discussion of four aspects of conversion: repentance, faith, baptism, and service. *Word in Deed: Theological Themes in Evangelism* (Grand Rapids: Eerdmans, 1975), 78–98.

11. Also Matthew 4:17.

12. Acts 3:19. See René Padilla's excellent discussion in *Mission between the Times,* 80–81.

13. That is not to make repentance a good work we do that earns divine forgiveness. John Calvin distinguished "evangelical repentance" (a necessary response to God's forgiveness) from "legal repentance" (an effort to earn God's forgiveness). See James Torrance, "The Ministry of Reconciliation Today," in Kettler and Speidell, eds., *Incarnational Ministry,* 137.

14. "Evangelism and the World," in Douglas, ed., *Let the Earth Hear His Voice,* 129.

15. See Stott, *Christian Mission,* 53, following Padilla. This is part of what Carl Henry meant (and Peter Wagner wrongly criticized) when he said "social concern is an indispensable ingredient of the evangelistic message." Quoted in Wagner, *Church Growth,* 143.

16. See chapter 8, 148–52, for the notion of social sin.

17. See also Ephesians 4:30–32; Colossians 3:13ff.; Romans 15:7.

222

18. Cf. Vinay Samuel's and Chris Sugden's comment that "There are no laws for loving God in the Old Testament which can be broken independently of one's relationship to other people." "Evangelism and Social Responsibility," in Nicholls, ed., *In Word and Deed*, 200.

19. Cf. also 2 Corinthians 5:15; Romans 6:4; Titus 2:14; Matthew 5:16; 1 Peter 2:12.

20. J. Deotis Roberts, *A Black Political Theology* (Philadelphia: Westminster, 1974), 219.

21. Webster, *Passion for Christ,* 49.

22. Hathaway, *Beyond Renewal,* 102.

23. Boff and Boff, *Salvation and Liberation,* 91–92, tend in this direction.

24. Wagner cites many of his critics in *Church Growth,* 133–34.

25. Ibid., 134, 138.

26. Ibid., 136.

27. Newbigin, *Open Secret,* 152.

28. See the important article by Anglican Bishop David Gitari of Kenya: "The Church and Polygamy," *Transformation* 1, no. 1 (January–March 1984): 3–10.

29. Newbigin, *Open Secret,* 152.

30. See McGavran, *Understanding Church Growth,* 169; and Wagner, *Church Growth,* 130–45.

31. E.g., Donald Anderson McGavran, *The Bridges of God: A Study in the Strategy of Mission* (New York: Friendship Press, 1955), 13–16.

32. So (rightly) Costas, *The Church and Its Mission,* 142. Wagner attempts (following a Fuller dissertation) to argue that "to obey" rather than "all things" is the object of the participle "teaching." It is quite clear grammatically that the whole clause "to obey all things . . ." is an object clause depending on the verb "teaching." To try to pull the two parts of the object clause apart makes no grammatical sense. See Wagner's *Christian Growth,* 135–36.

33. Costas, *Church and Its Mission,* 142.

34. *TDNT,* 441 (see all of 441–61).

35. Wagner argues *(Church Growth),* 133, that (1) since the word *disciple* is used only in the Gospels and Acts but not the Epistles; and (2) the Gospels and Acts are books of "origin and growth" but the Epistles are "chiefly nurture books"; therefore the most common biblical use of "disciple" or "to make disciples" is the D1 and/or D2 sense [i.e., initial conversion], not the D3 [ethical growth sense]. . . . The Bible does not use discipling as Christian nurture, rather as winning non-Christians to the faith" (ibid., 132–33). This is simply wrong. The fact that the Epistles may be largely devoted to the nurture of Christians does not lead to Wagner's conclusion about the meaning of the word *disciple.* Nor is it the case that the Gospels are focused on "winning non-Christians" rather than "Christian nurture." One must understand how the word functions where it is used. And careful scholarship (e.g., *TDNT,* IV, 441–61) clearly shows that the central thrust of the word *disciple* is on total, obedient submission to Jesus' entire person and teaching.

36. Wagner provides an illustration when he says the evangelist "is concerned more with discipling than perfecting" and should keep "the ethical content of discipling to a minimum" (*Church Growth,* 140).

37. For a short biographical sketch, see Sugden, "A Critical and Comparative Study," 176–90.

38. Quoted in ibid., 219.

39. Ibid., 221–47 (equally 226–27). Also, Vinay Samuel and Chris Sugden, *Evangelism and the Poor* (Oxford: Regnum, 1982), 55.

40. Stephen Neill, "Looking Toward the Fifth Assembly," McGavran, ed., *Conciliar-Evangelical Debate,* 321.

41. José Miguez Bonino, "Christianity and Democracy in Latin America," an unpublished workshop paper delivered on November 15, 1991, at the International Conference on Christianity and Democracy held at Emory University. See also David Martin's discussion of Protestantism in Latin America: *Tongues of Fire: The Explosion of Protestantism in Latin America* (Oxford: Blackwell, 1990).

42. Roberts, *Black Political Theology,* 88. Also James Cone, *The Spirituals and the Blues: An Interpretation* (New York: Seabury, 1972), 67–68.

43. James Q. Wilson, "Crime and American Culture," *The Public Interest* 70 (winter 1983): 22. See also Charles Colson, *Kingdoms in Conflict* (Grand Rapids: Zondervan, 1987), chap. 16.

44. Cited in ibid., 238.

45. David O. Moberg, *Wholistic Christianity* (Elgin: Brethren Press, 1985), 108. See also two recent books: George H. Gallup Jr., *The Saints Among Us* (Ridgefield, Conn.: Morehouse, 1992); and Robert Wuthnow, *Acts of Compassion: Caring for Others and Helping Ourselves* (Princeton: Princeton University Press, 1991).

Chapter 7

1. Anastasios of Androussa, "Address by the Conference Moderator," in Wilson, ed., *The San Antonio Report,* 107. I would not, however, make material goods and hope after death an either/or but a both/and.

2. In this sense, it is right to speak of mission as first of all *missio dei.* See Bosch, *Transforming Mission,* 389–93, for a good discussion and the literature. But that in no way excludes inviting people to a personal saving relationship with Jesus Christ.

3. See, for instance, Borg, *Jesus: A New Vision;* and John Hick and Paul F. Knitter, eds., *The Myth of Christian Uniqueness: Towards a Pluralistic Theology of Religions* (Maryknoll: Orbis, 1987); and the extensive citation of the literature in Clark Pinnock, *A Wideness in God's Mercy: The Finality of Jesus Christ in a World of Religions* (Grand Rapids: Zondervan, 1992), especially the introduction and chapter 2.

4. See, for example, Paul F. Knitter, *No Other Name? A Critical Survey of Christian Attitudes toward Other Religions* (Maryknoll: Orbis, 1985), and the literature cited in Pinnock, *Wideness in God's Mercy.* Pinnock's chapter 2 is a strong reaffirmation of Christ as the only way to salvation. On this and many

other related topics, see also Michael Green's superb book, *Evangelism through the Local Church* (London: Hodder and Stoughton, 1990).

5. So, too, with equal clarity Pope John Paul II's recent encyclical, *Redemptoris Missio*, sect. 5. The World Council of Churches' *Mission and Evangelism*, sect. 42, however, acknowledges that the WCC cannot make this its official position.

6. Meeking and Stott, eds., *Evangelical-Roman Catholic Dialogue*, 44.

7. See J. Verkuyl, *Contemporary Missiology: An Introduction,* trans. Dale Cooper (Grand Rapids: Eerdmans, 1978), 164, for a good discussion of this motive and the missiologists who emphasize it.

8. See Michael Green, *Evangelism in the Early Church* (London: Hodder and Stoughton, 1970).

9. Verkuyl, *Contemporary Missiology,* 164.

10. See Donald McGavran's frequent reminder that faith in Christ is the way to a more humane world (e.g., *Understanding Church Growth,* 127); and John Paul II's insistence that only Christ brings true liberation; *Redemptoris Missio,* sect. 11.

11. E.g., Matthew 3:7; John 3:36; Romans 1:18; 4:15; 5:9; Ephesians 2:3; 1 Thessalonians 5:9; Revelation 16:1.

12. Also Luke 14:15–20; 16:19–31.

13. C. S. Lewis, *The Problem of Pain* (London: Fontana Books, 1957), chap. 8 (106–16).

14. See the literature cited and Pinnock's discussion in chapter 5 of *Wideness in God's Mercy.*

15. Others include Philip Hughes, John Wenham, and Stephen Travis. See David Edwards and John Stott, *Essentials: A Liberal-Evangelical Dialogue* (London: Hodder and Stoughton, 1988), 313–20; Clark Pinnock, "The Destruction of the Finally Impenitent," *Criswell Theological Review* 4 (1990): 243–59; Edward Fudge, *The Fire That Consumes* (Houston: Providential Press, 1982).

16. Nor did it affirm Stott's view. A majority preferred to leave the question open as an issue on which evangelicals legitimately disagree. See Kenneth S. Kantzer and Carl F. H. Henry, eds., *Evangelical Affirmations* (Grand Rapids: Zondervan, 1990), sect. 9 (36).

17. See the literature in Pinnock, *Wideness in God's Mercy,* chap. 5 and footnotes (especially footnotes 30–31). Cf. also John Sanders, *No Other Name: A Biblical, Historical, and Theological Investigation into the Destiny of the Unevangelized* (Grand Rapids: Eerdmans, 1992).

18. See Pinnock, *Wideness,* 168–72 and footnotes for the literature.

19. It is possible, as some argue, that 1 Peter 3:19–20 refers to an encounter with Christ after death. Similarly, in 1 Corinthians 15:29 Paul mentions (without criticism) the fact that people at Corinth are being baptized for others who had died. First Peter only refers to those who died before the time of Christ. There is no indication in 1 Corinthians 15 about the identity of the dead for whom Christians are being baptized. Many questions come to mind. Were they "good pagans"? People who confessed Christ and died before they

received baptism? Should Christians today be baptized for the billions who die without knowing Christ? Neither of these texts is clear enough to build a positive, certain teaching that people who die without knowing Christ will have an opportunity to meet and accept him after death. On the other hand, they certainly raise doubts about a positive, certain teaching that God never gives people an opportunity to meet Christ after death. Humble agnosticism is the way to be most faithful to biblical truth.

20. See Pinnock's criticism of Stott's "agnosticism" at just this point in *Wideness*, 150. I think Stott is right.

21. Verkuyl, *Contemporary Missiology*, 166, stresses this motivation.

22. But we should be careful not to link our specific evangelistic strategies to the Lord's return. I get very uneasy, for example, when Jim Montgomery concludes that when we reach his very worthy goal of planting a church in every group of 400–1000 people in every country, then "we can almost hear the trumpet sound." *Dawn 2000: 7 Million Churches to Go* (Pasadena: William Carey Library, 1989), 13.

23. Verkuyl, *Contemporary Missiology*, 165–66, has a good discussion of this motivation.

Chapter 8

1. "Evangelist Banned," *The Christian Century* XCVII, no. 37 (November 19, 1980): 1121. (The South African government forced him to leave!)

2. See Grace Gitari, "Evangelical Development in Mount Kenya East," *Transformation* 5, no. 4 (October–December 1988): 44–46.

3. See David Gitari, "Church and Politics in Kenya," *Transformation* 8, no. 3 (July–September, 1991): 7–17.

4. Ronald J. Sider, "Interview with Rev. Frank Chikane," *Transformation* 5, no. 2 (April–June 1988): 9–12. Chikane's denomination was the Apostolic Faith Mission and the white deacon was from the home congregation of David Du Plessis.

5. A more equitable sharing of productive resources is what John Perkins points to with his third "R" (redistribution); see, for example, his *With Justice for All* (Ventura: Regal, 1982), 14–15, 145–97. Voluntary development programs (e.g., wide-scale micro loans) can produce substantial redistribution but unless the legal, economic, and political structures are at least partly open to that change, major, lasting redistribution of power is extremely difficult.

6. See the masterful way that Richard J. Mouw does this in *Politics and the Biblical Drama* (Grand Rapids: Eerdmans, 1976) and *Political Evangelism* (Grand Rapids: Eerdmans, 1973).

7. Ronald J. Sider, ed., *For They Shall Be Fed* (Dallas: Word, 1997). The earlier edition was *Cry Justice: The Bible Speaks on Hunger and Poverty* (Downers Grove, Ill.: InterVarsity, 1980). See also my *Rich Christians in an Age of Hunger*, chap. 3, and my "An Evangelical Theology of Liberation," in Kenneth Kantzer and Stanley N. Gundry, eds., *Perspectives on Evangelical Theology* (Grand Rapids: Baker, 1979), 117–33.

8. See above, chapter 4, 61–66.

9. See the many texts in Sider, ed., *Cry Justice,* 174–87.

10. Ibid., 69–75.

11. E.g., Boff and Boff, *Salvation and Liberation,* 48.

12. E.g., Castro, "Reflection after Melbourne," *Your Kingdom Come,* 28 (but see chap. 4, footnote 3). Also, Eugene L. Stockwell's claim that "our fundamental clue to a mission in Christ's way continues to be the experience of the poor" ("Mission Issues for Today and Tomorrow," in Wilson, ed., *The San Antonio Report,* 118); and Andrew Kirk's statement that "it is assumed, however, that *only* the poor will respond favorably to the message" of Jesus (*New World,* 100). Some have thought that by stating that God is "on the side of the poor" (*Rich Christians,* chap. 3), I have made the same mistake. From the first edition of *Rich Christians,* however, I have insisted that God is not biased and that it is only in contrast with our sinful neglect of the poor that God's equal concern for all looks like bias toward the poor.

13. Section 32 (my emphasis).

14. *Manila Manifesto,* A–2. See Samuel Escobar, "From Lausanne 1974 to Manila 1989," *Urban Mission* (March 1990): 25 for a good statement on how important God's concern for the poor became at Lausanne II.

15. Stott, *Christian Mission,* 30.

16. John Perkins, *A Call to Wholistic Ministry* (St. Louis: Open Door Press, 1980), 43–44.

17. Valdir Steuernagel is certainly correct that one dare not base one's social concern only on compassion. Unless the justice motif (see below on social sin) is also present, social concern will easily become too individualistic. "The Theology of Mission," 240–44.

18. So, too, Matthew 15:32; 20:34; Mark 1:41.

19. That is not to suggest some "divine spark" in everyone. Rather, it means that God in Christ so identifies with the poor and marginalized that it is true to say that when we minister to them, we minister to Christ. Cf. the similar statement in Proverbs 19:17.

20. Charlotte Waterlow, *Superpowers and Victims* (Englewood Cliffs, N.J.: Prentice Hall, 1974), 60.

21. That is not to reject divine healing today.

22. Interestingly, in the Evangelical-Roman Catholic dialogue, this was one of the many points of agreement; Meeking and Stott, eds., *Evangelical-Roman Catholic Dialogue on Mission,* 33.

23. See the excellent discussion of "social reality" in Mott, *Biblical Ethics and Social Change,* 10–15.

24. Exact figures are unavailable. From 1780–1860, about 4.5 million slaves were forcibly brought to the Americas. See David Eltis, *Economic Growth and the Ending of the Transatlantic Slave Trade* (London: Oxford, 1987), 249.

25. E.g., William Rainey Harper, *A Critical and Exegetical Commentary on Amos and Hosea* (Edinburgh: T & T Clark, 1905), 49.

26. Cf. also Isaiah 5:8–11, 22–23.

27. Cf. also 1 Kings 21. See also my *Rich Christians,* 103–8, and my "Racism," *United Evangelical Action* 36, no. 2 (spring 1977): 11–12, 26–28.

28. If we have absolutely no understanding or awareness of how a system is evil and how we participate in it, then I would argue that we do not incur guilt before God. God holds us accountable for what we know (John 15:22–24; Rom. 2:12–13). That of course does not in any way detract from the fact that the system is very evil and destroys people. Usually, however, we know enough about the evil character of the system and the way it benefits us to know that we *do not want to know more!* We are morally responsible for what we choose not to know (Zech. 7:11–12).

29. See Mott, *Biblical Ethics and Social Change,* 4–6.

30. Mott, ibid., 4, and *TDNT,* III, 868.

31. Quoted in Mott, *Biblical Ethics and Social Change,* 6. Sometimes, of course, *cosmos* simply means God's good creation (e.g., John 1:9, 10a). See Richard Mouw's delightful distinction in *Called to Holy Worldliness* (Philadelphia: Fortress, 1980), 75.

32. Clinton E. Arnold, *Powers of Darkness: Principalities and Powers in Paul's Letters* (Downers Grove, Ill.: InterVarsity, 1992), 203.

33. See Mott, *Biblical Ethics and Social Change,* 6–10; Arnold, *Powers of Darkness,* especially 87–210; and the massive, three-volume work by Walter Wink published by Fortress Press: *Naming the Powers* (1984); *Unmasking the Powers* (1986); *Engaging the Powers* (forthcoming).

34. I have always carefully insisted that behind the corrupt social structures we experience are personal fallen supernatural powers (e.g., Sider, *Christ and Violence,* 50–57). Therefore I find Arnold's interpretation of my references to the powers (*Powers of Darkness,* 195, 234, fn. 3 [he mistakenly refers to p. 51 rather than p. 57 of my *Christ and Violence*]) puzzling. With him, I have always rejected a reductionistic (anti-supernatural) approach that saw the principalities and powers only as social structures in our world. Walter Wink's brilliant work on the powers, unfortunately, is reductionist. He rejects the notion of "a personal entity: an angel, demon or devil" (*Unmasking the Powers,* 4–5).

35. See the examples cited in C. Peter Wagner, *Warfare Prayer: How to Seek God's Power and Protection in the Battle to Build His Kingdom* (Ventura: Regal, 1992), chap. 1. I would be more cautious, however, than Wagner, and would claim far less detailed information about "territorial spirits."

36. John Paul II, *Sollicitudo Rei Socialis* (December 30, 1987), sect. 36.

37. See especially Raymond Fung, "Human Sinned-Againstness," *International Review of Mission* 69 (July 1980): 332–36; "Compassion for the Sinned Against," *Theology Today* 37 (July 1980): 162–69; "The Forgotten Side of Evangelism," *The Other Side* 15 (October 1979): 16–25; "Mission in Christ's Way: The Strachan Lectures," *International Review of Mission* 78 (January 1989): 18–19. My Josephine So Memorial Lecture III at the China Graduate School of Theology in Hong Kong was called "The Sinner and the Sinned Against" and published (only in Chinese) in *Evangelical Faith and Social Ethics* (Hong Kong: China Graduate School of Theology, 1986), 49–69.

38. It is at this point that I find the discussion of the "sinned against" at the Melbourne Conference of the WCC quite inadequate. I quote from section I, 4:

> The poor who are sinned against are rendered less human by being deprived. The rich are rendered less human by the sinful act of depriving others. The judgment of God thus comes as a verdict in favor of the poor. This verdict enables the poor to struggle to overthrow the powers that bind them, which then releases the rich from the necessity to dominate. Once this has happened, it is possible for both the humbled rich and the poor to become human, capable to respond to the challenge of the kingdom (quoted in Anderson, ed., *Witness to the Kingdom,* 106–7).

There is much that is true here, but the suggested solution is wrong. It would appear that the first and primary way that the rich are released from oppression is by the social action of the poor who demand just structures. Only after that change has occurred can the rich and poor respond to the kingdom. That is unbiblical nonsense. Only if both oppressed and oppressor can respond to the kingdom's free grace while they are still oppressed and oppressor is there any hope of fundamental change. Personal conversion of both, although not mentioned here at all, is crucial. (The WCC's *Mission and Evangelism,* section 32, is much better.) Secondarily, of course, it is true that more just structures do impact everyone and foster more human relationships. But to make our response to the kingdom depend on prior structural change is totally unacceptable. It is astonishing, therefore, to find evangelical political activist Tim LaHaye stating that the "only way to have genuine spiritual revival is to have legislative reform." Quoted in James Skillen, *The Scattered Voice: Christians at Odds in the Public Square* (Grand Rapids: Zondervan, 1990), 55.

39. See David Bosch's comments on this in *Transforming Mission,* 401.

Chapter 9

1. C. H. Dodd, *The Apostolic Teaching and Its Development* (London: Hodder and Stoughton, 1963), 7. Alan Richardson, "Preaching," in *A Theological Word Book of the Bible* (London: S.C.M. Press, 1975), 172.

2. Sect. 12; cf. also sect. 15.

3. David Lowes Watson, "Prophetic Evangelism," in Theodore Runyon, ed., *Wesleyan Theology Today* (Nashville: Kingswood Books, 1985), 222. So too Costas, *Christ outside the Gate,* 168–72.

4. David M. Paton, ed., *Breaking Barriers: The Official Report of the Fifth Assembly of the World Council of Churches,* Nairobi, 1975 (London: SPCK, 1976), 233. The WCC's *Mission and Evangelism* says that conversion involves an "invitation to recognize and accept in a personal decision the saving lordship of Christ" (sect. 10). That seems to be incompatible with addressing the call to conversion to nations (sects. 12, 15).

5. McGavran, *Understanding Church Growth,* 333–52.

6. David Gitari, "Kenya: Evangelism Among Nomadic Communities," in Wright and Sugden, eds., *One Gospel*, 63.

7. See Samuel's subtly developed approach in Sugden, "Critical and Comparative Study," 313–15. Mortimer Arias notes that "Jesus' call is personal but not individualistic or privatistic" (*Announcing the Reign*, 112).

8. Cf. David Bosch's important insistence that "individualism" in this sense is not a creation of the West, but the fruit of the gospel. *Transforming Mission*, 416.

9. That is why one can speak of evangelizing a village but not General Motors. In the first case, one does not mean that the village itself or even necessarily every single person in the village comes to personal faith in Christ. Rather one means that the corporate village leadership with the people together ponder and accept the gospel invitation—but in such a way that each person also makes a genuine decision (and a few may say no). Furthermore, one does not mean that the specific village as a specific social structure will live forever in the presence of Christ whereas that is true of each person who becomes a disciple of Christ. We have seen how Romans 8 and Revelation 21–22 show that the glory of human civilizations and the nonhuman creation will be purged of evil and be part of the eternal kingdom. But that does not mean that every individual tree and flower or every individual human artifact will be in the eternal kingdom. In the case of persons, however, we do mean precisely that. Every specific individual who becomes a disciple of Christ will be bodily resurrected and live forever as a distinct person with Christ.

10. Nazir-Ali, *From Everywhere to Everywhere*, 185.

11. In his recent encyclical, Pope John Paul II is concerned to insist on this distinction. He distinguishes "mission ad gentes" (to the nations) from other mission work and insists that "missionary activity proper, namely the mission ad gentes, is directed to peoples or groups who do not yet believe in Christ." He warns against letting this specific task "become an indistinguishable part of the overall mission of the whole People of God and as a result become neglected or forgotten" (*Redemptoris missio*, sect. 34). John Paul agrees with the Lausanne Covenant's insistence that "reconciliation with man is not reconciliation with God, nor is social action evangelism" (sect. 5).

12. That is what Andrew Kirk wrongly argues (*New World*, 103–4). He is, however, at least partly right in thinking that the CRESR report often puts it that way.

13. Stott, "The Biblical Basis of Evangelism," in Douglas, ed., *Let the Earth Hear His Voice*, 69.

14. See the similar definition in William J. Abraham, *The Logic of Evangelism* (Grand Rapids: Eerdmans, 1989), 95. See Stott, *Christian Mission*, 38–40, who insists on defining evangelism in terms of the message, not the results. Cf. Wagner, *Church Growth*, 55–57, which indicates that the Lausanne movement has concluded that the goal of evangelism is making disciples.

15. Costas, *Liberating News*, 136ff.

16. See James J. Stamoolis, *Eastern Orthodox Mission Theology Today* (Maryknoll: Orbis, 1986), especially chap. 11.

17. *Liberating News,* 136 (his emphasis). This would seem to be a modification of his earlier thinking.

18. *Evangelism and Social Responsibility: An Evangelical Commitment* (LCWE and WEF, 1982), 24 (hereafter cited as CRESR). Unlike Kirk (*New World,* 105), who labels this statement a lack of courage, I consider it the result of clarity. For similar statements to that of CRESR, see Leslie Newbigin, *One Body, One Gospel, One World* (London: IMC, 1958), 43; and Nazir-Ali, *From Everywhere to Everywhere,* 182–85.

19. Stott (at Lausanne I), "The Biblical Basis of Evangelism," in Douglas, ed., *Let the Earth Hear His Voice,* 68.

20. See David J. Hesselgrave's critique of this use of John 20:21; "Holes in Holistic Mission," *Trinity World Forum* (spring 1990): 1–5 (especially 4). I agree with John Stott's response, "An Open Letter to David Hesselgrave," *Trinity World Forum* (spring 1991): 1–2.

21. See Stott, *Christian Mission,* 16–25.

22. Arthur Johnston has severely criticized Stott (in *Battle for World Evangelism,* 300–306). But his arguments are not persuasive and the mainstream of the evangelical movement has accepted Stott's position. See CRESR; the *Manila Report* (from Lausanne II in 1989); and Kwame Bediako, "Evangelization and the Future of Christian World Mission," in Samuel and Hauser, eds., *Proclaiming Christ,* 56.

23. Kirk's objection that this means that "Christian people only become aware of and committed to social concerns as a result of evangelism" (*New World,* 91) is simply wrong. Non-Christians may already have a powerful social conscience and excellent social engagement before they become Christians. But their activity cannot be Christian social concern (although it may be excellent activity pleasing to God and helpful to neighbor) until these persons are evangelized, accept Christ, and their social action is part of their commitment to Christ.

24. See Kirk, *New World,* 92; and Graham King's "Evangelicals in Search of Catholicity," *Anvil* 7, no. 2 (1990): 120–21.

25. It is also true that a (transformed) creation (Rom. 8) and the (purified) glory of the nations (Rev. 21:24–22:2) will share in the coming kingdom. But there is no biblical indication that God intends to bring every particular tree or artifact of civilization into the New Jerusalem in the way that God longs for every single person created in the image of God to be saved and enjoy eternal life. See above, n. 9.

26. Steuernagel, "Theology of Mission," 257.

27. Cf. also Acts 6:1ff. and the discussion in CRESR, 21.

28. Peter Wagner (*Church Growth,* chap. 4) agrees.

29. Hence it is puzzling that Wagner would say that it is good for every different person to consider his or her own task the most important one (*Church Growth,* 189).

30. Wagner, ibid., 110, and CRESR, 20–21. This should not, however, provide an excuse for congregations or denominations to persist in long-term one-sidedness.

31. CRESR, 25.

32. Walter Bauer, *A Greek-English Lexicon of the New Testament and Other Early Christian Literature,* trans. William Arndt, F. Wilbur Gingrich, and Frederick Danker, 5th ed. (Chicago: University of Chicago, 1979), 566–67; see also Mott, *Biblical Ethics and Social Change,* 126.

33. McGavran is right, for instance, that normally when there are just a tiny number of Christians, they usually have less opportunity and responsibility to work for just structures than when Christians become a sizeable percent of the population. See his *Understanding Church Growth,* 26, 172–73.

34. Peter Wagner (*Church Growth and the Whole Gospel,* 118–26) argues that the history of the Student Volunteer Movement and the decline of mainline churches in the 1960s–1990s shows that the evangelistic mandate must have priority. I would argue that the most important reason for the decline of both was the theological liberalism (and the resulting tendency to make social action more important than evangelism), not an "equal" emphasis on both. In fact, Dean Hoge's study has shown that theological liberalism has the highest negative correlation with the growth of the church ("A Test of Theories of Denominational Growth and Decline," in *Understanding Church Growth and Decline,* 1950–1978), ed. Dean R. Hoge and David A. Roozen (Philadelphia: Pilgrim Press, 1979), 191. And Wagner himself says elsewhere that "churches can be very active socially and still enjoy vigorous membership growth if they do not give the cultural mandate a higher priority than the evangelistic mandate" (*Church Growth,* 123).

Chapter 10

1. See Perkins's *With Justice for All.*

2. *Manila Manifesto,* sect. 4. Obviously, the drafters of the *Manila Manifesto* did not mean, nor do I, that one can never do evangelism or social action without the other. By an inseparable partnership, I mean that there are numerous ways that they are very closely interrelated. Cf. also Samuel Escobar, "The Social Responsibility of the Church in Latin America," *Evangelical Missions Quarterly* (spring 1970): 144–45; "Statement of the Stuttgart Consultation on Evangelism" (1989), in Samuel and Hauser, eds., *Proclaiming Christ,* 215; and David Evans, "Evangelism with Theological Credibility," in Wright and Sugden, eds., *One Gospel,* 33 (my view of the overall relationship is quite similar to Evans's).

3. See Donald Dayton, *Discovering an Evangelical Heritage* (New York: Harper, 1976), 19.

4. See Richard J. Mouw, "Evangelism and Social Ethics," *TSF Bulletin* (January–February 1982): 7.

5. Also Romans 10:8–16; Philippians 2:9–11. Cf. also Stott, *Christian Mission,* 54.

6. Samuel and Sugden, *Christian Mission in the Eighties: A Third World Perspective* (Bangalore: Partnership in Mission–Asia, 1981), 12.

7. Ibid., 25.

8. This is what CRESR (21–22) means by social activity as a consequence of evangelism.

9. See chap. 6, 113–18.

10. See also Philippe Maury, *Politics and Evangelism* (Garden City, N.Y.: Doubleday, 1959), 107.

11. Delos Miles, *Evangelism and Social Involvement* (Nashville: Broadman, 1986), 132.

12. Cf. Donald McGavran's statement (*Understanding Church Growth,* 292) that missionaries should "teach submission to existing governments as ordained by God."

13. This third point is really a sub-point of the previous one since it deals with the way the (evangelized) church impacts society.

14. H. Richard Niebuhr, "The Responsibility of the Church for Society," in *The Gospel, the Church and the World,* ed. Kenneth Scott Latourette (New York: Harper, 1946), 130–32.

15. Fackre, *Word in Deed,* 68. Cf. also Kirk, *New World,* 103–4.

16. Michael Green, "Methods and Strategy in the Evangelism of the Early Church," in Douglas, ed., *Let the Earth Hear His Voice,* 169.

17. That is why I cannot accept Peter Wagner's argument for homogeneous churches. Peter argues: "Homogeneity aids the evangelistic mandate, heterogeneity aids the cultural mandate" (*Church Growth and the Whole Gospel,* 170). Since evangelism is more important, Wagner argues, homogeneous churches should not disturb us. That is wrong on two counts. First of all, if Ephesians 3:1–7 is right, then the multi-racial character of the church is part of the gospel. The very essence of the gospel is at stake, not merely our "cultural mandate." Second, as I argued above, Wagner lacks an adequate basis for giving the "cultural mandate" that kind of secondary role.

18. In his speech at Lausanne I, Green said "the church is in a very real sense part of the Gospel" ("Methods and Strategy," in Douglas, ed., *Let the Earth Hear His Voice,* 169). In the Evangelical-Roman Catholic dialogue, there was agreement on this issue; Meeking and Stott, eds., *Evangelical-Roman Catholic Dialogue,* 66.

19. Arthur Johnston is quite right in reminding us that fallen society will never be able to follow fully the model lived by regenerating grace in the church ("The Kingdom in Relation to the Church and the World," in Nicholls, ed., *In Word and Deed,* 125). Because of grace, the church should be far ahead of the world. On the other hand, the existence of common grace and general revelation enables even non-Christians (and unredeemed social systems) to do many good things and imitate good models (however inadequately).

20. Cf., for example, the sixteenth-century Anabaptists' costly championing of religious freedom and separation of church and state. It cost thousands of martyrs and took several centuries, but the modern world finally accepted their view. See, for example, Franklin Littell, *The Free Church* (Boston: Starr King Press, 1957).

21. Matthew 5:13–16; 13:33. See CRESR, 34.

22. CRESR, 22–23, speaks of social concern as a "bridge" to evangelism.

23. See Samuel and Sugden, *Lambeth,* 73.

24. Escobar and Driver, *Christian Mission,* 44–45.

25. Arthur Johnston is also rightly concerned that we not make the power of the gospel depend primarily on our good social action. Thank God, as Johnston insists, the gospel is self-authenticating even when we fail to show the full compassion of Christ ("The Kingdom," in Nicholls, ed., *In Word and Deed,* 303). At the same time God has chosen to allow our faithfulness to have some impact on others' receptivity to the gospel. Jesus said that our love and care for each other would convince the world that he came from the Father (John 17:20–23). In Acts 6:1–7, the demonstration of concern for the material needs of minority widows led to church growth.

26. I do not mean to argue that official church structures are the right institutional location for all or even most Christian political engagement. Often parachurch structures like Evangelicals for Social Action or Bread for the World are more appropriate.

27. Mott, *Biblical Ethics and Social Change,* 125–26.

28. Quoted in ibid., 126.

29. Consequently, we should not think in terms of simply adding evangelism to social action or vice versa as if they were totally unrelated things. They are not identical, but they are so interrelated that they belong together, as CRESR said, like the two wings of a bird (23).

30. This fifth model is very similar to that of the "Statement of the Stuttgart Consultation on Evangelism" (1989) that Vinay Samuel and Albrecht Hauser summarize as "an understanding of mission and evangelism which integrates proclaiming the gospel and inviting people to respond to Christ as Savior and Lord with involvement in action for justice, bringing social transformation to structures and communities." Samuel and Hauser, eds., *Proclaiming Christ in Christ's Way,* 10. In the Stuttgart Consultation, evangelism and social concern are not identical but they are "inseparably related" (215). It would seem to me, however, to be clearer to speak of integral or wholistic mission rather than "integral evangelism" as the comprehensive category.

31. McGavran discusses the problem in *Understanding Church Growth,* chap. 15. "Redemptive lift," however, is my term. I doubt the validity of his distinction between "redemption" and "lift."

32. Ibid., 297–309.

33. Ronald J. Sider, "Religious Faith and Public Policy," *ESA/Advocate* (April 1992): 2.

Chapter 11

1. *Redemptoris missio,* 86.

2. David B. Barrett, "Annual Statistical Table on Global Mission: 1992," *International Bulletin of Missionary Research* 16, no. 1 (January 1992): 27.

3. David B. Barrett and Todd M. Johnson, *Our Globe and How to Reach It* (Birmingham: New Hope, 1990), 32.

4. See, for example, Robert T. Coote, "The Numbers Game in Evangelism," *Transformation* 8, no. 1 (January–March 1991): 1–5. See also Ralph Winter's response in the same issue, 6–8.

5. A Lausanne Statistics Task Force headed by David Barrett did the basic analysis. See Ralph Winter, "The Diminishing Task," *Mission Frontiers* (January–February 1992): 5. Winter's category of "Bible Believing" Christians is similar to Barrett's category of "Great Commission" Christians.

6. Barrett, "Annual Statistical Table . . . 1992," 27.

7. Ibid.

8. MARC Newsletter, March 1992, 2.

9. David Hesselgrave's estimate in "Today's Choices for Tomorrow's Mission," 190.

10. Barrett, "Annual Statistical Table . . . 1992," 27.

11. See both the 1982 Grand Rapids Report, *Evangelism and Social Responsibility: An Evangelical Commitment,* published by the WEF and the LCWE, and the 1989 *Manila Manifesto* from the LCWE's Lausanne II in Manila, *1989: The Manila Manifesto* (Pasadena: LCWE, 1989).

12. See the WCC's *Mission and Evangelism: An Ecumenical Affirmation* (1983) and John Paul II's *Redemptoris missio* (1991).

13. Resolution #43; *The Truth Shall Make You Free: The Lambeth Conference 1988* (London: Church House Publishing, 1988), 231. See also the analysis in Samuel and Sugden, *Lambeth,* 50.

14. *RM,* 83. For other statements, see Barrett and Johnson, *Our Globe,* 3.

15. William A. Dyrness, "A Unique Opportunity," in W. Dayton Roberts and John A. Siewert, *Mission Handbook,* 14th ed. (Monrovia: MARC, 1989), 17.

16. Evangelicals have long challenged the anti-supernaturalism of modern secularism, but they have just begun to grapple seriously with the larger problem of modernity. Andrew Walker's *Enemy Territory: The Christian Struggle for the Modern World* (London: Hodder and Stoughton, 1987) and Os Guinness's *The Gravedigger File* (London: Hodder and Stoughton, 1983) are two excellent exceptions to our larger neglect. In recent years, Leslie Newbigin has also produced excellent analyses of modernity in *The Other Side of 1984* (Geneva: WCC, 1984) and *Foolishness to the Greeks: The Gospel and Western Culture* (Geneva: WCC, 1986).

17. George Barna, *The Barna Report: What Americans Believe* (Ventura: Regal, 1991), 234.

18. See Walker, *Enemy Territory,* for a superb discussion.

19. See, for example, his foreword to the third edition of Sider, *Rich Christians in an Age of Hunger* (Dallas: Word, 1990), xi-xiii.

20. Phil Bogosian, "The Time Has Not Yet Come!" *Mission Frontiers* (March–April 1992): 39.

21. David B. Barrett, *Cosmos, Chaos and Gospel: A Chronology of World Evangelization from Creation to New Creation* (Birmingham: New Hope, 1987), 75.

22. Ibid.

23. From statistics in Barrett, "Annual Statistical Table . . . 1992," 27, and Barrett and Johnson, *Our Globe,* 32. The vast majority of even that 5.4 per-

cent goes for "foreign missions to other Christian lands" rather than to unreached people (ibid., 27).

24. According to FAO estimates, 51 million people (139,726 per day) died of malnutrition and related diseases in 1990. For the numbers in near absolute poverty, see Michael P. Todaro, *Economic Development in the Third World*, 4th ed. (New York: Longman, 1989), 31–32.

25. Barrett, *Cosmos, Chaos and Gospel*, 75.

26. "Evangelism and the World," in Douglas, ed., *Let the Earth Hear His Voice*, 132.

27. Jim Wallis has sought to move toward this kind of "wholistic revival" in the series of one-day events ("Let Justice Roll") that he and Ken Medema have done around the United States.

28. For Dr. Kriengsak, see Carolyn Boyd, *The Apostle of Hope: The Dr. Kriengsak Story* (Chichester: Sovereign World, 1991). Dr. Kriengsak is the chair of the Charismatic Fellowship of Asia. For shalom revivals, see my article in *Gospel Herald* (March 17, 1992): 1–4. For the interrelationship of earlier revivals and social concern, see Donald Dayton, *Discovering an Evangelical Heritage* (New York: Harper, 1976); Timothy L. Smith, *Revivalism and Social Reform* (New York: Harper Torch Books, 1965); and J. Edwin Orr, "Evangelical Dynamic and Social Action," in A. R. Tippett, ed., *God, Man and Church Growth* (Grand Rapids: Eerdmans, 1973), chap. 18.

29. A national survey recently posed the question: "What would make the church more attractive?" The second most common answer was a church helping the poor and needy. See *Never on a Sunday: The Challenge of the Unchurched* (Glendale, Calif.: The Barna Research Group, 1990), 24.

30. For some brief attempts to spell out what this would mean, see my *Completely Pro-Life* (Downers Grove, Ill.: InterVarsity, 1987); "Toward a Biblical Perspective on Equality," *Interpretation* (April 1989): 156–69; and my articles on political philosophy in the *ESA/Advocate* (September, October, and November–December 1988).

31. I have tried to spell this out in far more detail in my *Rich Christians in an Age of Hunger*.

32. For more information, write Network 9:35, ESA, 10 E. Lancaster Avenue, Wynnewood, PA 19096 (800-650-6600 [for orders only]; fax: 610-649-8090; e-mail: esa@esa-online.org).

Appendix

1. Gustavo Gutiérrez, *A Theology of Liberation* (Maryknoll: Orbis, 1973), 178. For a discussion of Gutiérrez and other liberation theologians who use the broader definition of salvation, see Emilio Nuñez, *Liberation Theology* (Chicago: Moody, 1985), chap. 7. For the notion of social salvation in the earlier Social Gospel movement, see, for example, Walter Rauschenbusch, *A Theology for the Social Gospel* (New York: Abingdon, 1945), 110 ff. For the WCC, see, for example, section II, "Salvation and Social Justice," in *Bangkok Assembly, 1973* (Geneva: WCC, n.d.).

2. For the official document, see *Evangelism and Social Responsibility: An Evangelical Commitment.* WEF and LCWE, 1982. For the papers presented at CRESR, see Nicholls, ed., *In Word and Deed.*

3. *Evangelism and Social Responsibility,* 28–29.

4. For example, Richard J. Mouw (e.g., *Political Evangelism* [Grand Rapids: Eerdmans, 1973]), now president at Fuller Theological Seminary, and Vinay Samuel (see nn. 16, 19 below), General Secretary of the International Fellowship of Evangelical Missions Theologians.

5. David J. Bosch, *Witness to the World* (Atlanta: John Knox, 1980), 209. I said the same in 1977: Ronald J. Sider, *Evangelism, Salvation and Social Justice* (Bramcote Notts: Grove Books, 1977), 11. See also Vinay Samuel and Chris Sugden, "Evangelism and Social Responsibility," in Nicholls, ed., *In Word and Deed,* 210.

6. Braaten, *Flaming Center,* 149.

7. Arias, *Announcing the Reign,* 11.

8. Braaten, *Flaming Center,* 150.

9. E.g., Costas, *Christ Outside the Gate,* 30, and the Report on Section II of the WCC's Bangkok Conference in "Salvation Today," in *International Review of Mission* 62, no. 246 (April 1973): 199.

10. See chap. 8, 148–51.

11. See chap. 6, 105–7, and Samuel and Sugden, "Evangelism and Social Responsibility," in Nicholls, ed., *In Word and Deed,* 199–209.

12. Costas, *Christ Outside the Gate,* 41.

13. See chap. 6 on conversion.

14. Vinay Samuel and Chris Sugden, "Toward a Theology of Social Change," in Sider, ed., *Evangelicals and Development,* 58.

15. I use the word *spill-over* to underline the distinction between the church and the world. But this image is not adequate to capture all the ways the salvation experienced in the church impacts the world. See further, chapter 10, 178.

16. So Samuel and Sugden, "God's Intention for the World," in Samuel and Sugden, eds., *Response to Human Need,* 141–42.

17. Ibid., 142. But does this not contradict the claim on p. 141 that they "share in God's saving work" unless all they mean here is the "spill-over" I want to affirm?

18. This distinction is used in the CRESR document; see *Evangelism and Social Responsibility,* 33.

19. Many theologians have debated this issue. In the following section, I will interact especially with Samuel and Sugden, "Theology of Social Change," in Sider, ed., *Evangelicals and Development,* 50–61, and Samuel and Sugden, "Evangelism and Social Responsibility," in Nicholls, ed., *In Word and Deed,* 189–214. But see also Costas, *Christ Outside the Gate,* 29–42 (especially p. 41), and Braaten, *Flaming Center,* 57–62.

20. Samuel and Sugden, "Theology of Social Change," in Sider, ed., *Evangelicals and Development,* 51–52; Sugden, "A Critical and Comparative Study," 271; and Braaten, *Flaming Center,* 61; who notes that this problem has been especially true of Lutherans with their particular two-kingdom theology.

237

21. Braaten, *Flaming Center,* 61; Samuel and Sugden, "Social Change," in Sider, ed., *Evangelicals and Development,* 52.

22. Ibid., 51.

23. Ibid.

24. Ibid., 54; Sugden, "A Critical and Comparative Study," 301–2.

25. Samuel and Sugden, "Evangelism and Social Responsibility," in Nicholls, ed., *In Word and Deed,* 203.

26. It is not clear if Samuel and Sugden mean these different ways of acting are simply distinct or contradictory. If the latter, then the objection is valid. But if they are only distinct (as I argue below), then I fail to see a problem.

27. Cf. Martin Luther's statement that public officials who are Christians "do not have to ask Christ about your duty." Quoted in John R. W. Stott, *Christian Counter-Culture* (Downers Grove, Ill.: InterVarsity, 1978), 113. See Luther's commentary on the Sermon on the Mount in Jaroslav Pelikan, ed., *Luther's Works,* vol. 21 (St. Louis: Concordia, 1956), 110–13. I think this kind of ethical dualism is wrong; see Ronald J. Sider and Richard K. Taylor, *Nuclear Holocaust and Christian Hope* (Downers Grove, Ill.: InterVarsity, 1982), 114–17.

28. Braaten, *Flaming Center,* 59.

29. Ibid., 58.

30. See Sider, *Christ and Violence,* 50–57, and the literature cited there. See also the three-volume work by Walter Wink, *The Powers* (see chap. 8, n. 33). A very different view is taken by Wesley Carr, *Angels and Principalities* (Cambridge: Cambridge University Press, 1981).

31. See Albert van den Heuvel, *The Rebellious Powers* (Naperville: SCM Book Club, 1966), 44.

32. See above, chap. 4, 61.

33. Unless the universalists are correct (which I do not believe to be the case).

34. I did not see this point clearly in my earlier discussion in "How Broad Is Salvation?" in Nicholls, ed., *In Word and Deed,* 102–3, and consequently granted a stronger case for the broader terminology than I now do.

35. Vinay Samuel also argues that advocates of the narrower view assume that "everything that is 'spiritual' in this life is perfect, and that therefore any experience we have of redemption cannot be mingled with imperfection." Quoted in Sugden, "A Comparative Study," 276. Samuel is surely correct that any such claim is wrongheaded. There is much imperfection in believers and the church about which the New Testament uses salvation language. But it does not follow that because both church and world are a mixture of good and evil, therefore there is no difference and salvation language applies to both. Three important things are true of the church and not the larger society: (1) Christians enjoy forgiveness of sins; (2) they experience now the sanctifying power of the Holy Spirit who lives in believers; (3) because of 1 and 2, the church is a new redeemed community enjoying the presence, power, and transformation of God as a community in a way not experienced by the world. Consequently it is understandable why the New Testament applies salvation language to the church and not the world.

36. Samuel and Sugden, "Theology of Social Change," in Sider, ed., *Evangelicals and Development,* 54; also Samuel and Sugden, "Evangelism and Social Responsibility," in Nicholls, ed., *In Word and Deed,* 211.

37. Gutiérrez, *A Theology of Liberation,* 176–77. For an excellent critique of Gutiérrez's doctrine of salvation, see Emilio A. Nuñez, *Liberation Theology* (Chicago: Moody, 1985), chap. 7.

38. Isaiah 45 is instructive. The pagan king Cyrus is called God's "anointed" (v. 1) and God uses him to save Israel (vv. 13, 17). But the prophet explicitly says that Cyrus does not know Yahweh (vv. 4–5). Salvation language is only used with reference to Israel (v. 17). And the passage ends with a ringing monotheistic declaration and appeal to all nations to "turn to me and be saved . . . for I am God and there is no other" (v. 22). God in his providence uses Cyrus, but the text does not say unbelieving Cyrus experienced salvation.

39. Part but not all of Christ's intention in this process is to prepare the way for explicit confession of Christ. Sometimes Samuel states this point in too sweeping a fashion. Sugden summarizes Samuel's view thus: "The goal of God's work outside the church is always to bring people into the Kingdom of God and membership of the body of Christ" (Sugden, "A Comparative Study," 288). That is one part of God's intention but not all of it. Precisely the creation/redemption distinction allows one to say that God's work outside the church is also to preserve the goodness of creation and enable people to enjoy that goodness during this life even if they never accept Christ. Simply on the basis of creation, social action designed to enable people to enjoy food and justice for this life has its own independent foundation. Of course God longs for everyone to accept Christ. But we should not ground God's action in the world solely on his desire to bring people to Christ. (See chap. 8, 141.)

40. Padilla, *Mission Between the Times,* 41; also Scherer, *Gospel, Church and Kingdom,* 86–87.

41. Commentary on Acts 28:31 quoted in Robert Doyle, "The Search for Theological Models," in Webb, ed., *Christians in Society,* 38 (see all of 36–38). So too, Wagner, *Church Growth,* 5–10.

42. I do not, however, consider people like Orlando Costas, Richard Mouw, Vinay Samuel, and Chris Sugden (all of whom use the broader usage) guilty of "theological error." They all vigorously affirm the importance of evangelism as well as social action and maintain a solid biblical theology avoiding universalism and the blurring of the church and the world.

Bibliography

Abraham, William J. *The Logic of Evangelism*. Grand Rapids: Eerdmans, 1989.

Aeschliman, Gordon. *Global Trends: Ten Changes Affecting Christians Everywhere*. Downers Grove, Ill.: InterVarsity, 1990.

Anderson, Gerald H., ed. *Witnessing to the Kingdom: Melbourne and Beyond*. Maryknoll: Orbis, 1982.

Arias, Mortimer. *Evangelization and the Subversive Memory of Jesus: Announcing the Reign of God*. Philadelphia: Fortress, 1984.

Armstrong, James. *From the Underside: Evangelism from a Third World Vantage Point*. Maryknoll: Orbis, 1981.

Arnold, Clinton E. *Powers of Darkness: Principalities and Powers in Paul's Letters*. Downers Grove, Ill.: InterVarsity, 1992.

Barna, George. *What Americans Believe: An Annual Survey of Values and Religious Views in the United States*. Ventura: Regal, 1991.

Barna Research Group. *Never on a Sunday: The Challenge of the Unchurched*. Glendale, Calif.: Barna Research Group, 1990.

Barrett, David B. *Cosmos, Chaos and Gospel: A Chronology of World Evangelization from Creation to New Creation*. Birmingham: Foreign Mission Board of the Southern Baptist Convention, 1987.

Barrett, David B., and Todd M. Johnson. *Our Globe and How to Reach It*. Birmingham: New Hope, 1990.

Bevans, Steve, and James A. Scherer, eds. *New Directions in Mission and Evangelization: A Collection of Recent Mission Statements*. Maryknoll: Orbis, 1992.

Bloesch, Donald G. *Essentials of Evangelical Theology*. 2 vols. San Francisco: Harper, 1978–79.

Boff, Leonardo and Clodovis. *Salvation and Liberation*. Translated by Robert R. Barr. Maryknoll: Orbis, 1984.

Bohen, Marian. "The Future of Mission in a Pluralistic World." *Theological Education* (autumn 1990): 31–43.

Borg, Marcus J. *Jesus: A New Vision; Spirit, Culture, and the Life of Discipleship*. San Francisco: HarperCollins, 1991.

Borthwick, Paul. *How to Be a World Class Christian*. Wheaton: Victor, 1991.

Bosch, David J. "Toward Evangelism in Context." In *The Church in Response to Human Need*, edited by Vinay Samuel and Chris Sugden, 180–92. Grand Rapids: Eerdmans, 1987.

240

———. *Transforming Mission: Paradigm Shifts in Theology of Mission.* Maryknoll: Orbis, 1991.

———. *Witness to the World: The Christian Mission in Theological Perspective.* Atlanta: John Knox, 1980.

Braaten, Carl E. *The Flaming Center: A Theology of the Christian Mission.* Philadelphia: Fortress, 1977.

———. *Justification: The Article by Which the Church Stands or Falls.* Minneapolis: Augsburg, 1990.

Bria, Ion, ed. *Go Forth in Peace: Orthodox Perspectives on Mission.* Geneva: WCC, 1986.

Buttry, Daniel. *Bringing Your Church Back to Life: Beyond Survival Mentality.* Valley Forge: Judson, 1988.

Canberra 1991: Message, Report and Programme Policy Report of the WCC Seventh Assembly. Geneva: WCC, 1991.

Carpenter, Joel A., and Wilbert R. Shenk, eds. *Earthen Vessels: American Evangelicals and Foreign Missions, 1880–1980.* Grand Rapids: Eerdmans, 1990.

Coleman, Robert E. *The Master Plan of Evangelism.* Tarrytown, N.Y.: Revell, 1972.

Colson, Charles. *Kingdoms in Conflict.* Grand Rapids: Zondervan, 1987.

Concerned Evangelicals. *Evangelical Witness in South Africa: A Critique of Evangelical Theology and Practice by South African Evangelicals.* Grand Rapids: Eerdmans, 1986.

Costas, Orlando E. *Christ outside the Gate: Mission beyond Christendom.* Maryknoll: Orbis, 1982.

———. *The Church and Its Mission: A Shattering Critique from the Third World.* Wheaton: Tyndale, 1974.

———. *The Integrity of Mission.* San Francisco: Harper, 1979.

———. *Liberating News: A Theology of Contextual Evangelization.* Grand Rapids: Eerdmans, 1989.

Curry-Roper, Janel M. "Contemporary Christian Eschatologies and Their Relation to Environmental Stewardship." *The Professional Geographer* 42, no. 2 (1990): 157–69.

Dayton, Donald. *Discovering an Evangelical Heritage.* New York: Harper, 1976.

Douglas, J. D., ed. *Let the Earth Hear His Voice: International Congress on World Evangelization, Lausanne, Switzerland.* Minneapolis: World Wide Publications, 1975.

Driver, John. *Understanding the Atonement for the Mission of the Church.* Scottsdale, Penn.: Herald, 1986.

Dyrness, William A. *Learning about Theology from the Third World.* Grand Rapids: Zondervan, 1990.

———. *Let the Earth Rejoice: A Biblical Theology of Mission.* Westchester: Crossway, 1983.

Engel, James F., and Jerry D. Jones. *Baby Boomers and the Future of World Missions.* Orange, Calif.: Management Development Associates, 1989.

Escobar, Samuel. "Evangelical Theology in Latin America: The Development of a Missiological Christology." *Missiology: An International Review* XIX, no. 3 (July 1991): 315–32.

———. "From Lausanne 1974 to Manila 1989: The Pilgrimage of Urban Mission." *Urban Mission* 4 (March 1990): 21–29.

———. "Has McGavran's Missiology Been Devoured By a Lion?" *Missiology* XVII, no. 3 (July 1989): 349–52.

———. *Liberation Themes in Reformational Perspective.* Sioux Center, Iowa: Dordt College Press, 1989.

———. "The Social Responsibility of the Church in Latin America." *Evangelical Missions Quarterly* (spring 1970): 129–53.

Escobar, Samuel, and John Driver. *Christian Mission and Social Justice.* Scottsdale, Penn.: Herald, 1978.

Evangelism and Social Responsibility: An Evangelical Commitment. Lausanne Committee for World Evangelization and the World Evangelical Fellowship, 1982.

Fackre, Gabriel. *Word in Deed: Theological Themes in Evangelism.* Grand Rapids: Eerdmans, 1975.

Fung, Raymond. "Mission in Christ's Way: The Strachan Lectures." *International Review of Mission* 78, no. 309 (January 1989): 4–29.

Glasser, Arthur F., and Donald A. McGavran, eds. *Contemporary Theologies of Mission.* Grand Rapids: Baker, 1983.

Gnanakan, Ken R. *Kingdom Concerns: A Biblical Exploration towards a Theology of Mission.* Bangalore: Theological Book Trust, 1989.

Green, Michael. *Evangelism in the Early Church.* London: Hodder & Stoughton, 1970.

———. *Evangelism through the Local Church.* London: Hodder and Stoughton, 1990.

Gustafson, James W. "The Integration of Development and Evangelism." *International Journal of Frontier Missions* 8, no. 4 (October 1991): 115–20.

Gutiérrez, Gustavo. *A Theology of Liberation: History, Politics and Salvation.* Maryknoll: Orbis, 1973.

Haring, Bernard. *Evangelization Today.* Rev. ed. New York: Crossroad, 1991.

Harris, Murray J. *From Grave to Glory: Resurrection in the New Testament.* Grand Rapids: Zondervan, 1990.

Hathaway, Brian. *Beyond Renewal: The Kingdom of God.* Milton Keynes, England: Word (UK), 1990.

Hesselgrave, David J. *Today's Choices for Tomorrow's Mission: An Evangelical Perspective on Trends and Issues in Missions.* Grand Rapids: Zondervan, 1988.

Isaacson, Alan. *Deeper Life: The Extraordinary Growth of the Deeper Life Bible Church.* London: Hodder and Stoughton, 1990.

Jansen, Frank Kaleb, ed. *Target Earth: The Necessity of Diversity in a Holistic Perspective on World Mission.* Pasadena: Global Mapping International, 1989.

Jeremias, Joachim. *Jerusalem in the Time of Jesus: An Investigation into Economic and Social Conditions During the New Testament Period.* Philadelphia: Fortress, 1975.

John Paul II. *Redemptor Hominis* (March 4, 1979).

———. *Redemptoris missio* (January 22, 1991).

———. *Sollicitudo rei socialis* (December 30, 1987).

Johnston, Arthur. *The Battle for World Evangelism.* Wheaton: Tyndale, 1978.

———. "The Kingdom in Relation to the Church and the World." In *In Word and Deed,* edited by Bruce J. Nicholls. Grand Rapids: Eerdmans, 1985.

Kagawa, Toyohiko. *New Life through God.* Translated by Elizabeth Kilbara. New York: Revell, 1931.

Kettler, Christian D., and Todd H. Speidell, eds. *Incarnational Ministry: The Presence of Christ in Church, Society and Family.* Colorado Springs: Helmers and Howard, 1990.

Kings, Graham. "Evangelicals in Search of Catholicity: Theological Reflections on Lausanne II." *Anvil* 7, no. 2 (1990): 115–28.

Kirk, Andrew. *A New World Coming: A Fresh Look at the Gospel for Today.* London: Marshalls Paperbacks, 1983.

Kraft, Charles H. *Christianity with Power: Your Worldview and Your Experience of the Supernatural.* Ann Arbor: Servant, 1989.

Krass, Alfred C. *Five Lanterns at Sundown: Evangelism in a Chastened Mood.* Grand Rapids: Eerdmans, 1978.

The Manila Manifesto: An Elaboration of the Lausanne Covenant Fifteen Years Later. Pasadena: LCWE, 1989.

Maury, Philippe. *Politics and Evangelism.* Translated by Marguerite Wieser. Garden City: Doubleday, 1959.

McGavran, Donald A., ed. *The Conciliar-Evangelical Debate: The Crucial Documents 1964–1976.* Pasadena: William Carey, 1977.

———. "Missiology Faces the Lion." *Missiology: An International Review* XVII, no. 3 (July 1989): 335–41.

———. *Understanding Church Growth.* Rev. ed. Grand Rapids: Eerdmans, 1980.

McLoughlin, William G. *Revivals, Awakenings, and Reform.* Chicago: University of Chicago, 1978.

Meeking, Basil, and John Stott, eds. *The Evangelical-Roman Catholic Dialogue on Mission 1977–1984: A Report.* Exeter: Paternoster, 1986.

Miles, Delos. *Evangelism and Social Involvement.* Nashville: Broadman, 1986.

Moberg, David O. *Wholistic Christianity.* Elgin: Brethren Press, 1985.

Mohabir, Philip. *Building Bridges.* London: Hodder and Stoughton, 1988.

Moltmann, Jürgen. *The Way of Jesus Christ: Christology in Messianic Dimensions.* San Francisco: HarperCollins, 1990.

Montgomery, Jim. *Dawn 2000: 7 Million Churches to Go.* Pasadena: William Carey Library, 1989.

Mott, Stephen Charles. *Biblical Ethics and Social Change.* New York: Oxford, 1982.

Mouw, Richard J. *Called to Holy Worldliness.* Philadelphia: Fortress, 1980.

———. *Political Evangelism.* Grand Rapids: Eerdmans, 1973.

———. *Politics and the Biblical Drama.* Grand Rapids: Eerdmans, 1976.

Nazir-Ali, Michael. *From Everywhere to Everywhere: A World View of Christian Witness.* London: Collins, 1991.

Newbigin, Leslie. *Foolishness to the Greeks.* Geneva: WCC, 1986.

———. *The Gospel in a Pluralist Society.* Grand Rapids: Eerdmans, 1989.

———. *The Open Secret: Sketches for a Mission Theology.* Grand Rapids: Eerdmans, 1978.

———. *Unfinished Agenda: An Autobiography.* Grand Rapids: Eerdmans, 1985.

Nicholls, Bruce J., ed. *In Word and Deed: Evangelism and Social Responsibility.* Grand Rapids: Eerdmans, 1985.

Nuñez, Emilio A. *Liberation Theology.* Chicago: Moody, 1985.

Padilla, René. *Mission between the Times: Essays on the Kingdom.* Grand Rapids: Eerdmans, 1985.

Padilla, René, ed. *The New Face of Evangelicalism: An International Symposium on the Lausanne Covenant.* Downers Grove, Ill.: InterVarsity, 1976.

Pannell, William. *Evangelism from the Bottom Up.* Grand Rapids: Zondervan, 1992.

Perkins, John. *With Justice for All.* Ventura: Regal, 1982.

Pinnock, Clark H. *A Wideness in God's Mercy: The Finality of Jesus Christ in a World of Religions.* Grand Rapids: Zondervan, 1992.

Pullinger, Jackie. *Chasing the Dragon.* London: Hodder and Stoughton, 1980.

Roberts, J. Deotis. *A Black Political Theology.* Philadelphia: Westminster, 1974.

———. *Liberation and Reconciliation: A Black Theology.* Philadelphia: Westminster, 1971.

Samuel, Vinay, and Albrecht Hauser, eds. *Proclaiming Christ in Christ's Way: Studies in Integral Evangelism.* Oxford: Regnum, 1989.

Samuel, Vinay, and Christopher Sugden. *A.D. 2000 and Beyond: A Mission Agenda.* Oxford: Regnum, 1991.

———. *Christian Mission in the Eighties: A Third World Perspective.* Partnership booklet, no. 2. Bangalore: Partnership in Mission–Asia, 1981.

———, eds. *The Church in Response to Human Need.* Grand Rapids: Eerdmans, 1987.

———. "Evangelism and Social Responsibility: A Biblical Study on Priorities." In *In Word and Deed,* edited by Bruce J. Nicholls, 189–214. Grand Rapids: Eerdmans, 1985.

———. *Evangelism and the Poor: A Third World Study Guide.* Rev. ed. Oxford: Regnum, 1983.

————. *Lambeth: A View from the Two-Thirds World.* London: SPCK, 1989.

Scherer, James A. *Gospel, Church and Kingdom: Comparative Studies in World Mission Theology.* Minneapolis: Augsburg, 1987.

Scriven, Charles. *The Transformation of Culture.* Scottsdale, Penn.: Herald, 1988.

Shenk, David W., and Ervin R. Stutzman. *Creating Communities of the Kingdom: New Testament Models of Church Planting.* Scottsdale, Penn.: Herald, 1988.

Sider, Ronald J. *Christ and Violence.* Scottsdale, Penn.: Herald, 1979.

————. *Completely Pro-life.* Downers Grove, Ill.: InterVarsity, 1987.

————, ed. *Cry Justice: The Bible on Hunger and Poverty.* New York: Paulist, 1980.

————, ed. *Evangelicals and Development: Toward a Theology of Social Change.* Philadelphia: Westminster, 1981.

————, ed. *Lifestyle in the Eighties: An Evangelical Commitment to Simple Lifestyle.* Exeter: Paternoster, 1982.

————. *Nonviolence: The Invincible Weapon?* Dallas: Word, 1989.

————. *Rich Christians in an Age of Hunger.* 3rd ed. Dallas: Word, 1990.

Sinclair, Maurice. *Ripening Harvest, Gathering Storm: What Is the Relevance of the Christian Faith in a World Sliding into Crisis?* London: Church Missionary Society (and MARC), 1988.

Smith, Timothy. *Revivalism and Social Reform.* New York: Harper Torch Books, 1965.

Stamoolis, James J. *Eastern Orthodox Mission Theology Today.* Maryknoll: Orbis, 1986.

Steuernagel, Valdir Raul. "The Theology of Mission in Its Relation to Social Responsibility within the Lausanne Movement." Ph.D. diss., Lutheran School of Theology, Chicago, 1988.

Stott, John R. W. *Christian Mission in the Modern World.* Downers Grove, Ill.: InterVarsity, 1975.

————. *The Cross of Christ.* Downers Grove, Ill.: InterVarsity, 1986.

Stransky, Thomas F. "Evangelization, Mission and Social Action: A Roman Catholic Perspective." *Review and Expositor* (spring 1982): 343–50.

Sugden, Chris, and Oliver Barclay. *Kingdom and Creation in Social Ethics.* "Grove Booklets on Ethics," no. 79. Bramcote, Nottingham: Grove Books, 1990.

Sugden, Christopher, and Michael Neville. "A Critical and Comparative Study of the Practice and Theology of Christian Social Witness in Indonesia and India between 1974 and 1983 with Special Reference to the Work of Wayan Mastra . . . and Vinay Samuel. . . ." Ph.D. diss., Westminster College, Oxford, 1987.

Utuk, Efiung S. "From Wheaton to Lausanne: The Road to Modification of Contemporary Evangelical Mission Theology." *Missiology: An International Review* XIV, no. 2 (April 1986): 205–20.

Van Leeuwen, Arend Th. *Christianity in World History: The Meeting of the Faiths of East and West.* Translated by H. H. Hoskins. New York: Scribner's Sons, 1964.

Verkuyl, Johannes. *Contemporary Missiology: An Introduction.* Translated by Dale Cooper. Grand Rapids: Eerdmans, 1978.

Volf Miroslav. "Materiality of Salvation: An Investigation in the Soteriologies of Liberation and Pentecostal Theologies." *Journal of Ecumenical Studies* 26, no. 3 (summer 1989): 447–67.

WCC. *Mission and Evangelism: An Ecumenical Affirmation.* Geneva: WCC, 1982.

Wagner, C. Peter. *Church Growth and the Whole Gospel: A Biblical Mandate.* New York: Harper, 1981.

———. *Warfare Prayer.* Ventura: Regal, 1992.

Walker, Andrew. *Enemy Territory: The Christian Struggle for the Modern World.* London: Hodder and Stoughton, 1987.

Wallis, Jim. *Agenda for Biblical People.* New York: Harper, 1976.

———. *The Call to Conversion: Recovering the Gospel for These Times.* New York: Harper, 1981.

———. *Revive Us Again: A Sojourner's Story.* Nashville: Abingdon, 1983.

Webb, B. G., ed. *Christians in Society.* Explorations, 3. Homebush West, Australia: Lancer Books, 1988.

Webster, Douglas D. *A Passion for Christ: An Evangelical Christology.* Grand Rapids: Zondervan, 1987.

Will, James E. *A Christology of Peace.* Louisville: Westminster/John Knox Press, 1989.

Wilson, Frederick R., ed. *The San Antonio Report. Your Will Be Done: Mission in Christ's Way.* Geneva: WCC, 1990.

Wimber, John. *Power Evangelism.* San Francisco: Harper, 1986.

Winter, Ralph. "Crucial Issues in Missions: Working towards the Year 2000." "Momentum Building in Global Missions: Basic Concepts in Frontier Missiology." "Seeing the Basic Picture." Unpublished papers, 1990.

Winter, Ralph, and Steven C. Hawthorne, eds. *Perspectives on the World Christian Movement: A Reader.* Pasadena: William Carey, 1981.

Wolterstorff, Nicholas. *Until Justice and Peace Embrace.* Grand Rapids: Eerdmans, 1983.

Wright, Nigel. *The Radical Kingdom.* Eastbourne: Kingsway Publications, 1986.

Wright, Tom. *New Tasks for a Renewed Church.* London: Hodder and Stoughton, 1992.

Yoder, Perry B. *Shalom: The Bible's Word for Salvation, Justice and Peace.* Newton, Kans.: Faith and Life, 1987.

Your Kingdom Come: Mission Perspectives. Report on the World Conference on Mission and Evangelism. Melbourne, Australia, May 12–25, 1990. Geneva: WCC, 1980.

Name Index

SCRIPTURE INDEX

Ronald J. Sider (Ph.D., Yale University), professor of theology and culture at Eastern Baptist Theological Seminary in Philadelphia, is president of Evangelicals for Social Action and publisher for *Prism* and *Creation Care* magazines. He is the author of over twenty books, including *Living like Jesus* and the best-selling *Rich Christians in an Age of Hunger.*

Persons interested in further information about meetings, programs, and materials that seek to implement this book's call for wholistic mission that combines evangelism and social action are invited to contact:

Ron Sider
President
Evangelicals for Social Action
10 E. Lancaster Avenue
Wynnewood, PA 19096
215-645-9390
800-650-6600
Fax: 215-649-3834

EVANGELICALS FOR SOCIAL ACTION

ESA is a national association of Christians dedicated to "Living like Jesus"—living out a genuine faith in our lives and communities.

Jesus is Lord of our whole lives, and our lives must be subject to the whole of his gospel. ESA provides a network and resource for Christians committed to this kind of "wholistic" discipleship and ministry in our lost and hurting world. Together we can share the good news of Jesus Christ through word and deed.

Join ESA and become a part of an exciting movement including . . .

PRISM> ESA's bimonthly magazine will equip, empower, inform, and inspire you to live more like Jesus, growing a genuine faith in every part of your life. PRISM offers insightful, biblical reflection on the world in which we live—stories and strategies for effective outreach and ministry.

Christian Citizenship> ESA helps Christians to be active, engaged, and responsible citizens. PRISM features a regular "Washington Update," providing a biblical perspective on the latest political developments in our nation's capital. Our Crossroads program brings together Christian scholars for a deeper look at important issues of public policy.

Caring for Creation> ESA hosts the Evangelical Environmental Network (EEN), a network of Christian organizations making care for creation an integral part of their work. World Vision, Habitat for Humanity, and InterVarsity Christian Fellowship are among the members of this environmental network. ESA also produces *Creation Care* magazine, a biblical, environmental quarterly.

Ministry Networks> Becoming a member of ESA makes you a part of a dynamic network of Christians throughout America. Network 9:35 is our exciting new network of churches and pastors committed to the genuine faith and wholistic ministry described in Matthew 9:35. ESA's Generous Christians Campaign is a rapidly growing movement of individuals giving sacrificially of their time and resources to help share Jesus' love with the poor, the hungry, and the outcast.

Join Us!

**Evangelicals for Social Action • 10 Lancaster Avenue • Wynnewood, PA 19096
1-800-650-6600 • esa@esa-online.org**

PRISM
MAGAZINE

"America's Alternative Evangelical Voice"